NOTEBOOKS

by JACQUES MARITAIN

France, My Country, Through the Disaster – Approaches to God – Art and Scholasticism – Christianity and Democracy – Existence and the Existent – Creative Intuition in Art and Poetry – The Twilight of Civilization.

On the Grace and Humanity of Jesus – An Essay on Christian Philosophy – On the Church of Christ – God and the Permission of Evil – The Degrees of Knowledge – St. Thomas Aquinas – The Rights of Man and Natural Law.

Freedom in the Modern World – Education at the Crossroads – An Introduction to Philosophy – Formal Logic – Art and Poetry – Georges Rouault – Integral Humanism – Antisemitism – Man and the State.

Man's Approach to God – On the Philosophy of History – On the Use of Philosophy – The Peasant of the Garonne – The Living Thoughts of St. Paul – The Person and the Common Good – Bergsonian Philosophy and Thomism.

Philosophy of Nature – Moral Philosophy – The Things That Are Not Caesar's – The Range of Reason – Ransoming The Time – Reflections on America – Religion and Culture – Art and Faith – The Responsibility of the Artist.

Saint Thomas and the Problem of Evil – Scholasticism and Politics – Science and Wisdom – A Preface to Metaphysics – The Sin of the Angel – The Dream of Descartes – Theonas – Three Reformers – Truth and Human Fellowship.

with **RAISSA MARITAIN**

Prayer and Intelligence – The Situation of Poetry – Liturgy and Contemplation – Notes on the Lord's Prayer.

Jacques Maritain

NOTEBOOKS

Translated by
JOSEPH W. EVANS

MAGI BOOKS, INC.

33 BUCKINGHAM DR.   ALBANY, NEW YORK 12208

Copyright © 1984 by University of Notre Dame
Notre Dame, Indiana

This work is a translation of *Carnet de Notes*, published and copyright © 1965 by Desclee De Brouwer.
Photograph copyright © Yan Jean Dieusaide

Manufactured in the United States of America
Composition in Press Roman by Magi Books, Inc. Albany, New York
Printing and binding by Edwards Brothers, Inc., Ann Arbor, Michigan

Library of Congress Cataloging in Publication Data

Maritain, Jacques, 1882–1973.
Notebooks.

Translation of: Carnet de notes.
1. Maritain, Jacques, 1882–1973.   2. Philosophers – –
France – – Biography.   I. Title.
B2430.M34A313   1984   194 [B]   83-26743
ISBN 0-87343-050-6

J.M.

Yan Jean Dieuzaide   **JACQUES MARITAIN (1882–1973)**

FOREWORD

(1964)

Chapters I and II of these *Notebooks* were written, Chapter IV begun, in 1954. Then came a long interruption due to the resumption of my philosophical work, to the trials of health which visited us, and to the death of our little sister Vera, the 31st of December, 1959.

Now all things have been shattered or dislocated in me, since the thunderbolt which began the last illness of Raissa (precisely at the moment when, arriving from America, we were passing through the door of the hotel room, in Paris, the 7th of July, 1960). At the end of four months of suffering, the 4th of November, 1960, God took her with Him, and I am henceforth alone here on earth, at least according to the appearances of this visible world.

The old broken tree, which still has a few roots in the earth, some others already delivered to the winds of Heaven, is it perhaps going for a short time still to continue to bear a little fruit on half-detached branches which incline towards the ground? I thought of these things while passing, in the garden of Kolbsheim, before an old cherry tree ill-treated by the storm — it was during the summer of 1961 — without suspecting that a few days later I was going to read the intimate notes and notebooks of Raissa, and that it would be granted to me to be able to transcribe them and to publish them: which is the greatest blessing in all my life's work for which I have to give thanks.

Why have I returned after this to my own notes, which beside those of Raissa are nothing? It is because at their level they can, I believe, have some utility, as indicated in the Preface; and it is because it was fitting in any case to complete this first volume (it has much chance of also being the last). Originally, it was a posthumous work that I had in view. The publication of *Raissa's Journal* (private edition, 1962; commercial edition the following year) caused me to change my mind, for the things of which it is a question in this first volume form as it were an external framework in which certain pages of the *Journal* situate themselves; I prefer therefore that it appear at this time.

1

The publication of *Raissa's Journal* has also led me to modify the composition of this volume in question, by completing it with three chapters (Chapters VI, VII and VIII) which matter to me much more than the chronological order of my notes: one is devoted to the memory of our sweet Vera; the other touches on some fundamental themes for Christian life, on which the *Journal* has cast a great light for me. The last one treats of the Church of Heaven.

Chapter III was written in 1964; Chapter IV, part in 1954 and part in 1961; Chapter V in 1963 (and, for the last pages, in 1964), Chapter VI in 1964; Chapter VII in 1962; Chapter VIII in 1963.

I leave, without changing anything in it, the Preface which I had written in 1954, at a time when they were both there, and when the word «happiness» still had a meaning for me.

J.M.
Kolbsheim, 12th of September, 1964

PREFACE (1954)

These *Notebooks* are not a Journal. Of the things which composed the substance of our life, Raissa has spoken in *Les Grandes Amitiés* as she alone could do; a certain limpidity of memory, limpidity in depth, is the privilege of very pure souls. I hope that it will be granted to her to continue her memoirs, interrupted, alas, by a long series of trials of health. If I happen to touch in these notes on some of the subjects of a purely personal order which she will have to evoke in them, this will be in an extrinsic and merely documentary manner. I shall note however in the first fragments many of the memories which are dear to us and which happen to fit into what she has written or prepare for what she intends to say. Apart from these exceptions, my aim is above all to deposit in the dossier of the history of our time some data concerning external facts and external debates with which the events of our life found themselves intermingled. Even if it concerns secondary points, I thought that a testimony of this kind could have its utility.

The idea of writing these notebooks came to me during the long days of immobility which a coronary thrombosis suffered at the end of March 1954 made necessary. In thinking of it beforehand, my imagination envelopped it with the airy wings of dream, I filled it with details and with reflections to which the life of dream lent an illusory interest. At the instant of executing my purpose, all of this becomes very cold and very dry.

What am I, I asked myself then. A professor? I think not; I taught by necessity. A writer? Perhaps. A philosopher? I hope so. But also a kind of romantic of justice too prompt to imagine to himself, at each combat entered into, that justice and truth will have their day among men. And also perhaps a kind of spring-finder who presses his ear to the ground in order to hear the sound of hidden springs, and of invisible germinations. And also perhaps, like every Christian, despite and in the midst of the miseries and the failures and all the graces betrayed of which I am becoming conscious in the evening of my life, a beggar of Heaven disguised as a man of the world, a kind of secret agent of the King of Kings in the territories of the prince of this world, taking his risks like Kipling's cat, who walked by himself.

As a child I detested the idea of resembling, as the friends of the family used to delight in kindly pointing out, the bust of my grandfather which adorned the mantlepiece of my mother's drawing-room. It was not solely pride, nor revolt at not being «only myself.» I had the presentiment of a kind of fatal element, and of what there was of violence and of bitterness, mingled with much grandeur and much generosity, in my hereditary line. If all of this was able to find itself pacified and softened in me, and did not disturb too much the progress of the so marvellously united little flock of our three souls, I think, without speaking of Christian grace, which is clearly the essential, that it was due to the meeting of the traditions of spiritual refinement, of innocence and of nostalgia for the absolute, present in the ancestral line of Raissa and of Vera. I feel myself thus a debtor to Israel. I do not like, moreover, the grossness of the Gentiles, I would like to be as little as possible a *goïsche kop*, I would like to be a Jew by adoption, since I have been introduced by baptism into the dignity of the children of Israel.

The aid and the inspiration of my beloved Raissa have penetrated all my life and all my work. If there is something good in what I have done, it is to her, after God, that I owe it. The radiance of her love and the pure fervor of her wisdom, her force of soul, her exquisite sense of the true and of the just, the blessing of God on her prayer and her sufferings, have illumined my days. Our sister Vera has given both of us total devotion, the treasures of charity of an admirably magnanimous heart, and the incomparable support of the assistance which she receives from her intimacy with Jesus. I wish that my gratitude to both of them be inscribed at the front of this collection of remembrances.

J.M.
Princeton, N.J., 1st of August, 1954

In order to distinguish them from the notes stemming from inscriptions hastily made at the very moment in the kinds of diaries which I kept after a fashion, I have, in the first five chapters, placed between brackets the notes written according to the present testimony of my memory or expressing my present reflections.

My oldest notebooks were destroyed by me. From 1906 to 1911 my notebooks were quite regularly kept, and are rather voluminous. Afterwards, I used small pocket notebooks, more and more rapid and summary; several of these notebooks have been lost.

(Parenthetical translations of some foreign and classical words and phrases as well as English titles of works when different from the original French are additions of the publisher.)

CHAPTER ONE

OLD MEMORIES I: FROM BEFORE BAPTISM

1898

[My mother kept for a long time a letter which I had written, at sixteen, to François Baton, the husband of the good, stout and wholly devoted cook, Angèle (for me «Yeuyeule»), who was a pillar of the house and who watched over my childhood. Baton was a laborer, and enjoyed in my opinion all the prestige of the manual worker, the «conscious and organized proletarian»; it was in chatting with him, in the kitchen, where he came each evening with his newspaper, *La Petite République*, and where I used to take refuge in order to flee from the friends of my mother, that at about thirteen or fourteen I had become a Socialist. The articles of Jaurès and of Gérault-Richard inflamed me. Later a performance of *The Weavers*, of Gerhart Hauptmann, was to make an extremely profound impression on me. While waiting for me to read the Socialist literature of that time, for example, «Le Droit au Produit Intégral du Travail,» of Anton Menger, which was not, I believe, very orthodox, but was one of my preferred books, Baton explained to me that the Revolution would be accomplished when the Socialist deputies in the Chamber would have «half plus one» of the seats.

If I do not deny, far from it, the esteem and the love for the working people which had developed in me and which I have always kept, I abhor the bad passion and the commonplaces of the revolutionary cabarets on which it lived at that time. They appear only too well in the letter from which my mother had copied a long fragment (the original is lost). In spite of its gibberish and its falsity of tone, I publish this fragment here in order to give some idea of the state of mind in which a young «traitor to his class» bourgeois could find himself at the time — whose desire, moreover, to serve «the proletariat and humanity,» while taking, in order to realize itself, very unexpected forms, and while subordinating itself to that of serving God first, has never been revoked.]

From a letter to François Baton:

I will be a socialist and live for the revolution.
. . . There is no merit in working when this amuses you, no more than there is merit in eating when one is hungry. If there is someone whom it is necessary to thank for the progress that I can make, it is precisely the immense crowd of the proletarians who toil while I delight in reading, so that I may have bread and wine, clothes, a roof, a bed, a fire, books and time to read — it is also all the work of humanity, all the accumulated intellectual labor of earlier and contemporary generations which I can freely enjoy, which I can freely appropriate. Capitalist property will never be able to enroach upon that communism, the sublime and universal communism of human thought and of human suffering and of human hope. But do you think that I am not ashamed when I think that at my age the children of the people toil, sometimes 11 hours a day (only yesterday, 12, 13 and 14 hours a day), and that it is thanks to their work *not remunerated at its value* that I, idle, without doing anything, whithout creating anything, without sweating, feed with a lukewarm satisfaction on the bread of the body and on the bread of science! Ah, certainly, this will not be lost, but it is an enormous debt and one which will *never* be and which can never be paid, that I contract with regard to the proletariat. There are moments when I ask myself if I have indeed the *right* to be a socialist, to enjoy consequently the blessed socialist hope, I who enjoy at the same time bourgeois privileges, whereas socialist joy, the gaiety of revolutionary hope should be reserved for the oppressed workers only, for those who work, for those who suffer, for those who constitute the sole true humanity. It is for this that at this moment an anxiety and a remorse mingle in everything I do, mingle in the joy that I experience in learning. Most certainly, everything I will be able to think and to know, I will consecrate to the proletariat and to humanity: I will employ it in its entirety to prepare the revolution, to aid, however so little, in the happiness and in the education of humanity.

4th of November, 1901. «Friendship like love supports only beings who cannot fall. These sentiments are always in the measure of the persons who experience them and they are built on sand when on both sides there are not solid bonds of high intellectual conformity and of reciprocal esteem.» (Raissa Oumançoff, 22nd of June, 1901).

All of us therefore have only the destiny which we have made for ourselves. It is our soul projected in time which comes back to us under the form of concrete events. We are not deceived. We deceive ourselves.

And then we are wrong to hope. Always, in spite of us, hope insinuates itself. We do not recognize it, but it is there. It takes possession of us gently and hypocritically, so that later it can have a good laugh.

Is it therefore true that we are irremediably mired in baseness and misfortune?

And what does it matter after all? I will always set out. O Death, old captain! It is a sweet assurance to know that you steer the boat and that you will lead us to port.

Wrecks floating along the way. But will in the sails and light in the lanterns.

*

Impenetrability of consciences. Windows! But always closed. Story of the pike in an aquarium which constantly knocked its head against a glass partition placed in the middle of the water, which it did not see — but felt. They say it was perceptive enough, at the end of a few months of this exercise, to remain in its little home of its own accord.

But are there not some which would have finally broken their heads? By stubbornness precisely. . . .

The story adds that one day they took away the glass partition. But the pike never touched the fish which had been on the other side, so inseparably associated remained the memory of the shocks it had received.

But will *someone* ever take away the windows which limit souls? Something or someone, will, friendship, death? But we too, we will have definitively acquired the habit, and we will always strike against each other, we will always collide with the glass, even when absent, always.[1]

*

From Raissa:

«In order to be everything it is necessary to be able to be alone! and Brand is not alone. He has to inspire him, to guide him and to support him, faith in God, in himself, in the Beauty and the Goodness of his work.

«*Nothing* of all this can exist for us. We believe that there exists an Unknowable and as such we cannot busy ourselves with it. — To have confidence in ourselves? What irony! — In our work? What work? Why?

«We believe neither in duty, nor in merit, that way we lose all support within ourselves (until ressurection). . . .

«I would like us, detached from everything, free from every prejudice, free from duty, disdainful of merit, *without any illusion* and without any weakness, to find in ourselves the strength to be, for the Beauty of being! to be alone and nevertheless strong!»

(22nd of June, 1902)

*

To leave.

Towards the sun, the countries of life, of refound solitude and

1. The majority of the fragments contained in these ancient notebooks carry mention neither of the month nor of the day of the month.

of present beauty. In the great unlimited plains with fine sand. In the great shuddering woods. In the immense fields with eternal harvests.

> O the steppes; the deserts.
> Contemplation.
> To die in Jerusalem.

*

«Curious» attitude of people who seem to imagine that something is due to them. Ah yes, I am ready to jump into the water for you: why do you not do it for me? — Life is an *exchange* (of courtesies?). One takes offence, one is bitter, and, to be sure, one in truth perhaps suffers when what one «expected» does not happen. Fatuity and insupportable demand.

If one truly understood life, one would see that it is necessary to take what happens each day as a «grace» dispensed from day to day. Evil as well as the good; perhaps especially the good. It is a marvel that such and such a joy has happened to me. Life owes me nothing. No one owes me anything.

No more than I owe something to life.

*

From a certain point of view, life seems to be a perpetual and disconcerting leap into chance. The unexpected character of encounters, etc.

But on the other hand, what logic. It is something which one has seized in passage, felt in an instant, something imperceptible, unformulable and inaccessible — which develops with the rigor of an equation, and which, at the end of a more or less long time, succeeds definitely in realizing itself and passes into actual events. Nothing is lost, truly. Destiny proceeds in silence, for a long time, underneath. With great difficulty one can have for an instant a fugitive intuition of it, which one discards immediately. It is more patient than everything. *This* happens one fine day, because it *was necessary* that that happen. On what date? I could not say before-hand. But one was able to feel something *stronger*, which passed — and which had to materialize.

Rarely have I been deceived in these dangerous intuitions, which reveal themselves by quite particular characteristics. Precisely because they are an immediate view of a latency at work, they absolutely escape language and verbal affirmation, they remain outside acted life and beliefs, they float, so to speak, a moment on consciousness, and *we refuse* to admit them into the system of our opinions — precisely because it is an unseizable force, like the enormous machines which turn in my feverish nightmares.

It could be indeed, finally, that I had an intuition of this kind some years ago, at Crécy, when I had such a horrible fear[1] — like those fears in the dark in which one does not dare to cry out — such a horrible fear of life, of my life which was coming.

But now, truly, I no longer have fear. Destiny can pass that way. Destiny surely passes that way. But we shall be *stronger* than it.

For it can do nothing, nothing, nothing, absolutely nothing against us and our will.

*

The poor cripple
goes on.
He is ugly and disgusting to see.
He is pitied and allowed to think that he is
as beautiful as other men.
He is wicked without knowing it.
He is pitied; he is allowed to think that he is good,
that he loves and that someone loves him.
He limps and stumbles at all the brooks.
He is pitied; and he is allowed to think that he walks
straight, as other men walk straight.

1. [No doubt during vacation when one day, in a moment of bravado and of irrepressible dream, I wanted to escape by the window, by means of bedsheets tied together. They became untied while I was suspended in the air — I was badly hurt by the fall.]

He is blind and sees only foolish hallucinations.
He is pitied; he is allowed to think that he sees
as other men see.

He is deaf and hears only foolish hallucinations.
He is pitied and allowed to think that he hears
beautiful harmonies, and that such are the harmonies
that other men hear.

He is mute and utters only inarticulate sounds.
He is pitied; he is allowed to think that he speaks,
and that such is the speech of other men.

He is sick.
He is pitied and allowed to think that he is healthy
as other men are.

He is dead.
He is pitied; he is allowed to think that he is living,
and that such is true life.

But sometimes does he not hear, far away,
something like a laugh?

*

See, the garden is dying slowly under the rain;
        Do you see the great holes forming?
We shall bury there our soul and our life,
        Darkness will sleep near us.
See the flowers fading slowly under the rain.
See, the water runs through the broken roads
        Carrying along rotted leaves.
Such will be indeed the river in which our felicities
        Will scud along to the blessed cities.
See us pass among the broken roads.

See us pass amidst wasted youth.
        The fruits of the orchard have fallen.
The sun has set at the bottom of the valley.
        I hear freezing winds run
And I am afraid to leave towards the wasted dawn.

[I was passionately fond of Baudelaire. But this wretched pastiche expressed the very real background of my state of mind at that time.]

*

The void. Heap of combined forces. I am worth more than them, since I know them; and they do not know me.

Failed universe. What a poor instrument is the human brain! What good can one do with it? Animals, animals. . . . In perfecting itself humanity perfects the vices and ugliness which are proper to it — by definition. Suffering, grief, shame, always at the bottom. To shake that off! To feel the burden weigh upon oneself. We wish to seize beauty, to seize happiness, like a breath of breeze with a pincers. To make the beautiful with the ugly, this is still possible, since they are of the same order. But to make the successful with the *failed*, to transform one order into another order — something «supernatural.» What is to be done with the infinite? Peasants, to make fun of me, called me «the apostle». . . .

And then, always the void, ignorance. Objective truth fleeing like objective beauty. Doubt. True doubt, even concerning doubt. Reason revolting upon itself. Coffee mill which idles.

I pulled myself up by the hair. High. High towards countries which my eyes created, towards songs which my ears produced.

I made a great city on the void, a great brightness on the night. My will supports itself in nothingness.

And then I gave my soul and it is more beautiful. We are two to live in the eternal vibration which passes through the night. Alone!

But how can we reanimate this void below? Conquer, in their order of action, the brutal forces? I can scorn the universe, we laugh at it in our home, in which it can do nothing against us. NOTHING.

But it holds us by other bonds. Struggle! Struggle! It is necessary to be stronger than the infinite. Integrate everything to oneself.

But everything that remains outside. . . .

*

From Raissa:

L'Étivaz, *14th of August, 1902.*   Presence of the soul at each instant of life.
School
       in order to create the golden atmosphere of Swedenborg, environment of the soul and of sincerity.

*

Raissa and I clearly felt, after the reading of Maeterlinck, when we had returned into the room, and were resting on the window, penetrated with buoyant air and with the indistinct colors of the mountains, and with the pale and continuous and living line of the road, we both clearly felt — our souls happy — our truth, our definitive truth. I write this in order to fix in my memory the congenial setting and the external situation; but what took place on the inside is ineffable and divine. The absolute sincerity, the profound harmony of our souls filled us with an inexhaustible happiness. Life appeared to us, our life, such as it should be, and in silence we promised each other irrevocable promises. Fortitude, the luminous and clear School, the School of life, of sincerity, the School in which we will animate souls, in which we will cause by appeals, songs and rays, the soul and real life to come to the surface of existence. The School from which men and women of truth and of harmony will emerge. The School in which we shall do the divine, necessary expression of our life, and of the constant power which animates it. Clear!

*

Voulangis, *9th of September, 1902.*   What Maeterlinck says of silence applies to many other things. It seems that men are afraid of what is great, profound, violent and definitive. Their whole art contrives to avoid it.
Thus for the union of souls.
That is the real reason for moral chastity, and, insofar as it is implied by the latter — physical chastity. It is a question of pre-

serving intact this gift of supreme intuition through which souls communicate.

This communication of souls is a desire of our nature. *Dissipation* in boys, *upbringing* in girls, the *experience* of adults aim only at spoiling and rendering impossible such a desire. Shameful prudence and fear of great things. The consequence is that in losing their beauty so many human beings lose the sense of beauty. Doors close. There are things which they can no longer see and which they will never be able to see. A base practical approximation of experience has replaced truth. Will, desire, profound wish, satisfy themselves with chance encounters and external illusions. The external from now on has established itself at the very interior of being.

1903

The idealists.

Either they affrim nothing concerning existence but solely concerning our possible knowledge. Their discovery is then only this affirmation: «We know only the known, and we will never be able to know anything except the known.» Let them say therefore what it would be to know something which is not the known, which is not known.

Or else they are not content with this tautology, and affirm something concerning being: «There is only. . . .» I stop them. They do not have the right and go infinitely beyond their premises.

If we wish to speak of being, it is necessary to posit other postulates.

Communities.

So there will never be any means of being free! No sooner are three or four individuals together than the same bonds of authority and the same servitudes appear. The least group becomes a small *family*. One takes the place of the father, the other of the brother. . . . — This community has all the vices of bourgeois marriage.

The theoretical claim of solitude holds against those on the outside. But you do not notice that, practically, it is null in the small circle of which you are a part.

Same essential misappreciation of values, same loss of duration, common stupidity, same falsehood, same enroachments of authority, same closing of horizon, preconception, cliquishness, practical agreements, same mode of language and of thought by customary allusion and ready-made sympathy, same indulgences, same obtuseness, same servitudes as in the family (and without the household gods of the family). Same absence of shame. Same *facility*. Same *attachments*. Same neglects.

*

It is necessary to bear death with gaiety. He is happy
       forever; wants to dance always.

And perhaps there will be beautiful days; the games of
       life will want to imitate the memory.

His suffering is his own, it is the nothingness of the work,
       for the past, the present and the future.

His infinite suffering is the fury of servitudes,
       which arisen from the ages, make God Himself
         weep.

His will belongs to God. His liberty is total.

All that God gives, he receives with happiness.
If one day God believes him to be in His image, and calls him,
then, he will come.

Thus he is dead, and almost nothing is changed in his life,
nor in his action, nor in his happiness. It is like a man
who would continue wakefulness by dream, and would
go on doing the same things. He dreams nevertheless.

That's enough for him.

It is necessary that God be free.

*

26th of November, 1904.   Marriage of Jacques and Raissa.

1905

Raissa, *5th of June*: «All men are made of the same clay, but not of the same breath.»

Raissa, *9th of October*. In the middle of the night she was awakened by these words which she heard: «You are always looking for what must be done. There is only to love God and to serve Him with all your heart.»

*

Began to recite the Lord's Prayer at the beginning of November, 1905.

*

30th of November.

Métiers. Is is necessary, above all, to be a man. This is the métier. This is the real place of human *natural* communion, communion of action. The humanitarians make me laugh. Let them begin by properly exercising their métier. True definition of métier, would be approximately this: To contribute, as far as one's body is concerned, (practical activity), to the life of men, and to draw one's life from it. That which remains is for us and for God. But it is on another plane. It is necessary that there be a point of attachment, a a point of resistance and a point of support, through which the point of our action is attached to the duration of all men, to the practice of all men. To contribute to the life of men, I say, in all the meanings of the word «life.» To give the bread of the body and the bread of the soul.

Parody of métier: luxury.

Corruption of métier: lucre. The «métier» of the coupon clipper. *To earn money*, as prime end — the contrary of métier.

What is bad in industrialism is not the machine, it is the bourgeois spirit.

*

5th of December.

Method in history. In the sciences, a forgotten fact, a fact not considered by us, does not prevent the other facts from being valid. It spoils only the theory, not the other facts. Reality is present, and one takes *successively* different points of view concerning it, one knows successively parts of it. In history it is entirely different. A forgotten fact, an unknown fact, prevents the other facts from being «true.» It is necessary to recast them. For here one works on wholes, not on parts. The facts do not have therefore the same signification as in the sciences; because in the sciences the present reality is infinite, so that the ensemble of known facts is only a very small part of reality; whereas in history, reality is past; it is therefore, as it were, a limited whole, which has taken place, so that the ensemble of known facts is thought to present an image of reality, an image of the whole. So that a new fact does not superadd itself to the others while extending their field, but is forced, taking its place in a limited circumference, to repress all the other facts. As in a trial.

All of which amounts to saying that historical reality is altogether different from scientific reality. And that history is not a science and has no need of the symbolical. And that in the end it presupposes a metaphysics.

[It is not for their intrinsic value that I have drawn these notes of youth from the jumble of my old notebooks. It seems to me that they give some idea of the state of a soul which searches in the night, and of the spiritual journey of a young man hungry for the absolute who, until his meeting with Léon Bloy (1905), believed himself an atheist or completely agnostic (if he then happened to sometimes use the word «God,» the meaning of this word remained for him merely poetical or mythical).

It is once again as a document that I have noted in the following fragment (drawn from the notebook of 1906) some of the arrogant and naive lucubrations which in reality bear witness to the torment which my intelligence endured in the months prior to our conversion, in trying to find, in the very midst of the errors in which it was engaged, a path towards the truth of which God caused it to feel the attraction, but to which it did not wish to give itself right away. It was a question, to tell the truth — for up till then everything had been suspended for me to this absolute end: humanity, and to its temporal salvation symbolized by revolution — it was a question of *changing ultimate end*, and of justifying this act which entirely rent me. Hence the theories which I constructed in a little treatise, from which I copy a few paragraphs below — I was there trying to rediscover, with the help of a clumsy and sometimes riduculous[1] vocabulary, the ancient distinction between the spiritual and the temporal, and I still clung for a few moments to the old socialist Manichaeism of my student years in order to condemn those whom I called with disgust «the Christians» (while mixing together in the same confused ideology Nietzsche, Proudhon, Marx and Léon Bloy) at the instant when a supernatural thirst was carrying me towards the Church. To enter into the one and to remain separated from the others, standing like a beggar on the threshold without entering into the choir — such was the absurd notion of which I dreamed at that time, but which helped me to cross the bridge, to thread my way towards God.]

---

1. It was not without embarrassment that I copied the words of this unfortunate vocabulary. At least inventions like *prattique* and *zôtique* were droll enough for a comic to appreciate.

1906

January-March. On human action.

I.   Human duration knows two states which differ by nature: the state of peace and the state of war. The first proceeds as if salvation were assured, requires of each one that he contribute for his part to maintain, to continue salvation, already acquired (for example, in society, practice of métiers; in religion, practice of «religious duties,» going to Mass), tend to an organization, a regular functioning, a harmony, in which immediate salvation is no more than a condition of that which flowers above it. On the contrary, the state of war proceeds as if salvation were absolutely jeopardized, always in question, and requires of each one that he abandon everything in order to find salvation.

But there is in human actions another division, according to another dimension. Not having the time to seek the suitable words, I shall call one of these parts *prattique,* or earth; the other, *zôtique,* or religion. The actions which relate to *prattique,* to earth, tend always to a result, must succeed, cause to take root: always an earthly interest. The actions of the *zôtique,* of religion, bear on the essence itself, consequently do not tend to any external effect, do not cause to take root; they do not have any earthly interest, but the absolute interest of the salvation of the essence. There is between the *zôtique,* and the *prattique* a relation analogous to that of the soul and of the body: a relation of *whole* to *part,* this part being the point through which this whole realizes itself in action.

23

This being given, the earth is either in a state of peace or in a state of war. Religion is either in a state of peace or in a state of war.

For the earth, what is excellent in the state of peace is the exercise of métiers — baker, philosopher or poet. The state of peace divides then into two: time of work (tension, it is necessary to succeed) and repose after work (free exercise, sheer play). In the state of war all the privileges of métiers are suspended, in the state of war there are also two times: battle and camp-life.

In human life, intermediate by nature, the state of peace and the state of war compenetrate each other. War is always subjacent to peace; misery lies in wait behind the métiers; and wars have always a substructure of peace and of organization.

One could say that the natural state of the earth, the natural tendency of *prattique*, is the state of peace. The state of war is forced, foreign. On the contrary, the natural state of religion, the natural tendency of the *zôtique*, is the state of war. There is no true peace for it except absolute triumph, which is not of this life in any case.

The state of peace is a state of liberty. One is free when one recognizes by reason a certain order, which one respects and which one wishes to obey. Then everything can develop in harmony. And thus the more there is of liberty (true), the more there is of authority (true). The earth tends towards liberty and authority — towards peace.

The state of war is a state of force. The natural state of religion is force, the state of war. It pains it to undergo peace, not to always burn. The force of arms is a caricature of force, the true name of force is Love. The true name of liberty and of authority — Justice.

Mortal error to confuse the earth and religion, the *prattique* and the *zôtique*. Neither peace nor war on earth will ever be Salvation. Neither métiers nor combats will bring about Salvation. (This is, however, what this century believes.)

Métiers will always bring about a particular work, wars a particular salvation, which will never replace salvation. It is necessary only to ask that they be the instruments of the *zôtique*. (Excellence of métiers, the cathedrals; excellence of war, the Crusades.) Everything in Socialsim and the class-struggle which aims to replace salvation and to establish universal Happiness is false. But there is an unassailable truth: it is that the present condition of the earth is such that war against social iniquity is an absolute necessity.

Bourgeois peace is not a peace. We recognize nothing of their order.

A god descending upon earth preaching benignity brings however war, not peace.

. . . .

II.   I have spoken of human action in general. The *zôtique*, which I have also called religion, is a certain universal typical mode of human action. Accordingly it is a question here of the religious function in general; in this sense, there is no man without religion. If you say that you do not have any religion, it may be that you have a religion of the stomach, or of money, or of nothingness.

But by definition the *zôtique* presupposes that there is only a single true religion. The true life of the soul. The word «religion» then designates no longer a mode of action, but a particular concrete reality, a given reality. Religion which one does not «choose,» which one does not invent, in which one is born in spirit (and of the Spirit, *ex aqua et Spiritu*). The Church, body of Jesus Christ, renders the *zôtique* present to earth. Cuts out in the *prattique* a *prattique* which is the pure expression of the *zôtique*.

It is on the plane of the *zôtique*, not of the *prattique*, that priests differ from other men — through function. Such and such act of *zôtique*, for example, a sacrament, requires two agents: one in order to give it, the other in order to receive it. A bad priest can give it; if he is bad, he will go astray himself, but will not alter the act of *zôtique*, whose efficacy is no more in him than the efficacy of a remedy is in the doctor. Likewise, if one of the faithful is bad, he will go astray himself; but will not alter the act of *zôtique* in receiving it.

The nobility or the ignominy of the priest does nothing for or against the truth of religion, no more than that of the faithful.

Only one must not forget that the function of the priest is essentially a function of war (in the order of the *zôtique*). But since the law of war is force (love), there can be between the function of the priest and that of the faithful only a relation of force. This is why the faithful owe obedience to the priest. Through a consequence, a necessity of the function. Saints obey bad priests.

. . . .

There is another division between men than that of priests and of faithful. The division between «public men» and «private men.» A «public man» differs from a «private man» in the order of the *prattique*, not in that of the *zôtique*. It is necessary that there be men, special servants of the communion of métiers, who undertake to *maintain* or rather to *create* the state of peace, the other men *practicing* only the state of peace. This creation of peace is a métier; but a métier which differs from all other métiers; two kinds of complementary métiers.

Only, the métier of the public man is almost entirely masked by war (just as the function of war of the priest, in the order of the *zôtique*, is masked by the peace of worship and of organized works). The greatest part of their activity is employed in force. And their name itself is borrowed from war («public man» is indeed ridiculous. They are «governors,» they hold *power*). And yet in reality, it is not war, but peace, which is the essential thing for them. They are organizers and night-watchmen.

. . . .

III.   The preceding analysis shows that the pursuit of *power* in the things of earth is a corruption for the priest.

. . . .

It would be absurd to say that the Church is corrupt, that she is no longer with Jesus Christ. In order to say this it would be necessary at one and the same time to assert oneself a Christian (in order to believe in Jesus Christ) and to deny oneself a Christian (in order to condemn the Church; but if you condemn the Church you can no longer believe in Jesus Christ). It is the misery of Protestantism.

One does not choose a religion for good reasons. One is born into the true religion through grace.

All that I write here has to do with men, and with the difficulties of the world. But in order to speak to God it is necessary only to say: O my Father, give me the faith of a little child.

The great obstacle to Christianity is the Christians. This is the thorn which pierces me. The Christians have abandoned the poor − and the poor among the nations: the Jews − and Poverty of the soul: authentic Reason. They horrify me.

Bloy is in the Christian people like a prophet in the Jewish people: in a fury against his people. (But all the same in this people.)

In such a situation, it is necessary to redouble one's interior submission and one's waiting, and one's love for the Church.

The model to which reason tends is the life of the ancestors of Jesus, the life and the religion of Mary. But what reason thus requires is a supernatural life. The whole tree of Jesse is a continous miracle; and Mary was miraculously contemporary with Abraham and separated from the corrupted Jews. It would be necessary to be separated in the same way from the Christians of today. With a body present to this current age of the world, it would be necessary to really live with the first Christians, to rise above all the Christians of this time. Kind of miracle; supernatural operation. Tolstoyans or Protestants, those who think to effect this right off, easily and naturally, and while separating themselves from the Church, are silly idealists.

Reason requires that one be baptized, because it is necessary that life have its center in *faith*, and because to ask for baptism is the sign that one would like to live this way. What will happen after is the affair of God. For the moment, I do not know if I believe. . . .

Since worship stems so to speak from the conjunction of the absolute life of the soul with earthly life and earthly practice, it is necessary that acts of worship be sensible acts (to the body) — since it is earthly life; and that they be at the same time a «celestial» reality, acting according to the laws of absolute truth, not according to the laws of earth, a work of God, not of nature. We see, therefore, that the operations of worship must not be images or symbols, but real operations. Thus for Christian faith, God is really present at the sacrifice of the Mass, and the Mass is the center of the whole of Christianity. «I alone,» said Jesus to St. Mechtilda, «I alone understand perfectly in what manner I immolate myself every day on the altar for the salvation of the faithful; neither the Cherubim nor the Seraphim, or any celestial power can grasp it entirely.»

. . . .

In religion, therefore, in this unique and complex essence, there is nothing which I reject, but everything is equally accepted, without restriction or mental reservation. But this faith is indigent in me, repelled and thwarted by the consent of Christians to earthly injustice and by the horror which their history, their inclination, inspire in me. It will be necessary to be in the midst of them like strangers, come from elsewhere. Far from fleeing the earthly house of God, we shall turn towards it, and we shall enter it. But how can one mingle with the horrible children who feast in it? We shall remain separated, on the threshold. We do not reject any truth, we do not separate God from His Church, charity from worship; we keep the whole of the faith. But what is to be done in order not to enter at the same time into the family of the satisfied, who in the name of their eternal salvation have taken sides against the temporal salvation of the world?

[Three months after I had written these things the mirage which stopped me on the threshold had lost its force and only troubled me vaguely in my first steps with the priest who was to baptize us. Baptism immediately swept it away; I understood that the image of «Christians» which I had fashioned for myself during my years of unbelief was a myth,[1] and that it is they − to the extent at least that they know of what spirit they are, and show themselves faithful to it, and it is no doubt not the greatest number − who work in the most profound and the truest manner for the «temporal salvation of the world.»]

*

Beginning of 1906.   [From a Bergsonian essay presumptuously entitled «Preliminary Discourse on Intelligence and on Order;» and which came to a standstill, I retain these lines which show that under the mask of Bergsonian duration it was indeed the intuition of being which preoccupied me from that moment. (And I already related it to the *intelligence.*)]

As soon as leaving the surface he penetrates in depth − reality, living and substantial, astonishes him and takes possession of him.

---

1. A myth of bourgeois origin to tell the truth; for it only reflected the caricature of religion, as guarantee of the established order, which the practical atheism of the bourgeois world introduced for a time, in thousands of archetypes, into the reality of human history.

There everything is reciprocal compenetration and movement; yet not confusion. . . . The more he descends, the more he proceeds towards solitude, where his person is in its entirety — solitude full of echoes; and the more he proceeds also towards the intuition of a duration in which the instants do not follow one upon the other, which does not at all admit of separated instants, but which completely conserves itself in the powerful simplicity and the expansion of its inconceivable unity. He cannot express this or communicate it directly; but whoever, sufficiently endowed and exercised, will follow the same path, will arrive at the same point; and will feel, like him, that he is in the presence, not of an idea which seems true by its convenience, to be handled in discourse and explication, but of the real itself, which asserts itself royally, and makes itself known by its force, through which it enraptures the mind, and by its absolute nature, into which the most agile rapidities of thought hurl themselves in vain. He is like a swimmer who, having left the surface of the sea, plunges into the deep water, and who feels himself caught between powerful currents, irresistible and warm internal torrents, which ravish his body, all of whose agility — though swift as an ar-- row — cannot equal them in speed or break them apart. Thus in the violence of the intuition, duration takes possession of the intelligence.

Of this primary intuition he will retain, when he has returned to consciousness, only a primary truth, and he says: *I exist in an absolute manner*, that is to say, I perdure. . . .

*

10th of April.   Philosophers play with fire (poets also). Nothing is as comical as a course at the Sorbonne, in which an enervated professor expounds his historical views to some dunces, and discusses David Hume as peacefully as Plato. Does this seem dead to you? Fortunately, not the slightest spark flies! But just remember all that this has raised up!

*

Thurdsay evening, 19th of April.   Death of Curie, skull crushed by a truck. Brief notice in the *Temps*: «A pedestrian was run over
on rue Dauphine. Cards found on him bore the name of M. Curie.»
The imbeciles who laugh at Pascal and at his carriage accident! —
This means that the man of genius must be ready to die like every
man — as a poor person; that is to say that intelligence is NOTHING
before death. But no one believes it except the Christians.

*

11th of June, 1906, St. Barnabas.   Baptism of Jacques, Raissa
and Vera, in the Church of St. John the Evangelist (Montmartre).

CHAPTER TWO

OLD MEMORIES II: FROM AFTER BAPTISM

1906

Raissa and I arrive in Heidelberg the 27th of August, 1906. Settle in a house on Gaisbergstrasse the 30th of August.

*

Heidelberg, *27th of September, 1906.* Letter from our dear Vera, with good news. Her parents went to church (in Bures) and her father greeted the bishop. In whatever situation he finds himself, before the great of the earth or amidst the baskets of Les Halles (where he likes to go in the early morning for the family provisions) this simple, candid, and daring man is always in his place, full of ease and of nobility. He is now lord of Bures.

*

Heidelberg, *28th of October.* From an *Introduction to the Life of Raissa* [which I wished to write only for ourselves. – The Introduction alone was written, and I omit here an ideological jumble on «Woman,» unluckily modelled on Léon Bloy. But I wish to keep the pages about Raissa herself, because I now know, much better and more profoundly than before, how true they are.]

Goodness. Purity. Raissa always goes to the bitter end, with a direct intention and an upright will. Her courage is without calculation and her pity without defence. Where there is no beauty she suffocates and cannot live. She has always lived for truth, she has never resisted truth. She has never bent her mind, nor lied to her suffering. She always gives without retaining anything. For her heart, as for her understanding, it is the essential reality which matters; nothing accessory can cause her to hesitate. Her thought, her genius, tends always to intuition. As she is wholly interior, she is wholly free. Her reason can be content only with the real, her soul only with the absolute.

In her passion for concrete certitude, in her respect for Wisdom and her love for Justice, in her indomitable humor and her vigilance in dispute, as also in the ardor of her blood and the precision of her instinct, everywhere she bears with her the nobility and the privilege of the race from which she is born, of the elder Race, in which God confided and which contemplated His Angels, which, alone familiar with Heaven, alone depositary of the promise, is everywhere in its place on the earth, will perish only with the world, and which has a right to regard all peoples as guests late come into its patrimony, uncultured and without past, heirs of the Lord by adoption, not by birth. *Puella Hebraeorum!* Her native pride marches before her; I have heard Jews exclaim on the purity of her type. *Ecce vere Israelita, in quo dolus non est.* But do we know how deep the roots of a true Jew plunge? We know well that the true Jew is not the carnal Jew, eager for dispute, chained to the pride of the world; do we know well enough that the true Jew loves Poverty and loves Tears, is Pure of heart and Merciful, is hungry and thirsty for Justice and suffers persecution and death for Justice, unyieldingly? True lineage of Abraham, indomitable and faithful people, obedient and tenacious, harsh but against ordeal, which built the temple with sword in hand and which fell by thousands in order to defend it, men patient and charitable, women pious and strong, whose Hope watered the miraculous Stem, worthy finally that God, who did not shun the womb of a Virgin, did not shun either to fashion their descendants for Himself, and to choose them for fellow-citizens.

In her there is not only beauty, but that living spiritual light which is like a glance of God above beauty, and which we call grace, that grace which adds itself to beauty, said Plotinus,[1] and without which a beautiful face cannot attract the eye. Awe-inspiring and

1. *Enneads*, VI, 7, 22: Χάρις ἐπιθέουσα τῷ κάλλει.

magnificent gift, in which the primitive splendor of Eve is reflected, and which descends as a trial on a few women of this fallen world. And for her, as for all those women on whom grace was conferred, grace is not an exception which sets them apart from other women, but rather the very excellence and the mystical characteristic of their sex. There is no woman for whom anything is as desirable as grace, and is not every woman entitled to suppose herself gracious at some hour of her life?

It is this innocence of child grace, it is this perpetual effluence of the soul through the body which her great eyes magnificently proclaim.

Who will ever be able to express the freshness of her childhood, and the innocence which shines in her like the Milky Way in the depth of the sky? There is no innocence except supernatural innocence; and when this innocence perpetuates childhood through the whole of life, is it not the mark of the Spirit? — The ingenuous world of *Pifo*[1] always breaths around her; her gaiety is the companion of tears, her sadness is charitable and pure; and whether she is borne by poetry or by music, or whether she meditates on the Word of Truth, one always discerns in her that innocence which plays in the rays.

Who will measure her good will? Good will was given to her without measure, even in her taste for order and classical arrangement; in her frankness, in her pity, in her aversion for all complacencies and all worldly interests, in her goodness, in her confidence, which the Angels must see while trembling with compassion. . . . For good will makes us the brothers of the Angels.

Finally, she loves God, she has always loved God, even before knowing Him. It is because she loves God that evil horrifies her, and that there is for her no «truth of bad taste.» She loved truth with her whole heart; and suddenly she said to herself: «But the truth, there it is! Where would wisdom be, if it was not with Wisdom?» It is because she loves God that she gives with joy, and «God loves a cheerful giver.»[2] It is because she loves God that she «loves grandeur and that she loves the abandoned,» and it is for this that «passing near the abandoned, she will recognize grandeur, if grandeur is there.»[3] And because she loves God, she can rest only in Him!

1. Cf. further on, Chapter VI, p. 187.
2. Proverbs (22:9); St. Paul, II Corinthians (9:7).
3. Ernest Hello, *L'Homme.*

This vocation is that of humanity itself, I know; but those who are marked for the glory of God are not outside humanity, they are the very characteristic and the essence of humanity.

When you are afflicted, Raissa, remember my testimony.

And You, my God, Father of the poor, without Whom nothing exists, with Whom the humblest can do everything, in Whom all Grandeur resides, support her with Your strength, spread Your grace over her, *give her what you command, and command her what you will!*

*

Heidelberg, *12th of November*, St. Martin.   Today, or at least so we hope, for we are without news, little Eveline, our niece and goddaughter, will be baptized. This day will be devoted to prayer.

Letter from Bloy, announcing the death of the son of Termier, thirteen years old, crushed by an elevator.

15th of November.   Letter from Jeanne, confirming the baptism of Eveline.

Heidelberg, *25th of November.*   We ask God, although one can serve Him in every condition, to grant us the favor of bearing witness to His Name, and, if He wills to dispense us from misery, to help us embrace a state in which we may be in His grace, not in that of a godless world, and which keeps the simplicity, the purity and the poverty of the Gospel.

Heidelberg, *11th of December.*   Vera and her mother arrived this evening at half-past nine.

[From that time our little sister Vera always lived with us. The blessing of her presence was not withdrawn from us, until the day when, passing into the other life, this beloved presence became invisible and unimaginable, and when the corporeal absence broke, not the indomitable soul, but the physical forces of Raissa.]

Heidelberg, *27th of December.*   Saw Driesch. Welcoming, amiable, charming. He lends me many books. Seems to me very superior to the other German professors whom I have met, although he also seems to like «empirico-criticism» a little too much.

Heidelberg, *30th of December.*   Apropos of St. Paul, Gal. 4. — Thus, salvation is not only paradise opened. But it is also the liberation of the world, of this world in which we live, and this is why the stones and the animals, all which is and all which lives, rejoiced over the birth of the Savior. The children of the world await the liberation as a great feast. But this liberation, and this God who came to give man the enjoyment of the earth and kingship, is Bethlehem, is Jesus Christ. Who will understand this adorable transformation of man? It is wholly hidden. Only the humble know it. And we enjoy the earth and our liberty in hope, «we are saved in hope.» And how could it be otherwise? We enter by the Cross into the liberty of the sons of God. This way of feasting — *ecce homo vorax et potator vini* — is for the scandal of the proud and of the wise men of this world. Just as Incarnate Truth was also for their scandal — that Incarnate Truth Who gathered together all contradictions, whereas in their imbecility they believe that truth «will bring about agreement» between men. . . . This triumphant truth, as also this great rapture and this final outburst of free joy, no, it is not what they think! It will be, it can only be, Jesus in His glory, and the Spirit of fire, and the devouring flames of the Judgment, of Anger and of Love.

1907

Heidelberg, *13th of January, 1907.*   Raissa is ill.
[Terrible attack of amoebic enteritis.] Began novena in common to Our Lady of La Salette.

Heidelberg, *15th of January.*   Raissa is very ill. She wishes to receive the Anointing of the Sick.

Heidelberg, *16th of January.*   Extreme weakness. The doctor sees no hope except in an operation. No, not that! I go to see Chaplain Keck. He will hear Raissa's confession this evening at six o'clock, and will bring her Holy Communion and the Anointing of the Sick tomorrow.

Heidelberg, *Thursday, the 17th of January, 1907.*   Admirable day, which we shall always remember. The Anointing of the Sick is experienced by Raissa as a new baptism, she is suffused with grace and with peace. Ineffable grace of total abandonment to God and of the joy of suffering. Vera and I feel its victorious gushing forth; we are as it were enraptured in Paradise.

As for the body, the improvement is sudden and undeniable. The doctor is amazed. «Merkwurdig!»

Heidelberg, *18th of January.*   Letter of Raissa to my sister Jeanne:

«My sweet Nane, your letters have this beautiful privilege of bringing my soul nearer to our Savior. Today however your letter

36

found my heart so near to Him that it was exhausted with joy. — It is the state in which I have found myself since yesterday morning. In order to reassure you, I tell you immediately that my health is better. But these last days, feeling myself quite ill, I asked for the Anointing of the Sick. It was administered to me yesterday morning after Holy Communion. What to say to you, dear sister? My soul overflows with joy, with peace, with hope and with love. This has been like another baptism. My soul felt itself truly liberated from sin, wholly united with the will of God. Oh! how sweet the Lord is, His mercy is infinite. I no longer recognize my faith, it is no longer mine, it is that of the Heart of Jesus.[1] Oh, may Jesus keep me always with Him! O dear Jeanne, I am too weak to tell you everything I have learned this morning. But know only that the Lord never refuses and gives all the more as one asks Him more. I embrace you.

Raia»

Heidelberg, *20th of January.* For two days she lived in the continual rapture of the love of God. And all three of us were in the heart of Jesus, abandoning *everything* to Him and glad for everything which would please Him. Yesterday morning Raissa was like the sparrow on the roof, between Heaven and earth, in a kind of starry sadness at being thus suspended. «I suffer above myself,» she said, in seeing herself return to the world. And again: «I feel the weakness of the recovery, not of the illness.»

. . . . It is as if it was dead for an inappreciable instant, and that now purified and strengthened this soul has retaken possession of its temple and has re-erected it without effort. How she looked at us from afar, from the other side of the world! What beatitude in her eyes, what love and what detachment! Not only was her mouth unable to refrain from smiling constantly for two days, but her eyes seem transformed, even larger, with a more pacific light; chiefly it is the absence of all curiosity in the gaze, it no longer penetrates into objects, but settles gently on them, less in order to borrow light from them than to give it to them.

From a letter to Léon Bloy in which I relate what took place: «. . . . If God does not definitively cure Raissa, at least we are now

---

1. I did not know how to better express what I felt, and yet the Savior had *vision,* not faith.
   (Note of Riassa on the page of my diary where I had copied her letter.)

sure that this illness no longer threatens her life, and is only a trial for her patience; whereas before the Anointing of the Sick death seemed certain to her. . . . Today Raissa was able to kneel in her bed, to sit up, to speak loudly, which she had been unable to do for a long time.»

Heidelberg, *22nd of January.*   Raissa continues to improve. She tells me that before being so sick she had dreamt of seeing her dress covered with blood; and the same night, she believes, she awakened, still holding her neck as in her dream, as if suspended and gasping for a host held by two celestial hands.

During the anointings, she had only absolute happiness and perfect peace; she only prayed and told God her gratitude. Afterwards, she opened her eyes and looked at us, Vera and me, from far away, and only to show us that she was not dead. In this she understood in a sensible manner that beatitude is *gaudium de veritate* («joy in the truth» edit.).

Heidelberg, *14th of February.*   An event in relation to the preceding state of the world. There was in the preceding state *almost* all the reason for the present state. But that constitutes a limit. If there had been all the reason, then this event would have taken place at this moment. Simple remark which destroys mechanism and universal mathematics. In reality, something was lacking, which took place only at the moment of the introduction of this event and which is inseparable from it, because duration is living and because God always acts.

[I note these thoughts because they were in my mind like a teething ring of the doctrine of physical premotion, of which I was then completely ignorant.]

Heidelberg, *1st of March.*   I leave for Paris. (Mania Vilbou-chévitch wrote to us that Raissa's parents, extremely vexed by our conversion, sob all day.) I stay with them. Mania must have excited them. I succeed, not without difficulty, in appeasing them, in making it clear to them that their children have found happiness. Less luck with my mother.

The 3rd of March I have lunch at her place and tell her of our conversion; it is a catastrophe for her. Betrayal of all her hopes, and of her dream to see me carry on for Jules Favre. She answers me by her own history — she left the Church quite young (encouraged by her father), because she was scandalized by the questions of a priest in the confessional. Later, on a train, she met another bad priest, who made shameful remarks to her.

Paris, *5th of March.* Lunched with Péguy at my mother's. Overwhelmed with joy at what he tells me about himself (he has made the same journey as us). «The body of Christ is larger than one thinks.»

Back again in Heidelberg the 7th of March.

Heidelberg, *11th of March.* In reading the *Exercises* of St. Ignatius, Raissa was astonishingly moved by this passage of Baruch: *Howl, weak firs, for the cedars have fallen, the powers have been overturned.* These words awakened a great symphony at the bottom of her heart. During the hours which followed she was wholly absorbed in this dreamed of music. Yesterday, after fifteen or twenty days, she began to sing gently, and nothing was as touching as this plaint of the poor firs, exhaled fearfully by her pure and fresh voice.

Heidelberg, *25th of March.* All three of us make the Consecration to Mary recommended by Grignion de Montfort.

Heidelberg, *2nd of April.* Our dear godfather sends us as an «Easter egg» his chapter on *Paradise.*

Heidelberg, *11th of May.* Visit of Marix and his sister, who are going to Nauheim. Péguy told him of our conversion, he comes to show his friendship to us. This touches us a great deal. And he himself is seeking.

Our friendship grows with Chaplain Kech, our confessor (who always gives each of us the same exhortation, namely, to put up with the *Unannehmlichkeiten des Lebens* [«annoyances of life» edit.], this cliché becomes a refrain which amuses us very much).

Heidelberg, *6th of June.* Exceptionally important day for us. Raissa having gone to confession to Father Kollmann, he told her to receive Holy Communion every day. At the end of our retreat here, on the eve of our return to France, a new phase of our life is beginning.

Heidelberg, *8th of June.*   Letter from Jeanne, who hopes to receive Holy Communion soon. (There was *sanatio in radice* of her marriage.)

Heidelberg, *20th of June.*   Raissa takes me to the Castle, under the beautiful green trees, inexhaustibly green, whose shade is a paradise of freshness into which one plunges «like a good swimmer who abandons himself to the waves.» Joy of going out this way with my beloved friend, like two good spouses who go for a walk on a holiday among this crowd of dressed-in-their-Sunday-best bourgeois. My heart trembles to see Raissa so tender and so good, and to feel her innocent soul vibrate so to speak around her like these warm rays which make the air tremble.

Vera, ailing, remained at home. We never cease to admire her progress in endurance, in patience, and her marvelous devotion.

Heidelberg, *23rd of June.*   Last errands and last packages. Raissa drinks and eats straight from the pans, for want of plates and of glasses. We have caused her to make admirable progress in the paths of disorder and of domestic indifference. [Illusion: this progress did not last.]

Left Heidelberg the 24th of June. Basel. Geneva. Grenoble. The 26th we go from Grenoble to La Mure, then to Corps, then to La Salette. Astonishment.

La Salette, *Sunday, the 30th of June, 1907.*   Conversation with Abbé F., bursar. The name of Léon Bloy is mentioned. He wrinkles his brow. «Wait a bit! Have you seen him? Do you know him?» − «He is our godfather.» − «Really! How odd that is. He came here last year. I will tell you what I think: we took him at first to be a queer character. His first act was to insult the porter. And he has such a strange style, so peculiar. He gave us a book (*Le Salut par les Juifs*). M. Geray, who is a licentiate in Arts, a former teacher of rhetoric, and who must be an expert in it, couldn't get over it. At the outset he greatly astonished us and we judged him badly. But at the end of a few days we retraced our steps. He is a good Christian; his wife is very nice; we shall talk again about all this. It is very interesting.»

La Salette, *3rd of July.* Conversation with Abbé Noirey. He speaks of Mélanie with much respect, admires her sincerity and the preciseness of her recollections; when she came here (her last pilgrimage), each time one of those who accompanied her spoke in error, she corrected unfailingly and exactly.

Mélanie told Mlle des Brulais that after the Apparition she had «prayed much,» for a long time. . . . — And what did you say? — But nothing, I remained on my knees.

Mélanie writing on her desk: 1870, the Prussians. Her aversion for Napoleon, inexplicable except through a prophetic warning. With regard to the secret, Abbé Noirey does not at all display the hostility of Abbé F., he merely awaits the decision of Rome.

He tells us that Abbé Déléon submitted at the end of his life and resumed his life as a priest with humility; the first time that he said Mass again, the tomb of the altar collapsed. Abbé Noirey speaks of him with charity, saying only that he «was wrong-headed.»

Friday, the 5th of July, departure from La Salette. It is as if we were leaving the paradise and the house of our heart. I have noted here only the external circumstances, the rest will have to be written elsewhere than on paper.

Pierre Termier takes us by car from Saint-Georges de Commiers to Varces.

Saturday, the 6th of July, 1907. All three of us are confirmed at Grenoble, by Bishop Henry.

8th of July. Arrive in Paris. Raissa's parents are waiting for us at the station and «receive us in their arms.» We shall live with them, on the extension of the rue Jeanne d'Arc.

24th of August. Charged with a mission by Péguy, I arrive at the Isle of Wight, at the abbey of Appuldurcombe. Baillet. Dom Delatte. He says that Péguy must give everything, not wait. I am charged with a counter-mission, to tell him that he must have his children baptized.

(In Paris, *September, or October, 1907*):

From Raissa:

I am the guardian of a Kingdom which I do not see, but which I must defend, which I cannot find by myself but which I can lose; people enter and leave it without my will, but I have the power to close the door if I wish. If I keep the key I can open it again. But I can also throw away the key, and no longer find it again, and lose everything. It is indeed my kingdom, and I am responsible for all that happens in it, but nevertheless it does not belong to me. It is myself, and I belong to the great King. I am seated at the door; I do not *see* who enters and who leaves, but I must *distinguish* between those who present themselves, and let pass only him who should come. *Attollite portas principes vestras; elevamini, portae aeternales.* I am a very little point. My kingdom is behind me, at my back, I cannot turn my head. I see only the little point. A little point attached to an immense sun, a little point which guards this great sun and through which the sun can be penetrated. There is everything in my kingdom, the sun and the moon and the stars, and the animals and the plants – and the Saints! – since all this is in God and since God is in my soul. And all this is in my soul according to the reality of the divine essence, whereas in my senses and my intelligence, in what I see, this is disfigured. But what is in my soul, I do not see. I am seated at the door. When the King gives a great feast, only then the noise of it sometimes reaches me.

Second stay in Heidelberg. Raissa and I arrive there the 15th of October; 24, Blumenstrasse. Vera rejoins us the 17th.

Heidelberg, *20th of October, 1907.*   In November, 1906, at Heidelberg, Raissa wrote a melody for her on the *Veni Sancte Spiritus,* which she had never yet heard sung. Opening now the book of Gregorian chant which I have just bought, she plays the *Veni Sancte*; identity of the first measures (about ten).

Heidelberg, *8th of November.*   Our life is very monotonous on the outside, quite difficult to describe as regards the interior.

I believe we are learning many things these days. But how can one express them? It is the tissue of life. . . . It belongs to Our Lord, who leads us, to know how far we have got, it does not belong to us.

Here is the ordinary practice of our days. Rising at 6 o'clock. Mass and Holy Communion, at 7:15. We return, read a little while one of us prepares breakfast. Afterwards I set to work until 11:30. − Until 10 o'clock (the days when there is no market), Vera plays the harmonium or else reads; then prayer from 10 to 10:45. Afterwards, kitchen. − Until 10:45, Raissa mends, arranges, reads or works. Prayer from 10:45 to 11:30. Harmonium (or kitchen!). I pray from 11:30 to 12:15. − After lunch, Raissa and Vera rest a little, read or sew. When we can, we say a few psalms. Then work. Latin, German, diverse readings. Vera has the onus of reading a little history, and of giving us lectures. About 5 o'clock, all three of us go and pray before the Blessed Sacrament. We dine at 6:30 or 7, chat a little, tell each other the news of the day, the last conference of Father Faber or the last advice of Madame l'Abbesse (de Sainte-Cécile); we prepare the menu for the next day. − At 8 o'clock, Raissa and Vera are in bed. Compline. Rosary. They fall asleep. I go to the kitchen, by the light of a gas lamp, and I work a little more, in the peace of a father of a family who has put his children to bed. Then an hour of dogmatic reading. Bed at 11.

We devour the Lives of Saints (many are stupidly written, so edifying that they would have us believe that by our own forces we can copy the acts of the saints).

Invasion of Father Faber into our life. Raissa reads him with passion.

For prayer we follow the plan which Raissa made at Pontaubert, and which is ordered according to the liturgy.

Heidelberg, *19th of November.* My work in biology: Wasmann and Pauly. − Our books. Raissa: St. Francis de Sales, *Treatise on the Love of God*; Vera: Father Faber, *Bethlehem*; myself, Abbesse de Sainte-Cécile: *La Vie Spirituelle*, and the commentary of Denis the Carthusian on the fourth Gospel. All, *The Liturgical Year.* And, for prayer, St. Ignatius of Loyola. He seems to me less useful this year than last year. All these considerations are a hindrance. Better to have a single short text, a single verse, and to bring everything back to it while meditating.

Heidelberg, *23rd of November.*   The meditations on the first week of St. Ignatius are finished. Dear Vera has been terror-stricken by what he says about venial sin, particular judgment, etc. This book does not suit her at all. I advise her to take the Mother Abbess as a guide.

Heidelberg, *26th of November.*   On returning from church, Raissa sits down without saying anything; I question her; she answers me with difficulty that she «cannot speak,» that I am not to be frightened. She comes to the kitchen to eat; we want to force her to speak, she begins to cry, and returns to the room; lies down on the lounging chair, the crucifix in her hands, her eyes shut. At the end of a half-hour or three quarters of an hour she utters a few words, says that she was not able to *will* to speak.

She felt like this immediately after Holy Communion, she had time to recite the Magnificat, and to think: *In manus tuas, Domine, commendo spiritum meum*; then impossible to think or to say a single prayer, to make any voluntary movement: every effort in this direction seemed to tear her in two. She had much difficulty in returning home. She felt nothing particular, remaining as if empty. This is what she explains to us in the afternoon. In the morning, after having spoken a little, she had taken the Gospel and again became absorbed. She then had a very peaceful silent prayer, in which she understood the absolute gratuitousness of divine mercy, and that the *pardon* which God grants to us is a real *abandonment* of Himself, a *gift* of Himself to us. Today her eyes have an expression which recalls to mind the one which followed her Anointing of the Sick, and she feels a little in the same state.

Special examination concerning bad judgments about others. There is noticeable progress, but it is not brilliant. I have an average of seven a day; Raissa and Vera, of three or four. Those of Vera are of the aesthetic order, ours of the moralistic order.

Heidelberg, *27th of November.*   Raissa begins the morning feeling in the same state as yesterday. She struggles with all her might, and succeeds in keeping her will; but she remains a little vague the whole day, and again in the afternoon begins to become absorbed, while reading the *Imitation.*

Heidelberg, *28th of November.* Raissa's eyes continue to be strangely inattentive, or rather attentive to the interior; a beautiful gaze which settles on objects without penetrating them, and seems suspended. Her voice is clear and gentle, like that of a child, but one would say that it has a kind of imperceptible hesitation, which makes one think of the short instant of waiting in the flight of a bee, very near a flower, before settling on it. Everything seems insipid to her, she cannot formulate any precise prayer, but she feels affections as it were veiled, not lively nor violent, but more continually *present* than certain lively sentiments that one can have in prayer and which pass afterwards. A single thing moves her desire: to hear the *Imitation* or the Gospel read. I read her the Gospel of St. Luke. At certain moments she seems ready to weep, and yet says she experiences no pain; she is only sad at heart, wholly moved. — After this she emerges a little from her quiet absorption, and resumes the *Treatise on the Love of God.* She thinks, she tells me, that when Jesus said: «My Father, my Father, why have you abandoned me?» He was thinking of all the men who would be lost in spite of his Blood, and for whom the Pardon was of no use.

Heidelberg, *29th of November.* In the morning I go to see Driesch. Charming reception. He lends me Wigand, Radl, Friedmann. . . . We speak of Bergson, whose *Matter and Memory* has just been translated into German, and who is preparing, according to what a young Englishman told Driesch, a book on morality. Driesch will write a review of *Creative Evolution* soon.

Heidelberg, *31st of December.* Driesch pays a visit. I go out in the snow for a part of the afternoon, seeking a clue in all the confusions concerning science, the concept, intuition, etc.

[This meditation was to be continued in other solitary walks. Cf. the preface to the 2nd edition of *La Philosophie Bergsonienne* (English translation: *Bergsonian Philosophy and Thomism*, edit.).]

The Germans celebrate the 31st of December with loud pistol-shots.

1908

Heidelberg, *18th of January, 1908.*   Happy the poor in spirit. How can I be a philosopher, when all the happiness I desire is *poverty of spirit?*

I see that the world is fruitless and that death exists, and I act as if death did not exist. *I see death and I do not believe in death.*

But if I see, and do not believe what I see, I am sick or I am insane.

Heidelberg, *21st of January.*   Purchase of skates for Vera. First session on the Neckar. . . . Sunday we went for a walk on this amiable river, to the great joy of Raissa, walking on the back of this large serpent.

This same Sunday I resolved to abandon all «personal inquiry» in philosophy, all desire to know by myself, being sure to know everything essential and everything necessary by the Word of God, and trusting for the rest on the blessed night of faith. I am in the night, I know in an absolute manner what the Lord Himself has told me, and I will know also at such or such moment what it will please Him to show me for the refutation of error.

[At this time I thought that the essential task of philosophy was to refute error. I have made headway since, I have understood that refutation is only a secondary task, and one most often fruitless and useless (and which has so harmed Thomism). One must not refute, but «enlighten» and forge ahead.]

From the 25th of February to the 5th of March, sojourn in the Black Forest, at Rickenbach Amt Säckingen, where our friend Chaplain Kech is now parish priest. We stay with his two aunts, Hermine and Luise.

Back in Heidelberg the 6th of March. Raissa falls ill with an angina on Sunday the 15th (first Sunday of Lent). It is grave, a kind of diptheria. I fall ill in my turn (occasion to read Flavius Josephus and Émile Mâle). Cured by Dr. Ullrich and the Sisters of Niederbronn, to whom we are very grateful (Raissa becomes very attached to Sister Ingratia). Vera is marvellous, watches over everything, lavishes her attentions upon us in spite of a cruel facial neuralgia, then an influenza during which she refuses to go to bed (how could she?). Finally all three of us are ourselves again for Easter.

Since our arrival here, I do not think that three days in succession have passed in which the two sisters have been in good health at the same time.

And nevertheless the little caravan rolls along, and we do not have reason to complain. . . .

Some expressions of popular German. — I am lucky. Ich habe *Schwein*; It is all the same to me: Das ist mir ganz *Wurst*; To court: *poussieren*. When one speaks frankly, it comes from the liver (*von der Leber weg*); *Das Hauskreuz*, this is the nice way husbands refer to their wives.

*

We return to Paris the 4th of May.

Paris, *30th of May*.   I become acquainted at Saint-Sulpice with Abbé Deléage. He had noticed us, my sister Jeanne, Raissa and myself, at the Church of Saint-Marcel, the day of Jeanne's confirmation (the 27th of May).

[With much goodness he helped us for quite a long time with his advice.]

Paris, *5th of June.*   Exquisite evening at the Bloys', who now live rue Cortot, and whom we are going to ask for dinner.

They now have only three francs, but the peace and the fragrances of Paradise inhabit their house. Barbot, by dint of work, has finished printing *Celle qui pleure*; the book will appear soon with Mercure.

Paris, *10th of June.*   My beloved Raissa! I will know only in Paradise all I owe to her. Every good comes from God. But as earthly intermediary, *everything* has come to me through her, from her heart, from her reason, from her prayers, from her counsels, from her example, from her sufferings, from her virtues, from her love for God and from her tender love for miserable me.

This is what I wrote at Heidelberg the 19th of March, and I recopy it in Paris [and forty-six years later I recopy it in Princeton, because I have thought this all the days of my life].

Paris, *11th of June, 1908.*   Anniversary of our baptism. Afternoon and evening at the Bloys'. This studio, in which there is a high temperature of 25 or 30 degrees, is a place of incomparable refreshment for our souls. Léon Bloy, beautiful like an old lion full of furrows, reads us the pages of *L'Invendable* concerning Varces and La Salette. Raissa sings us her songs, she is happy to see that she can delight the hearts of those she loves. All are happy, encourage her. Jeanne Bloy, very grave, urges her not to let the gifts which are in her be lost. Our godfather removes the absurd scruples, the fear of the seductions of art, which troubled us in Germany. Let Raissa understand the value of what has been given to her, let her keep her soul in peace, let her devote herself to music.

[It was through melody and music that her vocation as poet first began to manifest itself in her.]

After dinner, reading of the *Fioretti*. They are at the end of their resources, without a penny. And what have we to help them? The microscope which I pawned, and for which I expected at least 50 francs, brought me only 20 francs.

Paris, *20th of July.*   We rent the apartment at 11, rue des Feuillantines. Agreed with Hachette (M. Desclosières) for the orthographical Lexicon *Tout en Un* (*Everything-in-One*). I shall receive 11 francs 50 per page, plus a third for «my assistant» (Vera), plus a third for the correction of the proofs. 350 pages at the most.

Our dear Absalom (Feinberg) tells us some heart-rending things concerning Mania. Misery of false moral grandeurs (and of psychological breakdown).

26th of July.   Lunched at the Péguys', in Lozère. There I meet Dr. Amieux.

[Beginning of a friendship which will be both confiding and stormy.]

5th of August.   All three of us go to Saint-Pierre-en-Port, where Mme Noël (ex-Mme Rousseau, if I remember well) who was my godmother when I was baptized at my birth (by a Protestant pastor) has rented a house for us, where we shall pass the vacation.

Saint-Pierre-en-Port, *14th of August.*   From Raissa:

It is the privilege of poor households to transform themselves joyously for the holidays; which is impossible for rich households, always ornate.

Death of Marix, during the last days of our vacation at Saint-Pierre.

Towards the end of August we return hastily from Saint-Pierre, Raissa's health becoming very bad.

*

Paris, *15th of October.*   We settle in rue des Feuillantines. Vera comes with us.

Raissa's parents are still closed to any word which would allude to Christianity, but they are more and more mild. Passion of Papka for the organ.

Relations with my mother have notably improved (thanks to the extraordinary patience and charity of Raissa). Nevertheless, she remains unalterably, unshakably attached to her ideas. Angèle lives with her, Baton is at Ville-Évrard, insane.

A few days before the beginning of Advent, we made the acquaintance of Father Clérissac, to whom we paid a visit in Versailles.

*

Paris, *25th of December.*   Christmas morning, invention of the «Knout» (this is what we call the one of us who, by turns, will give orders to the other two). The Knout governs, has a right to punish, to impose penances of his choice, and to require us at any moment to say whatever prayer or ejaculatory prayer he wishes. He serves the others, particularly at table.

[This rotation of authority was a most useful help for our little novitiate.]

1909

[It was in the first months of this year that Raissa began the reading of the *Summa Theologiae* (in the big Commentary of Father Pègues) and was overwhelmed with joy, with light and with love. Exultation of the intellect in an intuition once given forever, and which fulfills the desire of nature under the grace of the Holy Spirit.]

Paris, *20th of March, 1909.* Bloy comes to lunch at the house, and reads to us, for our joy, a great part of *Sang du Pauvre.*

22nd of March. Raissa has been bedridden for a month. Relapse of enteritis. She thus keeps her Lent by illness (once more). She is very weak, can hardly eat.

Two weeks ago, she composed, having the piano near her bed, a very sweet melody on the words of the Offertory of the twenty-first Sunday after Pentecost: «There was a man, in the land of Hus.»

Vera, since the month of February, following a successful interview with Dr. Walter, goes to the Hôpital de la Pitié three times a week, in the morning, to study as a nurse (department of surgery).

In the afternoon, she helps me prepare the orthographical lexicon.

I wrote an article on modern science, which Raissa copied, and which I shall present to *Correspondant.*

Raissa, before being interrupted by this illness, was not only plunged in the *Summa.* She read the life of St. Francis Xavier, that of St. Catherine of Genoa, the book in which Hello translated Ruysbroeck and Angela of Foligno; and above all she reads and cherishes St. Gertrude, who is our guide in the spiritual life.

22nd of April.   Concerning the beatification of Joan of Arc, we say to ourselves: It is the sign of an approaching war. God is giving France a protectress whom she will not invoke.

25th of April.   A few weeks ago Jeanne Bloy reminded Raissa, who had forgotten it, that at the time of her great illness, before our baptism, when Jeanne Bloy offered her a medal of the Blessed Vrigin, not only did Raissa accept it (while seeming vexed), but, thinking no one was watching, kissed it.

26th of April.   Suzanne Marx comes to see Raissa. Jean and Suzanne are, among our friends before Baptism, almost the *only ones* to come to see us. We believe that they have a secret sympathy for the faith.

Sunday, the 16th of May.   Last day of a triduum in honor of Joan of Arc, at Notre-Dame. We go to Vespers, Absalom accompanies us. Pitiful sermon.

Great health worries for Raissa and Vera.

10th of June.   Bloy lunches at the house, in honor of our baptism, whose anniversary is tomorrow. He is preparing a book on Napoleon.

In the evening, departure of Absalom for Darmstadt, then for Palestine. He accepts, before leaving, as a remembrance of me, a medal of Our Lady of Victories, and promises to keep it always. Scheduled to leave for Canada. Called home by the telegrams of his parents.

All this time Raissa and Vera are helping me with the Lexicon. Very anxious about what I will be able to do afterwards.

2nd of July.   I finally agree to begin the *Dictionary of Practical Life* next year; matter settled with Hachette (M. Desclosières). 500 francs per month; 2 1/2% after 1,5000 copies sold. 300 francs of gratuity if the dictionary is completed in four years. [The gratuity and the 2 1/2%'s were to evaporate because of my delays.]

We leave the 8th of July for Sainte-Mesme, where we pass the vacation, in the village inn, and where I work a great deal on the lexicon with Vera.

When we can, we go and sit on folding chairs near the church; peaceful and delicious place. Our readings: *Story of Sister Labouré, Life of St. Frances of Rome, Life of St. Catherine of Bologna; St. Mary Magdalen of Pazzi; Life of St. Lydwine; Dialogue of St. Catherine of Siena.*

Received *L'Invendable* at Sainte-Mesme.

Thurdsay, the 22nd of July.   Visit to Mme Baudouin and to Mme Péguy. Complete failure. Returned Friday morning, after spending the night on the rue de Rennes.

Sainte-Mesme, *28th of July.*   Why, asks Raissa, does one fast before the great feasts? Poenitentiam agite, *quoniam appropinquat regnum Dei* [Do penance, *because the kingdom of God is approaching*]. A feast is not of the earth, it is a gift from the Jerusalem of Heaven to the Church militant.

How we would like to have, not a director (what a strange word for people who believe in the Holy Spirit!), but a spiritual Father!

5th of August.   Lunched at my mother's, in Paris.

Saw Péguy before lunch. Conversation concerning my visit to Lozère, which the women had not mentioned. He promises me to see Mgr. Batiffol, asks only secrecy.

Sainte-Mesme, *14th of August.*   Stayed on the ground floor of 16 rue de l'Orangerie, in Versailles.

Sainte-Mesme, *16th of August.*   The Bloys come to settle in the Village.

Sainte-Mesme, *17th of August.*   From Raissa:

Like the Holy Spirit, humility can have as its symbols the dove and the tongues of fire. It makes our heart its home, it makes the simplicity and the sweetness of the Dove rise towards God. It tends upward, it causes the fire of divine love to descend. Humility is an image of the Purity of God in the soul. There is no crease in the divine Essence, it is entirely one and simple. Likewise the humble soul avoids all the creases that self love, by a return upon itself, would produce in it. It is in this sense of an absolute purity and of a simplicity of intention that one can speak of Humility as a divine attribute. This is why the Heart of Jesus is divinely gentle and humble.

Humility is not a virtue born of the fall of man. It is fundamentally different from humiliation. And it is better to acquire it by considering the purity of the divine Essence rather than our sins.

Sainte-Mesme, *22nd of August.*   Bloy tells us how deprived he is of all joy, without consolation and without refreshment, like a man continually under the knife, and not being able to pray, even after Holy Communion, except by saying: Our Lady of Compassion, have pity on me, I am exhausted.

Sainte-Mesme, *25th of August.*   From Raissa:

Man is like a ship laden with all kinds of treasures, which advances on a stormy sea. With the tempest pressing on all sides, we have to throw overboard what we can: and first we jettison our sins. But this is not sufficient: we have to throw overboard our preferences, and the conveniences of life, and a certain, even licit, use of creatures, finally, ourselves. All of these (except our sins, which are counterfeit goods) are true treasures, but we have to get rid of them, for our heart is too weak and too narrow to contain at the same time the love of God and of our neighbor and the care of ourselves. But whereas all these treasures are lost in the sea, all we throw into God He keeps and will return magnificently to us.

[How deep this image of the ship must have been in her! I think of this perfect poem, *Transfiguration,* written many years later:

> . . . . Like a fortunate ship
> Which returns to port with its cargo intact
> I shall approach Heaven with my heart transfigured
> Bearing human and stainless offerings.]

Sainte-Mesme, *30th of August.*   Yesterday, Vera told us that in spite of the admiration which she felt for St. Francis de Sales and for the Visitation, she nevertheless experienced, in reading the biography of St. Chantal, no attraction to the life of the Nuns of the Visitation; on the contrary, much attraction to the life of the Sisters of St. Vincent de Paul.

Sainte-Mesme, *31st of August.* After dinner we go to see the Bloys. After his book on Napoleon, Bloy would like to write a book on exegesis. Noted what he told us concerning the reading of the Holy Books, and apropos of the Parables in particular:

Our Lord, he says, is not a *fabulist.* Each of his parables is a truth with an absolute and infinite bearing, which is valid under all aspects, dogmatic, historical, anagogical, etc., and which, visible in a succession of diverse events since the origin of the world, traverses the whole of history like a torrent of fire. Bloy says that the parables of Our Lord are all literally true, that the Prodigal Son, the poor woman who gives her alms at the Temple, all the other persons who are mentioned in the parables are historical personages, who really did the things which Christ relates.

But these parables, like all the events related in the Holy Books, are true in many other senses, and higher ones. Everything is symbolic in Scripture. And God always speaks of Himself. The moral sense, in which the Fathers delighted, is insufficient, however useful it may be for personal sanctification. It is the *theological* sense which is the true one, and which gives glorious lights to the soul. *Ego sum Via, Veritas et Vita* [I am the Way, the Truth and the Life]. Each time that you come across the word *via* in Scripture, read *Jesus Christ.* . . . All the fathers mentioned in the sacred text can signify only the Father, all the sons can signify only the Son, all the women can signify only Mary. Gospel of the lunatic. This lunatic, Bloy tells us, is Jesus, son of the Father, and son of Mary (who has her feet on the moon). He falls now into fire (on the side of the Holy Spirit), now into water (on the side of the Father). He is cured and the demon is expelled from him. Just as Jesus by his death cured all his members, and delivered them from sin — which he had assumed, *factus est peccatum pro nobis* [He became sin for our sake]. . . .

Sunday, Bloy spoke to us of Herod (Luke 23:8). *Herodes autem viso Jesu, gavisus est valde. Erat enim cupiens ex multo tempore videre eum, eo quod audierat multa de eo, et sperabat signum aliquod videre ab eo fieri* [When Herod saw Jesus he was very glad. For he had desired to see him for a long time because he had heard many things about him, and he hoped to see some sign done by him]. These words apply textually to the waiting of the Patriarchs! To such a degree is everything figurative.

Sainte-Mesme, *2nd of September.*   In the evening we return to Paris; stay with Raissa's parents.

Paris, *8th of September,* Nativity of Mary.   I like to think of Raissa's birthday as today. She was born about this date [on the 31st of August in the Russian calendar, which corresponds to our 12th of September, the Feast of the Holy Name of Mary] on a Saturday, on the day called *Erste Schlichess*, the first day, always falling on a Sabbath, of the prayers the Jewish people make in preparation for the New Year.

10th of September.   The system of the «Knout» is functioning quite well, at the moment, as to obedience. It is fitting to ask the Knout for permission for everything. Raissa's parents delight in this exercise. We decide to replace the name Knout by that of *Captain* from now on.

11th of September.   Strange idle remarks of Raissa's father: «Who is a little girl of three to four years, knowing French, Russian, German, married five years?» He is thinking of Raissa, he understands without realizing it that life must be reckoned from baptism.

12th of September.   Last Sunday, Raissa said to me apropos of St. Mary Magdalen of Pazzi: «I too want to detach myself from myself, without this there will be no joy for me.» This is as it were a sign of our vocation. It is necessary for us to be like religious of a certain special Order, having in their rule to live in the world. It is necessary to deceive the world so to speak, by seeming to lead the life of the world. How difficult, then, not to be secularized monks, rather than «regular» laymen, or rather laymen given to God. We feel that what we say here is important for us.

15th of September.   End of the Lexicon.

21st of September. Saw Father Clérissac at Saint-Philippe-du-Roule. He tells me that we must not hesitate to follow the way of contemplation in the world.

26th of September. Vera eagerly reads the *Manuel des Infirmières*, of Dr. Vincent.

Paris, *17th of October.* Moved out of rue des Feuillantines. We move into a house in Versailles the next day. Very laborious move, which lasts three weeks. Every morning I go to serve the Mass of Father Clérissac. Precious conversations after Mass.

Versailles, *end of October.* Long conversations of Father Clérissac with the three of us. Shun the reflex spirit. Without charity there are truths which the mind is powerless to attain. Beauty of obedience, even when the order given is stupid; invisible fruit: agreement with the intentions of Providence; this is why the instinct of faith makes obedience superabound, even when it is not dogmatically required. Leo XIII was disobeyed when he advised rallying to the Republic; and however inopportune this advice may have seemed, who knows what would have happened if he had been listened to?

Versailles, *28th of October.* Learned of the death of Baton. The doctors have enormous worries concerning the health of Vera. Formerly she suffered from tuberculosis. I think that God cured her at baptism, He is stronger than the doctors.

6th of November. I accompany Vera to Beaujon, where she is examined. The lung is completely healed. No active microbes in the knee.

8th of November. Bloy brings Brou, who, it seems, has gathered in the course of his life a long experience of nature and of sickness, and who comes to give his attentions to Raissa. [He will remain for weeks, with much gentleness and affection. A great deal of good advice regarding diet.]

17th of November. Ernest Psichari comes to lunch. No obstacle to grace, inclined towards faith. Péguy told him, as he told my mother, that he had sent me to the Ile of Wight in order that I might get in touch with Catholics of better quality than Léon Bloy. Sad double play. Ernest takes *The Sorrowful Passion* [by Emmerich, edit.], accepts a «miraculous medal» when leaving.

19th of November.   We receive *Le Sang du Pauvre*, inscribed by our godfather.

30th of November.   I receive *The Philosophy of the Organism* from Driesch.

2nd of December.   Jeanne Bloy tells me that at Sacré-Coeur the adoring religious Sisters recite litanies before the Blessed Sacrament in which they say: «Because of your humiliations, because of your sufferings . . . *we console you, Lord.*» Come, everything is for the better, and we are indeed reassured.

12th of December.   Visit of Rouault and of his friend Lehmann. Long conversation concerning art, apropos of the preface that I am to write for his Exposition. To what point it is true that the precept of St. Paul, *Nolite conformari huic saeculo* [Do not conform to this world], is literally true for art. I greatly admire Rouault's force and genius.

14th of December.   All three of us go to see Father Clérissac. He tells us his preference for the great intellectual and contemplative saints, rather than for the affective saints, like St. Francis of Assisi.
Joinville, prisoner of the Saracens, and on the point of being put to death. «I inclined my neck, and I thought: this is the way St. Agnes died. . . .»

17th of December.   Visit of Father Clérissac after lunch. Long talk afterwards with Raissa. She regrets not having a good old Father who would guide her in understanding her heart. I remember that before visiting Father Clérissac, last year, she had dreamt that believing she was going to see an old hermit, whose wrinkles showed his long and paternal experience, she suddenly found herself — and with what surprise! — in the presence of a beautiful young girl, of a vestal virgin. We understand that God wanted above all to give us very perfect intellectual guidance.

Worked at my preface to the catalogue of the exposition which Rouault is going to give in January or February.

22nd of December.　　At the hospital, this morning, there were two patients who told Vera that they preferred to have their wounds dressed by her.

Christmas.　　Three Masses at Father Clérissac's. Raissa and Vera arrive in the middle of the second Mass. All three of us receive Holy Communion at the third. Breakfast at the Father's, who lends us various songs. Mass at the Cathedral at 11:30. Father comes to dine with us. After dinner he sings us a poem composed by Newman after his conversion. Raissa sings him some of her songs.

29th of December.　　I go to the Bloys'. Bloy reads me the preface which he has written for the poems of Jeanne Termier which he admires very much («Derniers Refuges»); he says that she has an extraordinary and magnificent feeling for the *suffering of the world.*

30th of December.　　Baillet sends us the commentary of Father Abbot on the words of St. Paul: *Gaudete in Domino semper,* etc. [Rejoice in the Lord, always.]

31st of December.　　After dinner, we sing hymn upon hymn, endlessly.

1910

Versailles, *7th of February, 1910.* Father Clérissac tells us how he was seeking with Father Abbott (Dom Delatte), and also with Father MacNabb, what could be, in spite of the poverty of human words, the equivalent of sadness in God. He thinks that it is the necessity — blissful in a sense, but all the same a necessity of nature — of creating only the limited; that which God produces which is unlimited is Himself, in the bosom of the trinitarian life, but every creature is necessarily limited, and therefore naturally subject to evil.

[Father Clérissac thought that the Incarnation is like a remedy for the sadness of God. At the same time that it redeemed sin, it rectified, infinitized the created (hypostatic union, beatific vision).]

He asks Raissa: Are you ready to do anything if you are sure that it is the will of God? — Yes, replies Raissa. — Well, that is all that is necessary.

9th of February, Ash-Wednesday. Father Clérissac tells Raissa that he has given and consecrated us to God as St. Benedict and St. Scholastica, that we belong absolutely to God.

10th of February. I do not know what idiot wrote to my mother that he had just read a book of M. Bloy in which there is a reference to Jacques Maritain, — «Tell me that it is not your son, the grandson of Jules Favre!» Another wrote to her beseeching her not to read *L'Invendable* before a year, it would cause her too much pain. Naturally, she hastened to read it. All tempests are unleashed, lamentations, reproaches, bitter accusations.

12th of February. Decision to make a little «chapter» each day, in the manner of the monks; each one in turn will be charged with making a short exhortation. Raissa begins, she speaks to us of the gentleness to be maintained between us. Poor captain (I have been kept in this office for several weeks), I very much need to gain in gentleness.

[I never cured myself of impatience. And if it were a question only of that! But in my frenzy of work what a hard life I made for the two beings whom I loved more than myself. As to others, they mattered to me at that time much less than ideas. Mad person for whom there existed only the world of truth and of falsehood. It took me time to discover men.]

17th of February. I have the very clear impression, in reading the Mother Abbess, that Raissa will never have happiness except in establishing herself in the state of contemplative souls, and in making prayer the permanent foundation of her life.

1st of March. Visit to Bergson. He speaks to me, smiling, of the book of his friend Lévy-Bruhl, which tends to establish that metaphysicians are retarded primitives. He has much esteem for Driesch. Evolutionism in biology is undemonstrable; but the *onus probandi* is incumbent on its adversaries, because it is a more economical hypothesis. It was on this ground that he accepted it in *Creative Evolution*.

He feels no repugnance for the idea of a creation (*ex nihilo*), and nothing opposes attaching his views to it. At the origin of the *élan vital* there is something superior, yes, this is true, something rational if you will, understanding by this *more* than our logic, an intuitive reason in the sense of Plotinus.

But how are we to understand that Being is unchangeable? The immutability of God is an idea of the ancient philosophers, a Greek prejudice. Who says life, says change. (I reply: it is because one thinks of the immobility of a stone. The divine unchangeableness is supreme life. The mystery of the Trinity reveals to us a life in God higher than anything the conceptions of the philosophers can attain.)

Even in taking evolution for granted in the kingdom of nature, there is, Bergson admits, an abyss between animals and man. It is

liberty which constitutes this abyss. In this sense, there is something which comes θύραθεν, [from outside] as Aristotle says. Nature
tries to assemble mechanisms rendering liberty possible, but only
the brain of man succeeds in rendering it possible.

He complains of the English and German translations of his
books. Only the author could translate his works, because it is a
question of rendering the entire body of thought.

14th of March.   Trogan rejects and returns my article. I am
hardly surprised to have been judged unworthy of *Correspondant.*
[This article on «La Science moderne et la Raison» will appear in
June in *Revue de Philosophie.*]

29th of March (Easter Tuesday).   Léon Bloy comes to see us.
«There are no sinners in Hell,» he tells us, «for sinners were the
friends of Jesus. There are only the *wicked.*»

30th of March.   The Dictionary overburdens me. I am enraged
at not having the time to study theology. But actually I am afraid
of it. I am ensnared in my ratiocinations.

13th of April.   I read the beginning of my article to Father
Clérissac. He quickly managed to pulverize my little production,
and my half-Kantian, half-Bergsonian vocabulary, on the intelligence
(so-called wholly constructive) and reason (considered as superior
and intuitive). I see clearly that I erred, because of my ignorance
of Scholasticism.

15th of April.   I took a new tack, having understood how
shameful it is to use the word «intelligence» in the sense in which
the moderns do. I bring my recantation to Father. He is satisfied
with my corrected article.

20th of April.   Father laughs a great deal at the horrified
feelings awakened in me by the photographs of our bishops I saw
yesterday at the Curé's.

Raissa continues to read St. Thomas with the same winged joy.
She also does an entire work on Bergson for me [from which I
greatly profited in my articles, and later in my book. If I had been
less *grob,* this book should have appeared under our two names.

And Raissa would doubtless have deterred me from many of those violences which I was to regret afterwards.]

24th of April. The Rouaults come to lunch with their little Geneviève.

About Rouault: Talent without knowledge can produce beautiful works. But as soon as knowledge begins it is necessary to persist, to push it to the last degree, in order to rediscover the liberty of inspiration. Otherwise, no mastery, one is crushed. After the forced rest caused by his exposition, he would like now to resume his work with a new spirit, to seek both a blond and transparent painting and constructions after the manner of Poussin.

30th of April, St. Catherine of Sienna. From the capitulum on Nones (in the Dominican rite): *Brevis in volatilibus est apis, et initium dulcoris habet fructus illius* [The bee is brief in flight, and its fruit is sweet]. Father entrusts me with bringing these lines to Raissa on his behalf.

15th of May, Pentecost. Raissa tells me that for her the sky seems to be a symbol of the Father; the earth, on which everything is founded, an image of the Son; and trees, which receive everything from the dew of the sky and from the essence of the earth, a symbol of the Holy Spirit; and that the idea of that which is most alien to the world − peace, unction, silence, sweetness, perfectly pure love, purity, innocence, liberty in light − is what helps one most in thinking of this divine Spirit.

20th of May. From a letter of Raissa to Father Clérissac: «. . . O my Father, how good God is! To think that He is more present to me than the things that I see. To think that I have a true thirst only for Him, and this desire is like a flower among stones, for I myself am vain and without courage. I only hope that the good God will cause this vanity to drop off like a garment; that He will give me His strength, and that He will re-establish order in me by His Love.»

3rd of June. Visit to Father with Raissa. He speaks to us of Lacordaire, who was a big child, a great, sensitive romantic, but candid; intense desire for corporal mortifications, desire to *feel* that one has conquered nature, covetousness, etc. It is just the opposite with the saints, whose penance is «to bear with each other.» St. Philip Neri: My God, help me, without this I am capable of becoming a Mohammedan. . . .

Father tells me not to be too «nice,» too easy-going and childish with people.

14th of July.   From Father Clérissac:
La Salette is a recall to integral Christianity, to the faith of the first centuries. Redemption is not a joke, the life of the Christian is a crucified life, priests who do not desire sanctity are cesspools of impurity. But who can understand this, except a *pusillus grex* [flock of little onesṛ? Thus the patience of God is explained. With others, He seems to content Himself with a minimum, and what a minimum! – to treat them like the smoking wick and the bruised reed.

29th of July.   In chapter, Raissa tells us that when one wishes to detach oneself from someone, one begins by leaving him, jouneying far from him; little by little one becomes indifferent to him. One does not begin by being indifferent, one journeys first. This applies to ourselves. We must begin by journeying far from ourselves, doing our daily tasks, making a start on the various things God asks. After this, but only after, we will begin to be detached from ourselves.

31st of July.   From Raissa: «In all things, to always give the important time to God.»

6th of August.   From Bloy: «The *veil* is passing from the Jews to the Christians.»

26th of August.   Vera goes to Paris; tomorrow she will accompany the Bloys to Binic for a two weeks vacation.
Our little sister feels herself more and more clearly «unsuited for the world.»

9th of September.   Letter from Bloy, imploring that Vera remain another week at Binic with them. – Of course; how can one resist him!

15th of September.   Finally! Thanks to Raissa, I begin to read the *Summa Theologiae*. As it was for her, it is a deliverance, an inundation of light. The intellect finds its home.

17th of September.   Raissa tells Father Clérissac that when her half-hour of prayer is finished, she cannot apply herself to anything, is for some time unable to read or to speak; once or twice this state continued the whole day. Father replies that it is absolutely necessary to reject this interior absorption and to struggle against it (except during the time reserved for prayer), and as soon as this time is finished to adapt oneself to one's ordinary occupations.

[Example of a certain lack of comprehension, from which Raissa suffered a great deal. In his aversion for the «reflex spirit» Father Clérissac precipitated matters, and did not recognize authentic demands of her spiritual life. After the death of Father, she prayed to him, in days of great interior trials, to come to her aid and to rectify this. A little later we met Father Dehau who, thanks to God, became our guide and liberated her. She found peace and took her flight as soon as she gave to silent prayer all the time that God asked.]

21st of September.   Every human act is a judgment passed on the divine nature.

23rd of September.   Mass at 7 o'clock at Father's. Today is the 22nd anniversary of his first Mass (1888).

5th of October.   Idiotizing influence of the theory of grouping. Watchword of the hierarchy in France (our dear Bishop Mgr. Gibier): «Let us group!» — Let us group souls, dogs, pigs! Let us group the dead! Let us group Christian owners! — «Union gives strength!» This motto can have only one meaning for a Christian: union *with God* gives strength.

25th of October.   Sent an article to *L'Univers*, in response to an article in *Débats* (on the decree concerning First Holy Communion) which Father showed me and which made my blood boil. It was Father Clérissac who launched me in this career of polemist.

My article on Neo-Vitalism in Germany has appeared in *Revue de Philosophie*.

29th of October.   It is always by an *impression* overwhelming reason that the devil seeks to entice the mind into error. Sentimentality of the atheists.

8th of November.   Father tells us that his Prior is recalling him to Angers, without delay, as early as December. Terrible blow for us.

14th of November.   Tragi-comedy of Noisiel. I go there with Bloy to see Amieux, who wrote to me yesterday: «Jacques, come with Bloy tomorrow afternoon. Leave everything in order to come» — and who convened seven pastors to confer with us before his baptism, which will take place tomorrow at the D.'s', in Breuil. Bloy, learning of this convocation, brandishes his cane and declares that it is the only suitable argument. Amieux becomes panic-stricken and locks us up in his study. [All of this will be related by Bloy in *Le Pèlerin de l'Absolu.*]

17th of November.   The cursed fig-tree. It was not the season for figs! No doubt; but when God approached it and asked it to refresh his thirst, it should have put forth a fruit (not it to be sure, poor vegetable, but the soul of which it was the symbol, and which can respond to grace). Nature, even if it is not defective in its own order, if it remains only nature when grace is at the door and wishes to transform it, withers, just as, figuratively, the cursed fig-tree withered.

From Raissa, apropos of the sin of the Angels, which is a sin of naturalism: Since nature, even the best, is in itself entirely different from the life of grace, and since the divine world of grace is truly for it *another world*, it is therefore a rigorously necessary truth that it is necessary *to die* first in order to live with the life of this other world; and that if we do not leave father, mother, spouse, etc., for Christ, we are not ready to follow Him. It is necessary that, at least at the hour of death, there be a voluntary sacrifice of nature.

18th of November.   Thought of Father Clérissac, reported by Father Baillet: The Benedictines also have a *folly* — the folly of confidence in God.

27th of November.   Journey to Breuil to the D.'s', persuaded on the word of Amieux that they are ready to aid Bloy magnificently. Total refusal, I meet upon the worst and the most glacial «Catholic» bourgeoisie. [Story also related by Bloy in his journal.]

Apropos of the absurd «religious science» of the D.'s,' supposedly founded on Le Play, I note: An authentic philosophy of history must be based on theology. As Raissa recently said to me, God alone can write history.

10th of December.   Raissa thinks a great deal about the conduct of Abraham with regard to Sarah, of the artifice of Rebecca and of Jacob. Scripture is not a code of morality; the supernatural flows in it fully, and nature also. Abraham was justified by his faith. Admirable candor of Abraham in all his actions. Prophetic spirit of Rebecca. . . .

[Thus began from this time the reflections which later, at the cost of great interior sufferings and in the light of prayer, were to give birth to *Histoire d'Abraham* (English translation: *Abraham and the Ascent of Conscience*).]

12th of December.   Letter from M. de Gaulle, proposing that I succeed him next year in the course of Philosophy at St. Geneviève School.

[I find in my notes that I went to see M. de Gaulle in Paris, the 20th of December. I have, unfortunately, no memory of this interview with the Father of General de Gaulle. And I did not note why I did not follow up his proposal.]

17th of December.   We assist at the Mass of Father Clérissac, at his place, Boulevard de la Reine, the last which he celebrates in this room, where I have served his Mass almost every morning for a year. Near us, in Versailles, he unceasingly nourished us with the treasures of his intelligence and of his heart. We are going to become orphans. (And we are as yet only little fish, as he enjoys saying.)

Inexpressible grandeur of this Mass, in which with his whole soul he gives himself and gives us. All three of us receive Holy Communion.

He leaves this same day for Angers.

22nd of December.   Went to Father's to get a chasuble. The doorkeeper tells me that a telegram arrived the 19th, in the evening, for Father Clérissac, telling that his brother is dying. The doorkeeper forwarded the telegram.

25th of December.   Raissa was able to go with me to Midnight Mass at the Cathedral; she is very happy about this achievement. (Vera, in pain, was able to go only to a morning Mass). — Letter from Father, who is in great melancholy. He found his brother dead, his mother shocked with grief. He alone remains of all his brothers. He says that with this death and his departure for Angers a new phase in his life begins. We understand that he wishes to prepare himself for death. May God preserve him for us.

[I think of the four and a half years passed since our baptism; of that kind of long novitiate, in which our little community took shape on a kind of monastic base — as not being of the world, in the world — and of the desire to advance towards the perfection of charity; of the privilege that our two years of seclusion in Heidelberg were for us — of the invention at Versailles of the daily «chapter» we held, following the invention of the «Knout» or «Captain» whose weekly functions (to give spiritual instruction and to assign tasks) were exercised by each in turn — of the discovery of the *Summa Theologiae* — of the teachings of Father Clérissac, that great master in the illuminative life. (Later will come those of Father Dehau, that great master of the unitive life).

It is a well-known fact that the most profound and the most lasting — definitive— impressions are those of the years during which the child accomplishes this prodigious task: to conquer the visible world. It is the same for the years of spiritual childhood which follow conversion, when the intelligence throws itself on the world of divine truth. For six or seven years we *devoured* the lives of the saints, books of spirituality and the works of the mystics.]

1911

Versailles, *9th of January, 1911.*   Raissa has undertaken to correct the proofs of the orthographical lexicon for me. Thankless task which she does with her whole heart, and which takes much of her time.

8th of February.   Vera buys, for 105 francs, a statue of Our Lady of La Salette (in terra-cotta, very beautiful, must have been made a short time after the Apparition) which Father Clérissac had discovered at an antiquary's (the latter claimed that it was from the fifteenth century and asked a great deal of money for it). The next day we install this statue in our little oratory, decorated and transformed by Raissa.

13th of February.   [In rereading some years later the diatribes in which I engaged in this notebook against the modern apostolate, modern Catholics, the consoling religious «manifestations» which the Religious Week at Versailles encourages, the degradation of Christian thought, etc., I wrote in the margin of a note dated February 13:] What fatuity in my zeal!

18th of February.   Letter from Jeanne Bloy, announcing that they have rented a house at Bourg-la-Reine.

22nd of February.   At the Bloys' (who are still in Paris) we make the acquaintance of Pierre and Christine van der Meer, and of their son Pierre, six years old. The two Pierres will be baptized the day after tomorrow. (Christine, baptized in her childhood, lost the faith, finds it again with them). Generous souls, open, in love with grandeur. Spring-like fragrances of baptism.

24th of February, St. Mathias.   Raissa suffers greatly from sciatica. I go to Paris alone, to be present at the baptism of Pierre-Mathias and of Pierre-Léon, at the Church of St. Médard. The little one is radiant with joy, holds his candle firmly, answers *yes* with a flabbergasting vigor.

30th of March.   Raissa's father and mother come to live in Versailles, rue Satory.
     Father Padé gives sermons at the Cathedral which Raissa and Vera greatly admire. He becomes a friend for Vera.

20th of April (Easter Thursday).   At the Bloys. He speaks of Holy Scripture. He recommends to Pierre van der Meer that he note in the Gospel all the names which are applied to Our Lord, and, once this list has been made, to read *Jesus* each time he comes across one of these names in Scripture. I ask him, apropos of the symbolism in *Le Sang du Pauvre*, in what text the name «Money» is thus applied to Christ? He answers me by Psalm 11: «Eloquia Domini, eloquia casta: *argentum* igne examinatum.» [«The words of the Lord are pure words: like *silver* tried by fire.]

     Spoke of my thoughts on the Jews. Just as their aberration was the salvation of the nations, will not the defection of the nations be the resurrection of Israel? Thus, we would complete the Passion of the Lord, and would suffer for them, until everything is consummated.

24th of April.   From little Pierre van der Meer (he is six, he wants to become a priest): «If you love Jesus Christ, it is necessary to suffer, it is necessary to go into the cage.»
     He said to Raissa's mother («Madame Kokoff»): «People think that I am playing, but I pray all the time — above all for 'the poor disobedient ones'.»

4th of May.   Returned *L'Ordination* of Benda to Bourgeois, with this note: «My dear Bourgeois, enclosed herewith *L'Ordination* of M. Benda. Please spare me henceforth the little blasphemies of this jester. Cordially, J.M.»

[Péguy said later that I had withdrawn my subscription to the *Cahiers*. Not at all; it was a question only of Benda, and of this book.]

6th of May.   Saw Rouault at the Moreau Museum. This man has a gift which none of the others possess, a frankness before reality and an *immediate awareness* of things which nothing can replace. He reads me something very beautiful which he has written on Ingres. How, with so much freshness of impression, and so much penetration of spirit, could he be blinded in his art? No, his obstinacy will get the better of his friends. He shows me astonishing sketches, repulsive at first and which one cannot help admiring. After all, the sole criterion of the work of art is the authority with which it imposes itself, whether it pleases or not, and which depends only on the depth to which the artist has been able to descend, in his rigorously solitary exploration of the sensible world. The greater an artist is, the more he chooses, the more he admits. But also, the more that he has seen and loved *will impose itself* by force as more *real*. . . . But in order that the soul be bent by force, so to speak, before his work, it is necessary that he surrender instinctively, like a brute, to the frankness of sensibility; and this is what is lacking in Gustave Moreau. Rouault reminds one of Bernard Palissy, but with how much more extraordinary a depth.

10th of May.   Father Abbott Dom Jean de Puniet comes to sees us, saying that we are a very little branch to Saint-Paul d'Oosterhout, and that St. Benedict loves all that is little. «It is not necessary to want to do anything outside of your life; your life is your work.» [Today begins our year of novitiate in order to be received as oblates of the abbey of Oosterhout.]

11th of May.   Abbé Serol (*Revue de Philosophie*) asks me for an article on the evolutionism of Bergson, for September.

14th of May.   Bloy asks himself in *Celle qui pleure* why the «apparent failure of the Redemption.»

The answer is very simple. The Redemption, fully, wholly, absolutely, perfectly succeeded, so as to satisfy God and men eternally. This perfect success of the Redemption is the Virgin Mary.

This is why she was, so to speak, necessary to God. It was necessary that the Blood of her Son not be fruitless. After this everything can come, all the crimes, the betrayals, the abominations. The Redemption succeeded once and for all and right away.

This is also why the Virgin Mary is infinitely merciful.

Vera discovers in *Le Vieux de la Montagne* (p. 295) a passage which alarms us, and in which Bloy speaks of our niece Eveline and of the antireligious feelings of her father in such poorly veiled terms that Charles Garnier will surely recognize himself in the «university pedant» stigmatized in these pages. Wrote to Bloy, but the evil is done.

31st of May.   First Communion of Eveline.

29th of June.   Profoundly discouraged by my work with Hachette and the *Dictionary of Practical Life*. Nourishment which insults the intellect and which it is necessary to vomit continually.

15th of July.   Papka and Mamka move into their new lodgings, rue de Vieux-Versailles.

9th of August.   In spite of incessant torments of health and while continuing her precious reading of St. Thomas, Raissa works with all her might at a long essay on Bergson (for «The Evolutionism of Bergson») which she began more than two months ago.

29th of August.   Exhausted with fatigue, she cannot finish writing her essay. It is a great sorrow for her. «I have only one thing to do,» she tells me, «which is to renounce every desire, since the good God does not permit me to realize any.»

3rd of October.   The whole month of September has been absorbed by the article on Bergson.

[Fear of established rules? Old masculine rudeness? It will appear only under my name. I *should* have demanded that Raissa sign it with me.]

15th of October.   Letter from Amieux. His nine children have been baptized − get out! − in spite of the opposition of their mother.

18th of October.   We receive, printed as a booklet, the triduum of Father Clérissac on Joan of Arc.

[The continuation of my notebook for the year 1911 is missing.
This year was a year of upheaval, of continual sufferings of health
for Raissa and for Vera, and of pecuniary difficulties, of odious
family discussions (with my mother, with my brother-in-law). Our
rule of life, however, continued after a fashion; but the novitiate
was at an end, we were in open country.

Perhaps in 1911, or was it in 1912, I was suddenly assailed by
violent temptations against the faith. Till then the graces of baptism
had been such that what I believed I seemed *to see*, it was certainty
itself. Now it was necessary for me to learn what the night of faith
is. No longer carried in arms, I was brutally dropped to the ground.
I remember long hours of interior torture, rue de l'Orangerie, alone
in the room on the fourth floor where I had made a kind of retreat
for work. I took care not to speak of it. I emerged from this trial,
by the grace of God, very strengthened; but I had lost my childhood.
I consoled myself by thinking that this had doubtless been necessary,
if I was to be of some service to others.

Shortly before this, Vera, betrayed by her health, had to renounce her hope of becoming a nurse. All her inclinations were
brought back little by little towards the sole desire of union with
God. In the end, she made, as she told us much later, a very clear
choice, which was to live with her sister and me *by religious vocation. — Princeton, 1954.*]

*

[I believe that we sometimes err in imagining that the unity
of a Christian community suppresses the incommunicable, and
should be thought of as a sort of pious camping retreat, where
effusions which supposedly would reveal all about everyone would
be put on the table, in a large soup-tureen all steaming with familial
gaiety.

Our experience, in any case, was very different.

I do not think that there ever was a closer and more profound
union between three human beings than that which existed between

us. Each was open to the other two with an entire sincerity. Each was extraordinarily sensitized to the other two, and ready to give everything for them. It was, so to speak, a single act of breathing which held us in life.

And yet, not only did the personality of each differ a great deal from that of the other two, and not only did each have a sacred respect for the liberty of the other two; but in the bosom of this marvellous union of love which the grace of God had made, each kept his solitude intact. What a mystery! The more we were united, the more each proceeded alone; the more each bore the burdens of the other two, the more each was alone in bearing his own burden. Thus the unity of the little flock only grew with the years, but the solitude of each of us only deepened at the same time, sometimes cruelly, to tell the truth. It was God's hand.

I shall not say more about it, except that the two sisters were very secret, each in her own manner, Raissa hiding her treasures and her sorrows in the brilliance of intelligence and the grace of winged words, Vera hiding hers in a silence in which the goodness, the princely vivacity and the dreams of a candid and adventurous spirit took refuge. The solitude of Raissa was that of a poet with incredibly sensitive and delicate fingers, lover of the beauties of the world and entered into the thickness of the Cross, wholly given up to the contemplative life and to the immolations of love; the solitude of Vera was that of a contemplative disguised as a sister of charity, singularly strong and compassionate to the miseries of souls, and tenderly received at the table of Jesus. And my own solitude? It seems to me that it was that of a kind of clumsy diver, advancing as best he could in the midst of the submarine fauna of captive truths and of the larvae of the time. One will never know to what temptations of black sadness and despair a philosopher can be exposed in proportion as he descends into the knowledge of himself and of the great pity which is in the world. His rest here on earth will finally be in the night, if in this night, which is nearer to God than the day, and more desolate too, an invisible hand which he loves leads him like a blind man. — *Kolbsheim, 1961.*]

Some Dates

In my journal of 1906, at Heidelberg, I had noted a certain number of dates which were of importance to us. I transcribe them here.

Raissa was born the 31st of August (Russian date) — the 12th of September 1883, at Nachitchivan (Rostoff-on-the-Don). Arrived in Paris at the age of ten, in July 1893. Jacques was born in Paris, the 18th of November, 1882. Vera was born at Marioupol, the 20th of June (Russian) — 2nd of July, 1886.

First meeting of Jacques and Raissa, during the winter of 1900. Russian affairs, school year 1900-1901. First course of Bergson, followed by us, school year 1901-1902. Engagement of Jacques and Raissa, 1902. Marriage, 26th of November 1904. We live at 25, rue de Jussieu.

Our first letter to Léon Bloy, 40 rue du Chevalier de la Barre, was received by him the feast day of St. Barnabas in the year 1905 (this feast had been put back to the 20th of June). — First visit to Bloy, 25th of June, 1905.

Visit to the cathedral of Chartres, September 1905.

30th of January, 1906. New edition of *Le Salut par les Juifs* (dedicated to Raissa).

Illness of Raissa during the whole month of February 1906. — From mid-April, at Bures. Relapse of Raissa. Monday, the 11th of June, 1906 (St. Barnabas), baptism of the three of us by Abbé Durantel and the sacramental marriage of Jacques and Raissa, in the Church of St. John the Evangelist. (I am baptized conditionally, and go to confession before Baptism.)

Raissa leaves the next day for Plombières and returns the 2nd of July.

First confession of Raissa and of Vera, the 22nd of July (St. Madeleine).

First Holy Communion of the three of us Friday, the 3rd of August, 1906 (Finding of the Relics of St. Stephen) at Sacré-Coeur in Paris. — Second Holy Communion, Sunday, the 12th of August, at Bures.

Arrival of Jacques and Raissa in Heidelberg the 27th of August; settle in a house on Gaisbergstrasse the 30th of August.

*

Vacation 1904. «Cum eo salvabor.» [With Him, I will be saved.]

9th of October, 1905. Words heard by Raissa (see above, p. 20).

June 1906, at Plombières. Dream of Raissa: a burning cross implanted on her back. (Vera had a similar dream the eve of the Precious Blood; someone was breaking her bones.)

Earlier dates:

First meeting with Ernest Psichari, at the Lycée Henri IV, in 1898.

In 1901, Robert Debré brings me to Péguy's, rue de la Sorbonne (he was then at Dick May's, not yet in the shop).

Death of my father, the 20th of February 1904.

*

[How many other dates important for us, since then. I indicate some of them below, for the time to which these «old memories» refer.

Baptism of Eveline, the 12th of November 1906. — Arrival of Vera in Heidelberg, 11th of December 1906.

Anointing of the Sick and cure of Raissa, 17th of January 1907. — Consecration to Mary (according to Grignion de Montfort) 25th of March 1907. — Confirmation of the three of us at Grenoble, 6th of July 1907 (after first pilgrimage to La Salette).

15th of October 1908: We go to live at 11, rue des Feuillantines (near the beloved convent on rue d'Ulm). — About the same time (a few days before the season of Advent), first visit to Father Clérissac, in Versailles.

In the first months of 1909, Raissa falls in love with the *Summa Theologiae*. — 14th of October 1909: we go to live in Versailles, 16 rue de l'Orangerie.

9th of February 1910 (Ash-Wednesday): during his Mass Father Clérissac consecrates us to God. Raissa and I receive Holy Commumion at the Cathedral at Versailles. . . . — 15th of September 1910: at the urging of Raissa I begin the reading of the *Summa Theologiae*, with which in my turn I fall in love.

8th of February 1911: We place in our little oratory the statue of Our Lady of La Salette which Father Clérissac had discovered at an antiquary's. — 22nd of February 1911: first meeting (at the Bloys') with Pierre and Christine van der Meer and with little Pierre, six years old. — 24th of February 1911 (St. Mathias): Baptism of Pierre and of little Pierre-Léon, at Saint-Médard.

Baptism of Raissa's father: 21st of February 1912. — He dies the 24th of February. — All three of us become oblates of Saint-Paul d'Oosterhout, 29th of September 1912. — Vow of R. and J., 2nd of October 1912. — Began my courses at Collège Stanislas, October 1912.

Ernest Psichari received into the Church, 4th of February 1913. — His first Holy Communion, 9th of February. — My conferences on Bergson at the Institut Catholique, April-May 1913. — Meeting with Charles Henrion, then with Louis Massignon, in this year 1913. — 15th of October 1913, go to live at 53, rue Neuve (later called rue Baillet-Reviron) following a grave illness of Raissa (cured by Dr. Conan, whom Louis Pichet brings to us). — December 1913, publication of «La Philosophie Bergsonienne.»

Spring 1914, conferences on the spirit of modern philosophy, at the Institut Catholique. — June 1914, I am named professor at the Institut Catholique, on the intervention of Cardinal Lorenzelli. — 22nd of August 1914, death of Ernest Psichari. — 5th of September 1914, death of Péguy. — Night of the 15th to the 16th of November 1914, death of Father Clérissac.

1914-1915, conferences on German philosophy at the Institut Catholique. (In 1915-1916 I shall add to my course at the Institut Catholique a course at Collège Stanislas; in 1916-1917 a course at the Petit Séminaire de Versailles, in which I shall have Michel Riquet and Maurice Dejean as pupils.) — 11th and 12th of November 1915, first meetings with Father Dehau, who attends my course at the Institut Catholique (it was Father Garrigou-Lagrange who spoke to him about me). — 13th of November, Raissa comes to the Institut Catholique to see him.

Ever since these first meetings, Father Dehau became a providential guide for us. He understood Raissa's vocation at once. I remember that at this time she was very troubled, not knowing what God wanted of her and why He pursued her, wondering even if she ought not to throw herself into external works. Father Dehau said to her: «When you feel an interior call to recollection, never resist. Let yourself be led at the very instant. And remain with God as long as it pleases Him, without yourself interrupting (unles you are obliged to do so by a duty of charity or some other necessity).» Raissa was delivered, she had found her way.

Vera also found her way thanks to Father Dehau. They prayed at length together. She confided everything to him. It was the secret of the King. We glimpsed later what intimacy with Jesus was involved there.

As for me, I passed hours – priceless hours – reading John of St. Thomas to Father Dehau, and listening to his commentaries. What keys he gave me, what enlightenments I received from this brilliant intelligence! (It went more quickly with the affairs of my «interior,» which moreover did not offer much that was remarkable. Is not a philosopher, moreover, intended for the common good of the republic of minds? Sometimes I bore a little grudge against this common good.)

For twenty-five years Father Dehau aided us in the great problems of our life by dispensing to us with an incomparable goodness the light of his lofty knowledge and of his rich and profound spiritual experience. He died Sunday, the 21st of October 1956, at Bouvines, where he had retired for several years. Hallowed be his memory. – *Kolbsheim, 1961.*]

OUR GUIDES, COMPANIONS AND PROTECTORS

[After the greatest of our benefactors, he who engendered us to faith, our godfather Léon Bloy, we have a great debt of gratitude to many envoys of God who aided and counseled us spiritually, like Dom Delatte, Abbé of Solesmes (during the first years of our Christian life, after our return from Heidelberg; afterwards our paths diverged, and finally his attachment to the *Action Française* caused him to break sharply with me at the time of «Primauté du Spirituel»), Dom Jean de Puniet, Abbot of Saint-Paul d'Oosterhout, Charles Henrion, who held a unique place in our life, Louis Massignon, Abbé Millot, Mother Marie-Thérèse of the Carmelite Convent of Avignon, Mgr. Vladimir Ghika, and above all Father Garrigou-Lagrange, whose theological teaching was a light of grace and a blessing for our intelligence.

But there are some to whom our gratitude goes in an absolutely eminent manner, as to saints whom Heaven put on our road here on earth in order to assist with their charity our innermost selves and in order to load our souls with their favors:

Father Clérissac,
Father Dehau,
Abbé Journet,
Dom Florent Miège, Prior of La Valsainte,
Father Vincent Lebbe,
the holy Curé of Courneuve (Abbé Lamy).

Raissa, in *Les Grandes Amitiés,* spoke of Father Clérissac —
see also my prefece to *The Mystery of the Church* — she spoke also
of Charles Henrion and of Louis Massignon. I wanted to mention
all these names here out of love and devotion.

On Abbé Lamy see my preface to the book of Paul Biver.

Father Dehau did not only wrap himself in shawls and in
blankets, but also in secret. Half blind, he walked among souls as
a friend of God charged with awakening them to the things of their
Father, it was important that men know of him only that he was
without importance. He had forbidden us to speak of him. I had
thought of him for the character of Theonas (in the book thus
titled), but limited myself to a few quite superficial and incidental
features, which did not jeopardize his incognito. — *Princeton, 1954.*

CHAPTER THREE

OUR FIRST TRIP TO ROME

This chapter relates to the trip which is mentioned in *Raissa's Journal* (pp. 68-71), and which she and I made to Rome in 1918, during the first World War, apropos of a manuscript of mine on La Salette, which remained unpublished. I have no intention at all of reopening here an ancient debate or of entering into any controversy whatever. I would only like to deposit in the dossier about an issue — that of the first great Marian Apparitions[1] of modern times — which for more than a century has greatly disturbed minds, a certain number of facts which relate to our own personal life and to my adventures as philosopher, and which have perhaps some interest for the historian, however slight it may be. A further remark in passing: not only has the manuscript which occasioned our trip, for the reasons that one will see, remained unpublished, but even if it happened, against all probability, that one day external circumstances permitted its publication, I do not want it published after my death — no more than any writing blemished with the awkwardness and the high-flown style proper to works of youth. Also, in this particular case, it is a question of the first state of an engraving which could not be taken up again and reworked so as to give complete satisfaction to its author.

---

1. I mean Apparitions in which the Blessed Virgin (who is not bound by the *taceat mulier in Ecclesia)* [a woman should not speak in church] caused a message to be transmitted to the entire Christian people. — On the Apparition of La Salette (19th of September 1846), cf. *Les Grandes Amitiés* (1941-1944; 4th ed., Paris: Desclée De Brouwer, 1949), pp. 195-204; 471-475; 494-499 (Eng. transl.: Vol I, *We Have Been Friends Together,* tr. by Julie Kernan, New York, Longmans, Green and Co., 1942, pp. 183-192; Vol II, *Adventures in Grace,* tr. by Julie Kernan, New York: Longmans, Green and Co., Inc., 1945, pp. 220-223; 241-245).

The story which I am going to tell begins in 1915. The war is at its height. We have known and loved La Salette for several years. We have read *Celle qui pleure* and *Vie de Mélanie par elle-même*. It was during a novena to La Salette, at Heidelberg, that Raissa, gravely ill, was cured, and experienced a marvellous joy in receiving the Anointing of the Sick. It was at La Salette that it was granted to us to pray with confidence for the conversion of Ernest Psichari. It was in descending from La Salette that we received the sacrament of Confirmation. The freshness of the impressions experienced up there, and, in order to employ a saying of Ruysbroeck, «the delicious taste of the Holy Spirit» which one has however fleetingly sensed there, are something ineffaceable. But before all and above all, the mystery which struck the heart and which one will never finish scrutinizing, is that of the tears shed by Her whom all generations must call blessed, the mystery of the suffering manifested by the incomparably glorious *Theotokos*, weeping before two shepherds over the hard-heartedness of men and announcing great misfortunes. «I have been suffering for you for so long! If I wish that my Son not abandon you, I am charged to pray to Him unceasingly. And as for you, you do not appreciate it. You can pray and try as you will, you will never be able to repay the suffering that I have accepted for you.»

The war — and this war was the first *total* war — is a time of extraordinary misfortune. Heaven seems to have closed, the norms of human existence to have capsized. The works of life are as it were petrified, while death gallops through the world and goes through it at a furious pace. How could the soul not think then of God, whom men do not cease to offend, and whose arm is «so heavy» that Mary can no longer restrain it?

It seemed to me that for myself these kinds of reflections ought not to remain theoretical. I was not mobilized,[1] the examining boards for recruits before which I had passed had kept me in a state of discharge (because of an old pleurisy, which had brought me near death). I tried to make myself useful in civil life by doing double duty as a professor. But when I heard people blaspheme God because of the war, and remembered the words which end

---

1. It was only in 1917 that I was declared "fit for duty," and mobilized — and soon discharged again. (Cf. *Raissa's Journal*, pp. 44 and 58).

the public Message: «Well! my children, you will make this known to *all my people*,» the idea came to me that the drama lived by the world at that moment contained a summons to make La Salette better known.

The situation in this respect was not cheering in France. The majority of the faithful were very ignorant of the issue. Among those who had studied it, certain ones (such as Léon Bloy, Pierre Termier, and some of our closest friends) mingled no hidden motives in their devotion. But in other respects there was on the one hand, in many, a marked hostility with regard to Mélanie, the sheperdess who, with the little Maximin, had been a witness of the Apparition; the reason for this was the secret message which she maintained that the Blessed Virgin had allowed her to make public from a certain date (1858) and which she persisted in wishing to make known, and which began with words offensive to the clergy. On the other hand, there was a small number of fanatics who made the Secret of La Salette a partisan affair, and whose aberrant interpretations, and their manner of using prophecies like a railway time-table, could only compromise the cause which they claimed to defend.

My idea was that in order to truly serve the Blessed Virgin it was important to take up again the question of La Salette in its entirety, in as objective a manner as possible, and without any other passion than that of truth; and, since everything depended on the value of the testimony of Mélanie, to gather all the information possible on her life, the first thing to be done in this regard being to gather without delay, before they left this earth, the observations and the memories of those who had known her well.

I add that I had still other reasons — very personal ones — to undertake this work on La Salette. If I nourished some resentment against my grandfather Jules Favre (above all, I felt very vexed to have inherited certain traits from him, particularly, I had to admit, a certain detestable taste for Donquixotism and for lost causes), I was however touched to think that in spite of his aversion for Catholicism (he was rationalist and Rousseauist in matters of religion, before becoming a Protestant at the end of his life, under the influence of his second wife), this generous man had not hesitated to disconcert his friends and to place himself, whatever the consequences, on the side of the *Beautiful Lady* of La Salette, in bur-

dening himself with the cause of Mlle de Lamerlière and in delivering
for her a famous pleading before the Imperial Court of Grenoble, the
27th of April 1857 — it was the time at which the controversies concerning the Apparition were raging, and when certain enemies of the
bishop of Grenoble, particularly the Abbés Déléon and Cartellier,
stupidly accused this old stout spinster of having played the role
of the Blessed Virgin and deceiving the two shepherds. It seemed to
me that I was making a certain gesture of filial piety and perhaps
doing something useful towards the supreme accomplishment of
my grandfather's destiny in succeeding him in an affair in which,
no doubt without his knowledge or desire (but does one ever know?)
he had acted so as to draw a compassionate glance from the *Omni-
potentia supplex*.

In consulting my notes I see that after having written to my
superior, Abbé Millot, vicar-general of Versailles, and after having
received his approval and encouragement, it was the 1st of August
1915 that I began my memoir on La Salette (the Apparition, the
Two witnesses, the public Message, the Secret of Mélanie). I had
also written to the Father Abbott of Solesmes, Dom Delatte — not
that I considered myself bound in his regard by any obligation, but
out of concern to seek counsel, and because at that time I put him
on a very high pedestal. In his response, dated the 29th of August,
he condemned my project (which ruined, he said, all the services
which I could have rendered to the Truth and to the Church, and
which would discredit me), but the condemnation was couched
in such violent terms that it had much more force to annoy me than
to influence my judgment. (This was only the first disagreement,
and the pedestal remained intact. It was much later, at the time of
Primauté du Spirituel and of the condemnation of *Action Française*,
that the rupture between the Father Abbot and myself took place.)
Dom Jean de Puniet, the Father Abbot of Saint-Paul d'Oosterhout,
consulted on my project, showed very different dispositions, and
replied to me the 15th of September: «I am most happy to fully
agree with it, sure of your prudence and of the wisdom with which
you will accomplish your task. . . .»
     The two priests whose testimony seemed to me the most useful
to gather for my work were Abbé H. Rigaux, curé of Argoeuvres,

with whom Mélanie stayed twice for a few days,[1] and especially Abbé Combe, curé of Diou (Allier), with whom she lived for several months and who was her confessor during this time. Both had been her friends and held her in great veneration. I had already visited Abbé Rigaux the 2nd of March 1914; Pierre van der Meer and I spent, in October 1915, two days with Abbé Combe. Both were men of an incontestable uprightness. Unfortunately Abbé Rigaux had, in addition to his great sacerdotal virtues, the hobby of Nostradamus; as to Abbé Combe (who for his part, alas, tried, according to the remark of Massignon, to «chronologize the Apocalypse») his devotion to Mélanie was accompanied by a great rudeness of character and by an obstinacy from which she surely suffered. To tell the truth, if was not in France, it was in Italy that she had her best friends, and those more interested in the depths of the soul than in the extraordinarily supernatural; it was the Italian bishops, Mgr. Petagna, bishop of Castellamare, Mgr. Zola, bishop of Lecce, and, in the last hours of her life, Mgr. Cecchini, bishop of Altamura, who gave her the most efficacious support; it was on the invitation of Canon Annibale di Francia that she stayed a little more than a year at Messina, at the Institute founded by the latter, and where she was considered to be a «mistress of sublime virtue»; it was Canon di Francia who delivered her funeral eulogy,[2] and it was in the chapel of the Daughters of Divine Zeal, at Altamura, that her tomb was erected, with an inscription in which the title of «co-foundress» is given to her as a token of gratitude and of veneration.

The fact remains that the information which I received from the curé of Argoeuvres and from the curé of Diou was very precious to me, and gave me a high idea of the character and of the virtues of the Sheperdess of La Salette. My regret is not to have been able, for want of time, to visit them again, nor to consult the Italian sources, nor to devote myself to the whole work of historical cross-checking which I would have liked to do. It was necessary to go quickly, and I was occupied by my work and my teaching. My memoir finally gathered together materials as well verified as I

1. From the 27th of September to the 2nd of October 1902, and from the 2nd to the 8th of October 1903. (Precisions given by Abbe Gouin, to whom I here express my thanks.
2. He delivered the eulogy on Melanie two times. (Cf. *Documents I, Pour servir à l'histoire réele de la Salette*, Nouvelles Editions Latines, Paris, 1963.)

was able, but it was not brought to the point of elaboration at which a work of this kind can be considered as truly finished.

Be that as it may, it was already very advanced (Vera typed it — making four or five copies — as it proceeded), when the cause of Mélanie and of her Secret found itself more than ever compromised by the foolish commentaries of the small number of fanatics of whom I spoke above, and their insults against the bishops of France. On the 12th of January 1916 *La Croix* published a decree of the Holy Office, under date of the 21st of December 1915, forbidding anyone to treat and to discuss the question of the Secret of La Salette «under any pretext and under any form whatever, such as books, brochures or signed or anonymous articles, or in any other manner.» I found myself suddenly well taken care of, with my memoir in hand, and my conviction, confirmed by all these months of examination and of meditation, that I had not been wrong to undertake it.

In the face of such a formal disciplinary decree, the only outlet, if one wished to try a last effort, was to go to Rome when my memoir was finished (or almost finished), and to seek information on the spot — perhaps someone would advise us to ask whether an exception could be made in favor of my work.

This idea took shape only little by little, and passed to execution only two years later. The reasons which one could raise against it were very serious ones: it was doubtful that the physical forces of Raissa could endure the fatigue of such a trip — at that time such a long one. The world was at war, there was talk at the beginning of 1918 of the possibility of an Austrian offensive, and the turn of events could suddenly make our return difficult. Finally, the step itself entailed evident risks. We were of an extreme naiveté (and I hope, indeed, that this has continued all our life); naiveté however is not stupidity or blindness, and we knew very well to what we were exposing ourselves. Behold a convert, a godchild of the *Mendiant Ingrat*, who has sided with St. Thomas and in whom the Church seems to have confidence; and the first movement of this imbecile, after Rome has given him the Doctor's cap, is to go to torment the Roman authorities with an enormous memoir concerning a Seer very little loved by the French clergy, and a controversy (there is nothing worse) concerning a prophetic message which she claims to have received. What is he troubling himself about?

He is going to discredit himself irremediably, disappoint all his friends in the ecclesiastical world, make himself pass for a visionary, throw himself into a wasps' nest.

All these considerations were valid. They were not decisive for someone who, if he had obeyed reasons of the same kind, would doubtless never have asked for baptism (he remembered that at that time he still imagined that in order to be a Christian it was necessary to renounce the intelligence and philosophy). When one has once left everything in order to find truth, there are arguments to which one becomes little susceptible. Raissa was similarly disposed; and after having thought at first that there was no hurry, she felt one day that it was time to make this trip to Rome. It was for truth, and with the intention of serving the wishes of the Blessed Virgin, that I had undertaken my work. It was not a question here of a whim. To obey was beyond question for me, and I was ready to renounce publication, but on condition of having done everything in my power to know whether the interdiction of the Holy Office could not allow an exception. Although knowing all of the human that can mingle in the exercise of ecclesiastical authority, I had moreover total confidence in the Church, and I knew that complete candor was the best attitude towards those who had received power in her from above. The instinct of faith informs us of it, but I must say that quite a long stay in Rome, like the one which I was to make much later, at the time of my mission to the Vatican, gives very vivid lights on this point. Those who in their relations with the vast machinery of the Roman administration count on human maneuvers, intrigues and contrivances, which are so manifest, and are apparently so formidable, are sure to lose the game in the end. Those who bet on candor and on grace will always win in the end — be it sometimes when they will have passed to the other side of the veil. . . .

Raissa and I left for Rome Holy Tuesday, the 26th of March (1918), without intending anything definite, except to submit my manuscript to Père Garrigou-Lagrange and to ask him for advice.

The trip, in that time of war, was excessively long, and we very much feared being further delayed at the Italian frontier if Customs had fancied to examine my voluminous manuscript. The latter was at the bottom of a suitcase, the custom-officers did not see it. At the railway-station our friend Jacques Froissart (the future Père Bruno de Jesus-Marie) awaited us. (He had already entered the Carmelites, but on the advice of Mère Marie-Thérèse had resumed the lay habit in order to study at the Angelicum.) He was our guide during the whole of our stay, and thanks to him this first visit to Rome was for us an unforgettable pilgrimage to the Basilicas in which so many martyrs lie, to the Catacombs, to the room in which St. Benedict Labre died. . . .

Father Garrigou-Lagrange was happy with my memoir. After having read it, he said to me: «The Blessed Virgin loves you very much. You will suffer much.»[1] The advice given was to go to see the Pope. Our audience with Benedict XV took place the 2nd of April, in the morning. He received us with much kindness and goodness; remembering the title which the Roman Universities had recently conferred on me, and calling me with a somewhat ironical pleasing smile «Monsieur le Docteur»; asking us many questions — concerning the health of Mgr. Gibier, bishop of Versailles, and above all concerning the Big Bertha which was shelling Paris from a distance; then concerning the manual I was working on, concerning my courses. . . . After which I took the plunge, and asked him for permission to «open my heart» to him like a child to its father. He then turns towards me with great benevolence and simplicity, bending his head as if in order to hear a confidence, and I tell him my story. — «La Salette!» he says, with a lively and interested glance. And he explains at length his own feelings on the question. «The Apparition is beyond doubt; but the words of the Blessed Virgin to Mélanie, in particular when in the secret message they express such a severity with regard to the clergy, are they entirely certain? This is what is debatable! That speaking in general she complained about the clergy — this is very possible, but the terms could be exaggerated by the «fancy» (the imagination) of Mélanie, whatever her sincerity and good dispositions might be. In short, if it is a question of the secret Message, *quoad substantiam concedo, quoad singula verba nego* [as to the basic meaning I agree,

1. I found the notes, in pencil, which I had taken during our stay. I am using them here to aid my memory.

as to the particular words I do not agree]. The Holy Office wishes to avoid scandal, to pacify minds, to prevent the Christian people from turning away from their priests, whom so many enemies are already ready to crush. No doubt at certain moments scandal is preferable, «necesse est ut vaniant scandala» [scandals must come]. But it does not seem that this is the case here. . . .»

Then, with a great kindness: «But you, do you believe that the Blessed Virgin has thus spoken, literally?»

(What to do? Contradict the Pope? All that I see is that I am going to displease someone in any case, the Pope or the Blessed Virgin. Then no hesitation: better to displease the Pope. And I reply like a great simpleton — but it is one of the rare moments in my life in which I had the impression of positing an act with which I could be truly satisfied):

— Yes, Most Holy Father, I believe that Mélanie was a saint and that what she reported is literally true. I had many details concerning her life. She was a stigmatist. She suffered much by fidelity to her mission. . . .

— Yes, I know, says the Pope, who does not seem offended by my reply. One cannot say of her all the things with which one reproaches the other Seer.

— But Maximin has also been greatly calumniated. He did not have the extraordinary graces with which Mélanie was favored. But he was a good Christian.

Raissa: — A simple heart.

— You believe in it also, Madame? You also have devotion to Notre Dame de la Salette?

— Yes, Most Holy Father (she says this in a voice full of conviction, in spite of the fear of having gone too far by intervening).

— Yes, I know, there are many persons in France who have a great devotion to Notre Dame de la Salette. Greater in some than to Notre Dame de Lourdes, is that not so?

I say: — It is because the Blessed Virgin wept at La Salette, it is because of her tears.

— The tears, adds Raissa, correspond well to the present state of the world.

The Pope remains silent; he appears touched, his face is serious. Then, after a moment, he says to me:

— Well, here is what you must do. Go to see Our Brother (a

slight smile passes on his lips — I knew that they scarcely loved one another) Cardinal Billot. He is in charge of studies, it is quite a natural introduction for you. When you have talked philosophy with him, do as you have just done with Us, open your heart to him. He will listen to you. Tell him that you do not wish to ask him anything concerning the secret of the Holy Office, but that you have written a work, and that you submit it humbly to the Church, ready to obey its judgment if you are mistaken. There is not, is there, any self-love on your part. If the good God wishes to use you in this matter, He will inspire in Cardinal Billot the reply which will be fitting.

Go to see the Cardinal. You have not seen him yet?

— No, Most Holy Father. And I intended to speak of this only to Your Holiness, for I am ready to suffer all that is necessary for La Salette, but I would not like to compromise my philosophical work unnecessarily.

— In proceeding as we have just told you, you will not compromise anything.

The audience is finished. We thank the Pope; he blesses us «and all those whom we have in our hearts,» all the more paternally as he was not unhappy, I believe, at the little trick played at the same time on the Cardinal and on my presumption by a solution incontestably wise in itself.

*

I had therefore replied to Benedict XV, in this audience of April 1918, that I believed that the words reported by Mélanie were literally true. Forty years later, while I write these pages, I question myself. Would I, being equally sincere with myself, make the same reply now? It seems to me that my reply would be formulated a little differently — let us note well that I am no longer speaking here only of the Secret of La Salette in particular (moreover, I have prohibited myself from speaking of it in this chapter), I am speaking in general of any message whatsoever passing judgments on persons or announcing events, and transmitted as coming from someone of the other world.

Supposing (as is moreover the case if one still questioned

me concerning Mélanie) that I believe in the entire veracity of the witness — thus excluding the hypothesis of an even involuntary exaggeration on his part — I would prefer to say: «I believe in the full authenticity of the reported words»: without implying, for all that, that everything said must be taken «literally,» according to the usual sense of this expression, that is to say, as to the essentially human measure or to the essentially human modality which our words entail in common earthly usage. During forty-six years one has time to reflect a little on the infinite transcendence of the perspectives of Heaven in comparison with those of earth. Not only is it in eternity that the saints of Heaven see the events of earth, so that if they speak of future things to someone here below it is not at all in the succession of time (to which our own interest naturally tends) that they are interested — the periods mentioned can in reality be very distant from each other and find themselves more or less telescoped in what is said, and the chronological order can not be observed in it; but in a still more general manner, it is clear that in order to be a little understood by men, it is necessary indeed that the people of Heaven employ human language, which cannot precisely signify purely and simply «literally» what they themselves mean to say; the literal sense of what they tell us surpasses our words and remains therefore essentially charged with mystery, whereas a kind of immoderation — in «too much» (*overstatement*) or in «not enough» (*understatement*) — introduces itself into our words such as they employ them. The voices of Joan of Arc in her prison told her that she was going to be delivered: — that is to say, «literally,» that she was going to escape from her enemies? Surely not! This meant to climb the funeral-pile, and to be delivered in this manner from the English and from their prelates, and also delivered from this perishable flesh, and *delivered from evil*, and free to see her God. . . .

Furthermore, the term *language* does not relate only to the words which we use, it covers also all that which serves us to make ourselves understood, and therefore the whole imagery which we use and which is that of the men to whom we speak, at such and such a moment of time and in such and such a place on earth. (Supposing that through some telephone through duration we could tell a contemporary of Julius Caesar something which concerns our epoch, could we speak to him of airplanes and of electronic machines, of the British Parliament, or of the Praesidium of the Communist Party? The other person would not understand anything; it would indeed be necessary to use the imagery furnished by his own type of culture, as well as his own words and his own syntax.)

One can still go further. We know that in Heaven the blessed do not use words and speech to converse among themselves. On the other hand, we also know that God uses instrumentally what is in the mind of the prophet. Let us suppose now that one of the blessed, speaking to someone of the earth, does not himself produce, as we do, sounds physically transmitted through the air; so that the words heard by the witness of the here-below, instead of being carried by sound waves, result within him from a divine activation exercised on the faculties of his soul. In other words, let us suppose that a person of heaven who appears and speaks, does not utter audible words, but rather *reads* — while moving his lips, as we some- times do — in the soul of the messenger, and at the very instant of their production, the words which he himself produces there by divine action, which uses, instrumentally, the human faculties of the messenger.[1] Then one can think that utterances coming from Heaven, and really heard, and authentically transmitted, have passed through the instrumentality of typical or «archetypal»[2] mental perspectives present in the unconscious of the spirit of the mes- senger, without, for all this, the meaning or the letter of the message being changed, such as it was intended from on high to reach us.

1. Thus he seems to speak like us — and he really speaks, but not like us.
2. I do not believe, as Jung seems to do, in a psychological heredity, thanks to which archetypal representations would be transmitted to our unconscious. Nor do I believe in a collective Unconscious as a supra-individual entity in which each would participate.
    I think rather that each of us, throughout the course of his life, but more particularly during his childhood, undergoes the influence or the "contagion," in what I call the *unconscious of the spirit*, of what stimulates, consciously or unconsciously, the mentality of his contemporaries, and which is expressed by *signs* whose impact can moreover be entirely fleeting and imperceptible — it is then that this impact is the most efficacious and the most penetrating, because it is *unconsciously* registered. More generally, I think that in each of us the unconscious of the spirit, throughout the course of life, but more particularly during childhood, receives the impact (all the more penetrating as it is itself unconsciously registered) of an infinitely multiple universe of forms, signs and symbols emanating from the cultural environment in which

When someone from Heaven speaks to some poor child of the here-below, we need only accept, such as they are, the words which he causes him to hear, but it is necessary to understand them (to understand their «literal sense») according to the spirit of him who causes these words to be heard, and whose intention is not to tell our fortunes nor to *inform* us as a secret agent would, but, as is the case for all revelation under the New Law, to draw our attention, by great signs capable of stirring hearts everywhere, to things which are of importance to our action, and which, of ourselves, we see more or less badly — shortcomings too real, hopes or threats with which the times are burdened, purposes of God which when realized will doubtless appear very different from the image which we could form of them — all of this designated in terms essentially mysterious which, even reported exactly as they were heard, are true «literally» as to the general practical sense which is intended to be communicated to us, but not as to the particular mental perspectives, nor to the particular imagery, nor to the words taken according to the human measure through whose instrumentality a transcendent thought is signified to us.

*

As the Pope had told me to do, I went, on the 4th of April, to the Collegio Pio Americano to see Cardinal Billot — not without

he is steeped. But such a universe of forms, signs and symbols is an historically constituted universe, it bears within it the still active vestiges of preceding cultural epochs and of an immense past.

It seems, therefore, that in the sense which I have just indicated, one should replace the notion of the collective unconscious with that of an influence unconsciously received by each one (to diverse degrees) of the cultural community, and one should replace the notion of psychological heredity with that of cultural heredity. One would then see how the mental perspectives or mental attitudes on which the *modus significandi* [the way of signifying] consciously employed by us depends can result from the impact, on the unconscious of our spirit, of the forms, signs and symbols emanating from the cultural community, and one would see at the same stroke how such and such of these signs, forms or symbols can be "archetypes" going back to the most distant past. (Without forgetting that the word "archetype" can refer, not only to historically transmitted primitive forms, but also to structures or to modalities of action fundamentally natural to the human mind, which can manifest themselves in all by mere spontaneous convergence, implying no historical influence and no historical transmission.)

some apprehension, for I knew him to be little agreeable in general, and poorly disposed towards Mélanie in particular. A few days previously he had received Father Garrigou-Lagrange, and, discussing theology with him, had declared that Cajetan was «a bastard» and John of Saint Thomas a «double bastard.» Upon which Father Garrigou, not being able to tolerate this offense to the great Commentators, had taken his hat — and the door.

Very embarrassed by my frightfully large manuscript, I leave it in the anteroom. The Cardinal receives me very graciously, speaks to me of Psichari, of Péguy, blasts the adversaries of St. Thomas, says much evil about the Jesuits, attacks Suarez and Cajetan, and displays much bitterness. I broach the object of my visit, speak to him of my work on La Salette. He declares that the sect of the Salettists horrifies him, that Mélanie was tormented by them, etc. I reply that I came to see him only because the Pope sent me, and asked me to submit my manuscript to him.

— I shall read it.

— It is here.

I go and fetch it. In seeing the thickness of the package, he laughs, and asks what chapter it is necessary to read, then he starts again to speak scornfully of Mélanie and of her Secret.

— Do with this work what you wish, I tell him. The Pope sends me to your Eminence in order that It may judge whether an exception to the decree prohibiting any publication in which the Secret of La Salette is discussed can or can not be made in its favor. Permit me to leave it with you.

The Cardinal replies that he will keep it two months and will give me his answer through Jacques Froissart. «You have not wasted your time,» he tells me when I take leave of him, «you have proceeded properly,» and he gives me his blessing. The audience lasted an hour.

Raissa and I left Rome of the 8th of April, in order to arrive at Versailles two days later. After having accompanied Raissa to Vernie, where her mother and Vera were already settled in the large presbytery of Abbé Gouin, with the van der Meers, I returned to Versailles and resumed, on April 15th, my courses at the Institut Catholique de Paris.

*

It was just before returning to Vernie for the summer vacation that I received the reply of Cardinal Billot, transmitted by Jacques Froissart in a letter under the date of the 7th of June 1918, and another under the date of the 16th.

This reply was negative. Nothing was said on the core of the question, and nothing objectionable was pointed out in my manuscript, but publication was judged decidedly inopportune and authorization was refused. It was certainly possible to attribute the thing to the bias which the Cardinal had not hidden from me, nevertheless, I was persuaded that, perfectly conscious himself of this bias, he had applied himself with all the more care to judge in an impartial manner and for motives which imposed themselves objectively on his mind; for this rough and violent man had an evident intellectual honesty. I myself, moreover, was inclined to think that it was now a little too late, or much too soon, for a publication of this kind. In his conversations with Jacques Froissart, the Cardinal had insisted on the intellectual confusion in France, the affair of Loublande, and on the state of a cast of mind which after four years of war was ready to grow feverish and to set out on false tracks.

With regard to myself, in any case, since the judgment which I had solicited was passed, and the authorization to publish refused, the only thing to do was to obey, as I was prepared to do from the beginning. I had done all that I could for La Salette; to undertake this piece of work had been for me an obligation of conscience. To now renounce all publication, and to let my manuscript remain in my files, was another such obligation. Raissa was as convinced of this as I was.[1] We have never felt any bitterness nor nourished any mental reservation concerning the matter.

In what are called the Roman circles our trip had been, as one had to expect, followed by some eddies. Cardinal Billot (who had read my manuscript from one end to the other) had, Jacques Froissart told me, consulted «two other» important persons about it (I knew the name of one of them). People had begun to gossip,

---

1. Speaking of myself, she wrote to Jacques Froissart, the 13th of June 1918: "He exercised a legitimate freedom in devoting more than two years to the work which you know. He obeyed a strict command of his conscience in bringing it to Rome. Henceforth his responsibility is discharged, and absolute silence is easy for him as long as the Church does not authorize him to speak."

they circulated writings against Léon Bloy and against me. All of this had scarcely any importance and was to abate of itself, not without Benedict XV, anxious for a moment, it appears, having himself contributed to calm minds by an equanimity which I greatly admired.

I maintained relations with Cardinal Billot, either directly or through the intermediary of Jacques Froissart. I am very grateful to him for the confidence and for the kindness which, in spite of our differences, he continued to show me. It was thanks to him, particularly, that I received communication of a report which two chaplains of La Salette[1] had sent to Rome by Mgr. Giray, bishop of Cahors, and in which, apropos of the *Vie de Mélanie* by herself (or, more precisely, apropos of the story of her childhood)[2] the text of which had been given by Abbé Combe to Léon Bloy and published by the latter, they endeavored to completely discredit the Seer. Their report denounced a multitude of erroneous assertions in Mélanie's narrative, and utilized to that effect the testimony of Mélanie's brother, Eugene Calvat, who had contradicted many things about which he had been questioned.

At first sight, and for someone who had not especially studied the question, this report, extremely well constructed, seemed overwhelming for the Seer. None of it held up, however, as soon as one looked at it closely, which I did not fail to do. I spent a great deal of time on this; checking each detail and drawing up a very

---

1. The chaplains have ceased to exist; after the war they were replaced by the Missionaires de la Salette, who returned to the mountain and resumed the care of the sanctuary.

2. It was on the order of Abbé Combe, then her confessor, that Mélanie wrote this story in 1900. She discontinued it moreover (after having brought it as far as the age of fourteen), as a result of praise which a priest, to whom Abbé Combe had shown it, lavished on her.

I note that in 1852, six years after the Apparition, Mélanie had already written for Père Sibilat a much shorter story, with which the more detailed story of 1900 agrees. M. Amédée Nicolas was acquainted with this first story. "It is impossible," he wrote in 1881, "to understand the Sheperdess if one does not know the story of her infancy and of her earliest youth, which cannot be given to the public until after the death of her mother and her own death. We have possessed this story for twenty-five years. We have had on these points the avowal of her parents, although these facts were not very admirable as concerns themselves." Amédée Nicolas, *Le Secret de la Bèrgere de la Salette, Complément de notre réponse du 19 octobre 1880*, Nimes, Clavel-Ballivet, 1881, note on p. 18.

long reply with all the pains of a minute historical critique (thanks to Pierre Termier I was even able to be enlightened on certain topographical details which were mentioned). I was constantly surprised myself to see so many so-called arguments of fact vanish into smoke. Let it suffice for me to indicate here that Eugène Calvat[1] was the junior of Mélanie by five years (he was the fifth child of the family), and that at the time of many of the events supposedly contradicted by him he was only four or five years old; at the time of certain others, he was not yet born.[2] His testimony did not exist as such.

It was a great satisfaction for me to be able to re-establish the truth, in the opinion of Cardinal Billot, and to send him an extremely precise report which, accompanied by quite a long letter, was delivered to him by Jacques Froissart on the 8th of November 1918.

I confess that regardless of the fragile forget-me-nots of my modesty, it seemed to me that I had never seen a so perfectly peremptory reply to such cleverly raised accusations.

1. Jacques Froissart himself was able to see Eugène Calvat on the 26th and the 28th of July 1918, and to question him at length, as well as his wife, concerning this affair. Both of them venerated Mélanie and declared her incapable of falsifying the truth. Neither of them knew that Mélanie had written her autobiography, and that the latter had been published by Léon Bloy. His interlocutors had told him nothing about it, and he had no idea that the story which was mentioned to him had been written by his sister. When he was questioned in 1912 (he was then seventy-six) he had moreover become "quite furious" when it was stated that the Secret was a lie and that Maximin was only a drunkard; and it was in this angry state that he had replied to what he believed were inventions of people from Paris seeking to blacken his family. He willingly agreed before Jacques Froissart that he could not remember facts which would have taken place when he was only four or five, or even younger. What was very important for him was the good reputation of his family, and he refused to believe in the harshness of his mother towards the little Mélanie, but he was then too young to remember the facts in question, or to have been present when they took place. The only clear thing is that the memory of this old man, who told Jacques Froissart something altogether different from what he had told the two chaplains, offered no guarantee of veracity.

2. As I wrote to Cardinal Billot, when I sent him my counter-report, "it is no longer there the *testes dormientes* of whom St. Augustine speaks apropos of the tomb of Our Lord. It is the *testis infans*, nay, it is the *testis inexistens*, the *testis nondum extra nihil positus*, the *testis antegenitus*; history will be indebted to the chaplains of La Salette for this useful discovery, which marvellously enlarges its methods and permits it all hopes." (The letter from which this amiable passage is taken was written on the 23rd of August, and given, together with my counter-report, to Cardinal Billot by Jacques Froissart, after vacation, on the 8th of November 1918.)

*

Many years later I again had an occasion to stand up for Mélanie apropos of an article signed Pierre Herbin, which had appeared in the August-September 1946 issue of *Vie Spirituelle*, and which attacked at one and the same time Léon Bloy, Mélanie (who was accused of fraud) — and the Secret (in violation of the Decree of the Holy Office prohibiting all discussion concerning the latter). The rectifying letter, rather harsh, but certainly merited, which I sent to the review, was published in the October issue. I had wished to add to it a postscript concerning a book by Père Jaouen, a missionary of La Salette, which I had read in the interval — I had to give this up at the request of the editorial staff of *Vie Spirituelle* (the book in question had been published by the same publisher as the magazine itself). It was my friend Louis Massignon who published this postscript (together with the letter — reprinted — which it completed), as an appendix to an important article of his own written for the centenary of the Apparition, and which appeared in *Cahier* 7 (1946) of the review *Dieu Vivant*.[1]

Père Jaouen's book merited a certain attention by the very fact of its evident partiality, and the author worked unintentionally, but with remarkable energy, to saw off the branch on which he himself and his brothers in religion were seated. For it is clear that if one held, not as a result of presumption and bias, but as a well-established conclusion, the idea that the principal witness of the Apparition was only an hysteric and a fabulator who was a victim of the worst illusions, the Apparition itself, in spite of all the miraculous cures of the body and of the soul which had taken place on the Holy Mountain, would be found suddenly exposed to the gravest doubts.[2]

This did not go unnoticed at Rome, where I was then the Ambassador of France to the Holy See. Pius XII, who was aware

1. Reproduced in the *Opera Minora* of Louis Massignon, Texts gathered by J. Moubarac under the patronage of the Cercle d'Etudes Dar El-Salam (Dar Maaref, Liban, 1943), t. III, pp. 752-766. [P. 752, under the title, read 1946 and not 1948.]
2. He who has fabulized today could fabulize yesterday; moreover, the hysterical temperament is a congenital disposition.

of my interest in La Salette, was so good as to warn me, at the beginning of 1947, that the recent controversies had raised doubts concerning the Apparition — it was the whole question of La Salette which now passed through a serious crisis. I understood that they were again going to submit everything to study, and that they would not hesitate before radical decisions if they seemed reasonably required.

For my part, I communicated Massignon's article, which had appeared in *Dieu Vivant*, to the Vatican. And it seemed to me that it would not be inopportune to make known to the Pope that I had formerly written a voluminous work on the question, which had remained unpublished for the reasons set forth in this chapter.

In March the competent commission asked to see this work, as well as my grandfather's Address to the Court in defence of Mlle de Lamerlière, in which it seemed to be particularly interested; the first document was delivered by me on the 24th of March, the second[1] towards the middle of April. The note in which I pointed out the existence of these two documents had been written at the end of January.

I have no illusions on the very minimal importance of the contribution which they were able to bring. It is clear that many other sources of information were available in Rome, which certainly played a greater role in the study which was then undertaken. Moreover, I spoke of the facts mentioned above only because they concern my personal recollections.

In the months which followed, and during which I naturally refrained from asking anything concerning matters which were not within my province, they no longer said anything to me about the question of La Salette, from which I concluded that the storm had passed. With regard to my memoir, with all the defects which render the works of youth so irritating, and which a hasty re-reading had just recalled mercilessly to my attention, but also with the good faith which it was not difficult to discern in it, and with the particulars of fact and the diverse restatements which it contained, I thanked Providence for having caused it to reach, by paths which I would never have been able to foresee, persons in whose hands it was doubtless most important that it be placed.

---

1. *Affaire de la Salette, Mademoiselle de Lamerlière contre MM. Déléon et Cartellier*, published by J. Sabatier, Paris, Librairie C. Barrain, 1857.

CHAPTER FOUR

MEETING WITH PIERRE VILLARD

I

LETTER FROM A STRANGER

[In the sequel to Les Grandes Amitiés *which Raissa so much desired to write, and which she was obliged to renounce, first by our stay in Rome and the burdens which it imposed on her, afterwards by the illnesses which did not cease to afflict us, it was to Pierre Villard, to the Thomist Circles, to our friends of Meudon that she intended to devote her first chapters. The notes which follow would like to satisfy in part the purpose which she was not able to accomplish. I regret their dryness, when I think of the gift which she had of again possessing the past in a kind of fresh-like-the-dawn melody which issued forth from the living sources of memory.]*

18th of April, 1917. Received from a stranger the following letter, which touches me very much.

Tours, the 16th of April 1917

Sir,

At the beginning of 1915, I was able to hear some of your lectures on «German Philosophy» which I have remembered with special vividness. In listening to you, every attentive listener discerned behind the philosopher, following with a lucid eye the chain of causes and of effects, the personality of a man for whom the difficult problem of living well had posed itself in all its gravity, and who had resolved it. It is to this man that I permit myself to

100

come to ask counsel in my profound intellectual isolation. I thought, Sir, that you cannot remain indifferent to the void of a soul if indeed you know the fecundity of the principle which delivers and also all the value of time.

I shall tell you more rapidly my modest intellectual history by naming to you the three authors to whom I am the most indebted: Charles Maurras, Georges Sorel and Pascal.

From the first, I have above all kept a taste for order, an accurate definition of politics (which is neither morality nor religion), the idea that we are governed more by historical laws than by our abstract constructions, and finally the sense of our historical participation.

From the second, I have loved the intense pessimism from which flow his conceptions on right and violence and on the genesis of every great realization of the human spirit.

But to Pascal especially I owe the revelation of the soul: sole stable point in the midst of our internal flow, sole fortress in which we can escape from our individuality and from contingencies, sole living principle capable of introducing a little order into our chaos. To show that the soul is absent from our natural life and that nevertheless it is the principle of all action and that consequently everything decays and falls without it: is this not the main point of the Pascalian argumentation? Then the value and the use of reason, the mistrust in which we must hold ourselves vis-à-vis ourselves, the necessity of the spirit of sacrifice and of the faith which creates, are explained.

In spite of these powerful aids I am more miserable than ever, because I have not been able to succeed in utilizing their method and in incorporating it into my personality. In the presence of events which demand the greatest strength of soul, I fluctuate in the worst moral uncertainty. What foolish pride would keep me from confessing that never having met a pure human affection, my heart wanders without refuge in hours of distress!

My difficulties in succeeding seem as insurmountable in the temporal order as in the spiritual order:

a) Causes of my lack of temporal certitude.

The catastrophic events which we are going through have taken from me, I dare not say all hope, but at least unshakable faith in the future of the great temporal works for which (in the absence of purely spiritual ends) it is beautiful and good to love and to sacrifice oneself. But the grace of joyous sacrifice is accorded only to him who dies with a thought of love inseparable from an absolute faith in a great realization of the future. What makes me doubt about the future is less the dreadful sum of the present destructions which are not yet wholly consummated, than the ignoring of the laws of all temporal construction in all domains. I, too, would like to ignore these laws, I would wish that those who taught them to me should have been mistaken in order to be able to hope for the impossible. Renan, after 1870, wrote *Réforme Intellectuelle et Morale*: what would he not write today? I can unfortunately not give to my thought all the developments and all the precisions which it would require, but in order to speak here only of the highest of temporal realities, the one for which so many of our friends have died: France, do you believe that France can recover its past glory and power with methods of government as primitive as those with which we are and apparently must remain afflicted?

If at least war brought us some progress in the moral order? It is an illusion which I no longer share. In order that «evil as suffering may triumph over evil as malignity,» it is necessary:

1. that an energetic will served by a rigorous method of interior life effect this transformation: this first condition is manifestly lacking;

2. that suffering not surpass a certain limit beyond which it can only brutalize man instead of elevating him: but the present war slowly empties the brain and even the heart of the combatants.

The majority of those who will come out of this war will experience only a formidable appetite for enjoyment which no instruction will come to temper and which will lead us more surely towards universal mediocrity.

Pascal was very struck by our smallness in the face of the grandeur of the universe; I experience the same fright in considering our weakness in the presence of social movements whose inexorable march no will seems to be able to check.

b) Causes of my lack of spiritual certitude.

Incapable of finding repose of soul in the pursuit of purely temporal ends, I am left to seek, in an issuing forth of spiritual life, a more profound explanation of present events. My heart, famished for a substantial good, seemed to have to lead me onto this path, if here again I had not met the most serious difficulties.

Religion has only one goal: it is to render to the soul its free movement; contingencies (of which our individuality is the center) tend constantly to let us ignore our soul — first principle of all profound life — and lead us to do without its action. But psychological observation proves that our nature is so clever at deceiving us that we can never distinguish what comes from our soul and what comes from nature. There remains a single solution: it is to withdraw ourselves from nature, to abdicate all self-will and, objectifying the term of the progress of the soul (God is only the purified and perfectly ordered soul), to anticipate our present state and to live in a continual conversation with God from Whom alone we await our strength and our inspiration. But we can escape from nature in order to elevate ourselves to the supernatural only by still relying on this nature. Moreover, the supernatural is not completely heterogeneous to nature: it is only purified and ordered nature. The relations which we shall maintain with God will therefore have nothing specifically different from human relations; on the contrary, they will take the form of the strongest of human sentiments, that of the family. Arrived at this point, the difficulty reappears. We shall in vain have wished to create for ourselves the framework of a purified nature (or Supernatural) in order to escape from impure nature, we shall receive no aid from this Supernatural if we have not first of all taken precautions not to reduce this Supernatural to the level of our impure nature. This is the permanent danger from which the present Church has unfortunately not been able to preserve the flock of her faithful. But the danger is as menacing in *solitary religious life*: this is where the real practical difficulty exists for me. We cannot maintain in solitude direct relations with the celestial world without fearing the worst aberrations of the intelligence and of the heart. It would be necessary to be of a truly naive optimism to believe that mystical inspiration can renew itself constantly by itself, and above all not to understand that such a wholly ideal life (which does not even enjoy the advantage which human relations have of being subject to the inestimable control of reality) leaves the door wide open to the malignity of nature. Inevitably the effort to triumph over individualism, over intellectualism, over sentimentalism and over idealism, would turn against itself.

Conclusion. Unless he is an exceptional genius no man can accomplish such a bold religious experience without the aid of a group of companions having adopted the same judicious and rigorous discipline.

This group of companions is lacking to me and this is the reason why I judge it useless to attempt such a capital experience without any chance of success.

You will object to me: And the Church?

I do not think that the Church in the state in which she finds herself can be of any help to me. Very young I left her; I do not think that I can enter her again. If solitary religious life is perilous if not impossible, religious life in society is as full of snags: the faithful relies on the spiritual society and on its leaders to take charge of maintaining pure and alive the hidden meaning of doctrine; he forgets that a personal and constant effort is alone capable of causing him to recover the inspiration which he is losing the thirst for; the materiality of his relations with his co-religionists leads him to allow himself equally easy relations with God; the letter kills the spirit in him and little by little the routine of practices enslaves him to the point of causing him to forget their reason and the great unique goal: to restore to the soul its free movement. How few Christians today have kept the sense of the soul and a profound comprehension of the Christian method? Such a contact could only cool me and weaken me instead of stimulating me. Why did the Church not understand that it was necessary to watch above all over the *purity* of doctrine and over *its practice* rather than to modernize it and to popularize it in the vain design of gaining the multitude of the mediocre? This politics was to lead her to the degree of abasement in which we see her.

Georges Sorel often returned to this idea that one cannot meditate too much: the fact is that it is the regular Orders which have made the grandeur and the astonishing youth of the Church. It is necessary that a few groups of severely selected men, perfectly trained thanks to the monastic life, be dedicated to the search for the absolute, in order to maintain the living religious tradition.

«There is no doubt,» writes Sorel, «that certain religious Orders have been very efficacious educators of heroism; unfortunately, for a number of years the monastic institutes seem to have made serious efforts to take on the secular spirit with a view to better succeeding with society people. As a result of this new situation the Church today lacks the conditions which have so long occasioned the appearance, maintained the energy, and popularized the direction of heroic leaders; conciliators no longer have much to fear from the spoil-sports.»

A second objection prevents me from embracing the Christian religion, although convinced of the eternal truth of the method of Christian life. I wish to be of my century: not in order to espouse its errors, but to understand its preoccupations, its needs, its tendencies, in order to be able to mingle with my contemporaries and to act on them by the strength of my convictions. But I doubt that the Christian myth can flourish again in the state of the present world; we will no longer know the high civilization of the Middle Ages. Then would it not be better to seek to utilize the Christian method in another manner?

I did not believe that I ought to disguise any of my thoughts or any of my judgments. I regret only that time did not permit me to give them a somewhat less imperfect form. But the main thing was to act by writing to you: already it seems to me that I am a little less ready to sink into despair because perhaps you will be able to give me the alms of some advice or to indicate to me some salutary reading.

Pardon the boldness which impelled me to write to you; but then who said: «Knock and it shall be opened to you.» Receive, Sir, the expression of my grateful sentiments.

P. Villard

Villard Pierre, volunteer in the 112th Infantry regiment, presently convalescing at Nice, Grand Palais, 2 Bd de Cimiez (Maritime Alps).

P.S. I will be arriving in Paris for a short stay on Thursday the 19th, in the evening. I shall remain there Friday the 20th, Saturday the 21st, and perhaps Sunday, before leaving again for Nice.

If I could have the opportunity of meeting you either in Paris or in Versailles, I believe that I would derive the greatest profit from it. If this were possible for you, you could let me know by leaving a word for me at General Delivery rue Vaugirard, opposite the Luxembourg (Paris-Luxembourg Office).

21st of April, 1917. Visit of Pierre Villard. In this poor soldier with the face of a contemplative one divines a soul eager for purity and for the absolute, for whom to *feel* the things of the spirit has become the great need, and whom the loss of faith (if indeed he truly lost it) has left in a vacillation without remedy; for he is too perspicacious to be content with a substitute. He is in great anxiety, which resembles a spiritual trial sent by God. He committed himself to follow a very vivid internal light which showed him with all the brilliance of evidence the value and the fecundity of sacrifice. Now this light has completely disappeared, and he finds himself caught as it were in a trap in the distressing miseries of that military life which he himself went to seek, and in the terrible reality of that total risk which he himself willed — no longer knowing (at least sensibly) if he was right to will it.

8th of May, 1917. Wrote to Pierre Villard, in answer to a letter from him dated the 3rd of May (see further on).

[I saw Pierre Villard again two or three times, in the course of leaves; correspondence with him continued regularly; his letters, especially the last ones, indicate an admirable and profoundly moving spiritual progress. In May 1918 he is sent to the front. He is killed the 28th of June 1918. (The military medal was granted to him posthumously in 1921.)]

6th of July, 1918. Learned of the death of Pierre Villard. The news of this death is given to us by Abbé Charles Rolin, the stretcher-bearer in the same regiment, in a letter (sent to Paris, it follows me to Vernie, then from there to Versailles) which both grieves us and shows us the mercies of God concerning a soul which was dear to us and for which we prayed a great deal. Friendship which took shape in a climate of eternal snows — we knew of him only his moral solitude, his high desires, and the heroism of his heart.

II

CORRESPONDENCE BETWEEN PIERRE VILLARD AND J. M.

[I received twenty-three letters from Pierre Villard (including the first, which was read above). I publish here this correspondence between him and me, cutting out some passages that are irksome or devoid of interest.

This correspondence exists (as also the letters which we received from Léon Bloy) in the archives of the Study Center at Kolbsheim.]

From Pierre Villard: Nice, *the 3rd of May, 1917.*

Dear Sir, in leaving you I felt entirely incapable of thanking you, so much did every human expression seem weak to me in comparison with the aid which you very kindly granted me in such a grave debate. Also, I thought that the best manner to show you my gratitude was to tell you that I was a little nearer to the Source of life to which you invite me, and that consequently I was able to better appreciate the wholly special quality of your solicitude. But I have waited in vain, and I can unfortunately not announce to you this good news.

I take refuge in vain in the «cell of self-knowledge,» the conviction of my natural weakness no longer appears to me as profound nor above all as rich in insights as formerly. I try in vain to gather together my ideas, to interrogate them, to squeeze them: I do not succeed in finding again their substantial reality. I suffer above all from not being able to know again the reality of that Idea which was at once all Sentiment and all Will so indissolubly united that emotion seemed to me to be in direct ratio to the precision and to the logical rigor of thought. Towards it, all realities caused my mind to converge, for it illuminated them all and assigned to each its just value: I had a «watch,» as Pascal says. I defined this Idea as follows: the soul become intoxicated with itself because having abdicated all intoxications; the soul attaching itself solely to Being and rejecting every germ of death; the soul having re-established its order and becoming conscious of all that it owed itself; and also: the soul having realized all measure and all spontaneity through the virtue of sacrifice. I now see well that all these forms of the same Idea fused into a sentiment of Love which vivified them all. But in vain I strive to go deeper into all these diverse expressions, to gather together all these scattered fragments, I cannot give re-birth to this Idea which gave them their whole reality.

Rereading notes taken at that time, I remember how much I was struck by this thought of Pascal: that an end could not be a true end if it is not the principle. Thought taken up again by Bergson and which Péguy and Sorel have so well illustrated. I discovered then that ends were not lacking (and most noble and most beautiful ends!) which proposed themselves to the activity of man, but that in actual fact man did not pursue any of them because he did not nourish his soul on them and had not realized them first in himself through love, and that thus he stove for great phantoms.

I remember also that having recognized how little man is inclined to good, how incapable he is of working at a great work for the sole glory of this work and not for his own, I judged that the main thing was to teach man to love and for this to know himself and to sacrifice himself. But at the same stroke I had perceived by a sudden illumination the soul as principle of action, and this soul which I envisaged first as a means of a great social work appeared to me as the only true end of every temporal work.

I know all of this by memory, but can no longer even repeat it with that perfect logic which convinced my mind. My soul has ceased to desire, and I am listless.

Perhaps at that time my heart was more sensitive to earthly goods: I sought to snatch my father from death and I knew better the value of life; I hoped that my country would again find the wise method of a realist politics and I loved France better, I thought of returning to service, and fearing this separation for my family I had a better sense of how disinterested a father's affection must become. Péguy had also helped me to admire all human greatness. Also, when I began to think that all this greatness was only miserable greatness if it did not have for its end the greatness of the soul, I understood at the same stroke the infinite value of this soul. Is this not an explanation of the reflective and cold (if I may venture to say so) enthusiasm which then supported me? Did not the passage of Pascal into worldly life (Méré, Miton) have a great influence on his conversion?

I could not bring back with me from Paris the books which you recommended to me (the bookshops closing at 6 o'clock). I received them only last Saturday.

Up to Chapter X, *The Life of St. Catherine*[1] disturbed me a little. I have little taste for these attempts at edification. Even if one considers that it is a question of a select creature in communication with the Absolute, there are stories which seem extravagant because they touch on the absurd.

On the contrary, the *Dialogue* of St. Catherine filled my mind with satisfaction: what admirable good sense allied to such boldness! What sureness of psychological observation! What incredible richness of life! How she knows how to lead us «with a firm step and with a light hand» as far as the highest summits of contemplation, this little saint who always repeats to us: «Act courageously!»

I also read the encyclicals: I would need elucidations and commentaries for them.

If I am to receive inspiration and strength from On High, I ask you, dear Sir, to please pray God to make Himself known to me under the form of Light. St. Catherine advises us indeed to renounce even «spiritual self-esteem»; but I am still very far from this perfection and indeed I must admit that I will be able to believe in this God whom I have already sought so long only in the measure in which He will be willing to reveal Himself to my intelligence. May I be able to prepare myself well to receive the fruit of your prayers!

I still have thirteen days before me and I desire with all my heart to employ them to the best of my ability in this search. When I am in the army, my mind will no longer be able to adhere to Truth if it has not already done so, for I would be afraid of believing in God under the pressure of events as in an object of consolation, whereas I wish first to see in Him only a creative principle.

Please accept, dear Sir, the expression of my most profoundly grateful sentiments.

From Jacques Maritain: Versailles, *8th of May, 1917* (St. Michael the Archangel).

1. [By Raymond of Capua.]

Dear Sir and friend,

Excuse me for not having replied to your good letter as rapidly as I would have wished. I have a multitude of urgent affairs to settle, having been assigned on the 30th of April to armed service (I have never been a soldier), and having to leave in a few days (unless I am granted a postponement until the end of the school year).

If I have not written to you, at least I have thought of you a great deal, and each morning at Mass I ask God to lead you into His admirable Light. Your soul, I believe I have well perceived, is made for contemplation, it will breathe only in the pure and virgin air of living Truth; and as well for God who loves you and wants you, as for you who wants life, I have an immense desire that you both find rapidly that which you seek — that you find each other.

For this I can only pray, and offer to Jesus the few troubles which He is pleased to send me — and I do it gladly. For the rest, it is He who acts, it is He who works within you, and who will show Himself to you at the bend of the road. And would you seek Him, if you had not found Him? It is asked of you only to prepare your soul and to hold it disposed, in waiting and desire. *Expectans expectavi — et consolatus sum* [I awaited with hope — and I was consoled]. I cannot remember without emotion, and without thinking of the days when I suffered like you, the words of that poor father who said to Jesus: *Credo, Domine, adjuva incredulitatem meam* [I do believe, Lord! Help my unbelief].

What you tell me of your interior state does not surprise me at all. You had for a moment — favored by a whole concurrence of natural circumstances, and by one of those marvellous coincidences of intellectual fecundity and of love's ardor which are so rare in ordinary life — a grace of illumination. I do not believe that you can regain it *just as it was*, for it was given to you for something else, and for something more beautiful and greater; so that wishing to seize it again artificially and by your own strength can only give you the impression of reassembling lifeless fragments.

It is because the Idea which you then lived, and that kind of revelation of the Soul, were only a messenger sent from very far before the face of the King, and charged with announcing His approach. *Ecce sponsus venit, exite obviam ei* [The Bridegroom is coming. Go to meet Him]. Once the Message had been brought, the Messenger went away again. It is not you whó had sent him, it is not you who can call him back. And if you took for an end or for a term this means and this call, you would exhaust yourself in a vain individualism, and in a kind of egoism. There is a truth infinitely more beautiful than what you guessed was there; or rather, what you sensed in an unstable intuition and which you will no doubt later find still very-dim and very-earthly, it is this same Truth which is wholly pure in the light of Revelation, and which lets us know in Himself the very-good Father from whom we come. There is only one means of possessing it in a stable, and truly divine, and deifying manner. It is to receive it from God through the public, universal, catholic, intellectually defined teaching of the Church, of the Mystical Body of Christ, of that mysterious Society, visible like the city built on the mountain, although secret in its profound life and in its spirit, which alone says: I have the deposit of the infallible Word and I am myself infallible, I engender for divine life, I can cure souls and remit their sins, I give them grace by my sacraments, I unceasingly produce Saints, I distribute the Blood of God, I offer without interruption a Sacrifice, not fictitious or symbolic, but true and real, in which every sacrifice has its exemplar and its power.

Then, when you have abandoned yourself, and when you have, by an act of rational submission, adhered by faith to the First Truth, then, under a new form, the spiritual joys of which you have had a foretaste will be given back to you, a hundredfold and with a superabounding measure. «Ah!» said Ruysbroeck the Admirable, «if we knew the sweetness that God gives, and the delicious taste of the Holy Spirit!»

— Certainly yes, I pray God that He will reveal himself to your intelligence, that He will make himself known to you under the form of Light, He who is Light par excellence. There is no «spiritual self-esteem» in asking for this, for we are made for Light.

I am happy that you like the *Dialogue* of St. Catherine of Sienna, which I also like so much. Do you have the Catechism of the Council of Trent? Do you also have a New Testament? I must finish this letter in haste. If you need any elucidations concerning the encyclicals or concerning another of your readings, do not hesitate to write, I shall reply to you as soon as I can.

Believe, dear Sir and friend, in my profound sympathy and

in my affectionate devotion.

I am sending you an article which now dates back several years and which will perhaps interest you, in spite of its imperfections. . . .

From Pierre Villard: *17th of May, 1917.*

I am leaving Nice in a few hours.

I hope that military life will be a purifying life for me. I am taking along the *Dialogue* of St. Catherine, and Pascal.

From Pierre Villard: *4th of June, 1917.*

I am now completing in a training-center behind the lines a period of instruction as grenadier, which is to conclude at the end of this week. Immediately afterwards, I will leave in support. I had taken along with me «Christ in the Church» (by Benson) in order to continue reading it, but on arriving here a comrade who was going up to the front asked me to give him this book. So I was very happy to receive the copy which you sent me.

I strive to follow my métier as a soldier gladly. I suffer above all from not finding around me any «faith» of métier. What has become of that conception of the army as school of pride and fortress of honor which Psichari revealed to us?

In hours of rest I try to find again some spiritual thought and to nourish myself on it. But how difficult it is to create in oneself a true interior silence! This silence which I have known, and which alone lets one perceive the voice of the soul: sensation having ceased to fascinate, the intelligence to stir and the heart to beat madly. Will I again taste this pure serenity? Sometimes I wonder if I am not pursuing a vain phantom and, with astonishment, watching other men live, if I have not lost contact with realities and abdicated my good sense. Then it seems to me that never was my intelligence so weak and my heart so dog-tired and so dry. Nevertheless, impelled as it were by the force of the memory of a lost good, I continue to seek in spite of my discouragement and my weakness.

From Jacques Maritain: *21st of June, 1917.*

The army Psichari was thinking of, the one he loved, was the *professional army. . . .*

How will you judge Benson's book? I do not know if its manner, quite specially English, will please you. What I would have wished you to discern is that the Church is not a material collection of individuals and of decrees, but a living mystery and a holy Person, incomprehensibly identified with Jesus Christ.

It pains me to think of your moral isolation, and for my part I do not cease to pray for you each day. Alone? No, you are not alone, for God stands at the door of your heart, and he knocks. You feel His presence, I believe, very near, behind this door: it takes so little for Him to enter, scarcely a heart-beat, a moment of kindness, a movement of surrender.

From Pierre Villard: *24th of June — 3rd of July, 1917.*

I do not exaggerate at all: for whoever reflects on the march of events and knows the immense internal misery of modern society, it clearly appears that the last human institutions are collapsing, that the end of a great civilization will soon be here and that barbarism is again going to cover the world.

How in these conditions is one to observe the first commandment of all Christian life: to live constantly in joy?

Suffering in the present war can only be *endured*: thus it loses all elevating value. From the first chapters of the *Dialogue*, St. Catherine puts us on guard against false interpretations of the role of suffering. She affirms with vigor: «I have shown you, very dear daughter, how fault is not expiated in this finite time by any suffering endured only as suffering. I have told you that it is expiated by suffering *endured with desire*, love, and contrition of heart, not by reason itself of the suffering, but by reason of the desire of the soul.»

I carry too tired a soul in a still more tired body to practice such a Christianity which demands the greatest vigor and the most constant courage.

Thanks for having thought of me on the occasion of the Feast of St. Peter.

I return exhausted with fatigue and with heat: we work the whole night a few hundred metres from the Germans. In order to get some rest we have to go through interminable kilometres of communication trenches every day. Sector moreover very tranquil except for the gas, against which we have to be perpetually on guard.

From Pierre Villard: *6th of July, 1917.*

I have just learned that I go up tomorrow in support: probably to the 26th Infantry regiment, crack regiment of the 20th Corps. I do not hide from you that I am a little affected by it: but not dejected. Never have I felt stronger, more resolved, more happy to have enlisted.

My sole fear is to meet death without having arrived at the full Light. May I die — if such is my destiny — in a thought of faith and of hope!

More than ever I need your help and your counsels.

From Pierre Villard: *9th of July, 1917.*

I hasten to tell you my new address: Soldat au 26ᵉ d'Infanterie, 10ᵉ Cie, S.P. 126.

Forty-four hours spent in the 26th Infantry regiment have sufficed to correct my pessimism: what lofty morale! What magnificent spirit of submission and of sacrifice!

Finally I breathe a pure air: a truly French air. I am profoundly happy.

From Jacques Maritain: *12th of July, 1917.*

I just now received your letter giving me your new address, and I write you this note in haste to tell you with what affection I follow you in my thoughts and in my heart.

The difficulties which you indicate to me in a preceding letter would vanish of themselves before an act of faith, for they stem now and always only from the observation of the radical powerlessness of man, left to his own strength, in the temporal order and in the spiritual order.

As to *suffering endured*, it is meritorious and elevating from the moment that it is endured *with love*; and this love which we cannot give to ourselves, God gives it to us gratuitously, the vigor and the courage required by Christianity do not come from us, it would be folly to expect them from ourselves. They come from God alone. Come quickly to my help, said St. Philip Neri to God, otherwise I am capable of becoming a Mohammedan! – Without Me, said Jesus, you can do nothing, *sine me nihil potestis facere.* You are asked, my dear friend, to turn away from yourself and to turn towards God, and to expect no good except from Him alone, from Him, I say, who is the living God, Being Itself, the Principle of all reality and of all goodness – and not an ideal projection of yourself – of Him without whom you can neither be, nor act, nor think, nor will.

I am sending you a medal of the Blessed Virgin, and it would be very nice if you would wear it on you, not through superstition, but as a sign of our spiritual affection, and because the humblest material signs can be the occasion of a blessing or of a grace from God.

From Pierre Villard: *2nd of August, 1917.*

Dear Sir, Just a word to tell you how much I appreciated your letter of the 12th. I have attached your medal of the Blessed Virgin to a rosary which my father always carried on him and from which I do not part through filial piety. It is with a sentiment of the same order, still wholly human, that I preciously keep this image of the Blessed Virgin.

I was not able to reply to you sooner although I often planned to. For three weeks I have been undergoing a very great physical effort, scarcely sleeping three hours a day, and besides in what conditions! I hope to go on leave soon and to be able to write to you in full liberty of spirit.

My first impressions of the 26th regiment were tinged with a little too much enthusiasm and my optimism resulted in great part as the effect of contrast with the 112th regiment. This is to tell you that I still live in a great moral solitude. Does there still exist a living faith of whatever nature it may be?

I feel very abandoned, not hoping for any temporal compensation for my efforts, of any kind, not even that (which would be, however, the only true one) of believing in the usefulness of my sacrifice. More than ever I discern in the course of my daily observations how much the human is incapable of sufficing for itself.

Nevertheless, I believe myself less incapable of abandoning the pure critical attitude in order to attain to and to participate in Life. I perhaps glimpse the dawn of Hope. . . .

Believe, Dear Sir, in my profoundly grateful and affectionate sentiments.

From Pierre Villard: *5th of August, 1917.*

I am planning to go and spend 24 hours in Paris. But I am not at all certain of being able to realize this plan.

From Pierre Villard: *27th of August, 1917.*

Received with joy your letter of the 20th.

Know only that I live in union of heart with you and believe myself closer to your thought. St. Catherine enlightened me on a grave error of method which you had already pointed out to me. I am more eager for spiritual enjoyments and spiritual consolations (of which I am moreover totally deprived: which is logical) than for the real progress of my soul. It seems to me that I am on the point of leaving the hell of doubt, of anxiety and of confusion to enter into the kingdom of certitude, of strong assurance and of free action. All that I suffer from grave anxieties, from indifference, from hatred and from ingratitude; above all, the frightful void of my acts which drove me to despair: all these griefs would therefore not be sterile.

From Jacques Maritain: *7th of September, 1917.*

All that I can tell you — in a very imperfect manner — is that I feel very vividly and very profoundly that God loves you.

I am sending you a little book which I like very much: a catechism written at the behest and according to the counsels of Saint Pope Pius X. You will perhaps be happy to have at hand this very simple résumé of a doctrine vast like the infinite.

From Pierre Villard: *26th of September, 1917.*

Although my reflection is annihilated by the tyranny of my métier, a profound and hidden work takes place in me which will cause you joy.

From Pierre Villard: *21st of October, 1917.*

You rightly guessed that I was in a new disposition of mind which rendered possible to me the understanding of the catechism. Arrived at the point where I am, this reading became opportune for me, even indispensable. How can one not be touched by the admirable wisdom of a doctrine which expresses itself in such full and such firm formulas! Thus the doctrine of distrust of ourselves is the one which has been able to conquer uncertainty of soul, the greatest evil of man.

I am infinitely grateful to you, dear Sir, for not having been afraid to speak to me the language of Faith and of Charity, in spite of my so great estrangement.

From Jacques Maritain: *21st of October, 1917.*

In these days in which you have perhaps to suffer more than usual, my thought goes towards you with a particular affection.

But yes, in the depths of your soul there is taking place between God and you things more important than the course of the earth and of the stars; for it is a question there of the Unique Necessary.

I wonder if sending some book would be acceptable to you? I have, however, the impression that in the lofty debate in which you are engaged, external helps are very little. The soul is alone in treading the wine-press, alone in making the decisive choice. Around it there is only the absolutely hidden presence of the prayers of Heaven and of earth.

From Pierre Villard: *27th of October, 1917.*

Dear Sir, My leave is advanced contrary to my expectations.

I hope to be in Paris on the 30th, barring hindrance still to be feared. I shall not fail to go to Versailles: true goal of my trip.

From Pierre Villard: Nice, *1st of November, 1917.*

Very dear Sir, I arrived this morning at my mother's. I found her in her bed paralyzed and voiceless, struck by an attack for five days. She retains however all her lucidity of mind: I was only too convinced of it when I met her gaze full of an inexpressible tenderness. You guess my distress. . . .

I no longer have anyone but her. And I have sacrificed her to my self-esteem perhaps more than to my duty.

What is the meaning of this new misfortune? May I be able to penetrate it and to inspire my whole life with it.

Thanks for your support which my weakness prevents me from appreciating as it merits.

I venture to hope that you will still keep Léon Bloy in spite of his great age. With all my heart to you.

From Pierre Villard: *3rd of November, 1917.*

Dear Sir, I lost my mother yesterday. With her has died the last profound affection which I kept on this earth.

I am transporting her body to Tours where my father already rests, while waiting until I can bring them back to Nancy after the war.

I have thought of you a great deal during these three days: your friendship is for me a refuge against despair.

It is at such times that I truly appreciate its unique quality. With all my heart to you.

From Jacques Maritain: *4th of November, 1917.*

My very dear friend, I find your letter[1] today on returning from Bourg-la-Reine, where I passed the night sitting up with the body of poor Léon Bloy, who died Saturday at 6 o'clock in the evening after a long agony. With all my heart, dear friend, I share in your suffering, and I pray to God for your mother and for you. God, by the very fact that He is God, treats us in a manner whose meaning our human gaze can scarcely penetrate, or rather which it understands only after the event, when time, and our experience of the graces that suffering brings, have been able to disengage for our eyes the tenderness which hides itself in this always strong and generous treatment. Without yet knowing in what manner, I am sure that this new misfortune, which brings you nearer to the living mystery of the Cross, which causes this mystery to throb at the very center of your heart, will increase the light and purity in your soul. But be strong, do not let yourself be shaken by scruples whose value is absolutely unverifiable, do not ask if you have acted through self-esteem or otherwise. Hurl all the past into God. Do we not know that we are nothing, that we can do nothing good by ourselves? Does not St. Paul affirm that everything, absolutely everything, even the faults which they have committed, cooperates for the good of those who love God? Diligentibus Deum *omnia* cooperantur in bonum [*all things* cooperate for the good of those who love God]. Turn yourself entirely towards Him from whom every hope comes; turn yourself entirely towards the light which is *before* you, not behind you, and whose promise is already present and active in you. Tell God that you do not want to refuse Him anything, and He will give you everything.

Tell me news of yourself, and of your dear invalid person. I hope that this letter written in haste will reach you in Nice before your departure. Believe in all my affection.

1. [Of November 1st.]

From Jacques Maritain: *9th of November, 1917.*

What to say to you in these sad days except that I am thinking of you with tenderness, and that I am praying for you with all my heart? Suffering has a power not only purifying, but illuminating, and there are truths which one sees better through tears. I ask God to give to your suffering the plenitude of this power, I ask you to *hope*, more than ever.

From Pierre Villard: Tours, *13th of November, 1917.*

Dear Sir, Before leaving this land of Touraine where my father and my mother now rest, where so many human grandeurs solicit the soul towards a Superior Order, an Order which is substantial and true, I wish to address to you a short note of remembrance.

I have tried in vain until this day to fortify my weak heart which devours itself in its aridity. However, I understand more what transformations these two little words could accomplish in me: God exists. Such a proposition, if it were believed, but believed with all the consequences of an absolute and total belief, must convulse the world. «I am Who am, you are the one who is not.» O immense wisdom expounded in brief syllables! said St. Catherine. All the divine mercy overflows from this Existence towards this nothingness: «If one intends to say that man is too little to merit communication with God, one must be very great to make this judgment.» Once again the inflexible logic of Pascal triumphs over my blind heart.

Shall I soon find the strength of abandonment into the arms of God? Or shall I never know anything but the weakness of abandonment to inhuman matter and to the chaos of events?

Shall I be stronger tomorrow than yesterday, when every human aid will have left me and when I shall bend under the weight of the horrible necessity of war?

I remain always very affectionately yours.

From Jacques Maritain: *10th of December, 1917.*

More than ever, my dear friend, you are alone with God.

With God who is more father, more mother, more brother and more friend to you than any creature. And who breaks everything in us in order that we love Him entirely. But in this solitude, think that the prayers of the whole Church invisibly envelop you.

From Pierre Villard: *4th of January, 1918.*

I can only deplore the absence of all intellectual life rendered totally impossible by the rigor of the temperature and the difficulties of the war. Virtue cannot increase without the exercise of the intelligence, and the latter necessitates a minimum of physical well-being. This experience makes it clearer to me what high moral intentions could inspire the proletarian claims and what civilizing power they acquired from this fact, even in their most violent explosions.

Military life has become for all of us soldiers a slow burial of all our faculties. This is perhaps what is most profoundly sad in this war. We act mechanically under the immediate influence of necessity or of an order, but without any spontaneity, because in our métier the principal motives which cause a man to be interested in his task are absent.

These conditions of existence constitute an obstacle to all life, however incomplete it may be: *a fortiori* to Christian life, life constantly gathered upon itself and tending towards action. I do not believe I form a false idea of Christian life in saying that it is the highest expression of artistic life; I mean that the Christian models the external works to which he devotes himself under the inspiration of the Truth which illuminates him, as the sculptor models the clay under the constant inspiration of his Idea. The Christian spirit is inventive because it does not abandon itself to habit, but constantly refers to the voice of God, from whom alone it awaits grace, that is to say, strength and inspiration. It is, by this very fact, unifying of all the moments of existence, anxious to have Truth penetrate into all its acts, even the most humble, even the most routine, precisely in order to take away from them this mechanical character and to fecundate them with a new meaning. A lively circulation establishes itself between [on the one hand] ourselves and all the moments of our life, which are so to speak the members — and [on the other hand] God, who is the heart. To cut oneself off from God for a single moment is strictly speaking to die, and this is indeed why the Christianity of our moderns who make two parts in their life — one for God, the other for the world — is a dead and sterile Christianity.

But this «artistic» conception presupposes that *all* our external acts lend themselves to receive this new meaning which divine inspiration confers on them and that in some manner we are free to fashion our external works as the sculptor models the clay. In other words, a material base is needed for our interior life. The external work is nothing by itself, but insofar as it incarnates the spirit and because it strengthens it and purifies it in contact with reality, it becomes the necessary condition for the rationality and for the enrichment of the interior life.

This impossibility of devoting myself to external works, of causing divine Truth to produce fruits outside of myself, to penetrate all my acts with it: this is precisely what prevents me from adhering to this Truth. I do not wish to fall into idealism. I do not feel any taste for a Christianity cut off from reality, which turns inevitably to sentimentalism and begets only powerlessness and debility.

From Jacques Maritain: *18th of January, 1918.*

This «burial of all faculties» caused by military fatigue could be compared, I believe, in a soul like yours, to one of those «passive purifications,» by interior darkness and interior aridity, of which the mystics speak. God does his own work, while the soul perceives in itself only nothingness and inertia. What you write to me about the Christian life is certainly very true, and we must indeed tend to be free, fresh and alert under the influence of grace. But do not forget that in this life we are not the first cause, but mere instruments of one stronger and wiser than we, and all the better the more we are instruments. This life is not our work, but that of God in us. There is therefore no reason at all to be disheartened if God wishes to use our heaviness and our powerlessness rather than our spiritual activity and our spiritual agility. Everything is equally good under His hand. A prayer, an act of faith, an act of love — these are very positive and very real works and fruits, and ones which we can produce in any situation. And nothing, absolutely nothing, can and should prevent us from adhering to divine Truth, because this adhesion is a matter between It and us, without any external consideration having to interfere with it, and because we must trust in this Truth, sure that it will indeed be able to transfigure our life when we will have abandoned ourselves to It. Who will separate me from the charity of Christ? said St. Paul.

From Pierre Villard: *17th of January, 1918.*

How can we not not feel a burning desire to introduce a little seriousness and order into our life? But can total confidence exist if an essential goal is not recognized and practiced?

My thoughts turn towards you with ever more confidence as towards the last fixed point capable of resisting the flux of events.

A week ago I sent you my new address in a letter which, I hope, has reached you.

From Jacques Maritain: *20th of January, 1918.*

I just now received your letter of the 17th of January, which crossed with the one which I just wrote to you. I would like to answer you today with a single remark: — Can total confidence exist if an *essential* goal is not recognized and practiced? Certainly not. But the *essential* goal is there: it is to do that for which we were made, that is to say, to save our soul, which is not made for the earth or for any terrestrial goal, but to be united with God in eternity. All the rest is purely secondary.

And the means of *recognizing* and of practicing this goal is there also. It is Faith, and it is the life of grace, which do not come and cannot come from us and from our efforts, but from God alone; and which we are assured of obtaining if we ask them of God through prayer and of the Church in the Sacraments. «I believe,

Lord, help my unbelief,» said the father of a family to Jesus. And this prayer pleased Jesus.

Believe, my dear friend, in all my affection.

[My letters after this date are missing in the packet which was given to me after the death of Pierre Villard.]

From Pierre Villard: *28th of March, 1918,* Holy Thursday.

Think a little for me who cannot find in my perpetual agitation a single hour of substantial and fruitful reflection. Ought not well-conducted thought always end in a prayer?

From Pierre Villard: *lst of May, 1918.* — Tours.

Dear Sir, I left you yesterday evening with my heart a little less charged with bitterness, joyous even, as I had not been for a long time.

I felt myself rejuvenated by contact with you, and as it were bathed with the tranquil lights of your intelligence.

But how not to curse once more this life which war imposes on us, which takes away from us the sense of the Absolute and the taste for the substantial happiness for which we are made?

I have begun reading the work of Father Clérissac[1] : my interest increases with each page.

Very respectfully yours.

From Pierre Villard: *10th of May, 1918.*

Dear Sir, I very much regretted not being able to bring back to you myself the work of Father Clérissac which you kindly entrusted to me. I returned it to you by mail before leaving Tours. My first too hasty reading left me longing to meditate as they deserve these strong and dense pages, several of which have awakened a

1. [The Mystery of the Church.]

profound echo in me. I neglected to make a note of the publisher: I would ask you when the opportunity arises to tell me the name so that I can have this work sent to me as soon as it is published.

Although still too distracted from myself by extraneous pre-occupations, I have been able however during my leave to enjoy a few hours of fruitful solitude and to renew the thread of my abandoned reflections. In proportion as my hungry intelligience bit into the substantial truths for which it is made, I experienced from them a more profound serenity.

First result: I succeeded in getting rid of a doubt concerning the orientation of my life. I often wondered if my search for an interior life was not solely and in the last analysis the sign of a weakness: my inaptitude to lend myself to events and to society, and to move in the midst of them. Certainly this inaptitude is a weakness; but I augmented it with another weakness which consisted not in the search for an interior and substantial good, but in doubt concerning the legitimacy of this search.

This baneful doubt could only prevent me from developing my proper virtualities, leading me into a way which I was not destined to follow. Is my lot so bad? I am refused the knowledge of how to enjoy contingencies and to dominate them (temporally), but I am given the taste for spiritual goods. The first power would reserve for me, it is true, immediate satisfactions and the esteem of men: but which is more desirable: the world or God?

I was confirmed in this sentiment by the reading of a chapter on «Maine de Biran» in the beautiful posthumous work of Victor Delbos, *Figures et doctrines de philosophes.* I can only be very sympathetic to the thought of Maine de Biran because he ran into the same difficulty as I: that of maintaining that subtle and unstable harmony between what he calls «his self» and his internal or external impressions. Incapable of abandonment to external events, yet too passionately fond of life not to feel the void of a Stoic will, he had inevitably to seek the proper Object of his soul. Object to which the soul can abandon itself without fearing to lose itself, Object source of life.

If the Germans allow me, I promise to follow through his *Journal Intime* that long and sorrowful elaboration of the sense of God of which Maine de Biran has left us a precious testimony.

I desire with all my heart, dear Sir, to be able, during this period of four months, to work a little in order to draw nearer to your thought whose lights and fruitful sweetness I envy.

Very respectfully yours.

From Pierre Villard: *18th of June, 1918.*

Dear Sir, I came out alive from Courcelles; but many of my comrades found a cruel end there. My Company Commander,[1] of whom I thought very highly, was killed first. Of the eight officers in our two engaged Companies, only one returned from the lines. . .

During these frightful hours I felt myself in the hand of God; and I thought at what infinite value should be esteemed the time granted for the work of God, by those whom death avoids.

The distress of my body smothered that foolish Stoic pride which prevented me from praying to God for an end which is not solely spiritual; remembering that other great distress, the one which impelled Péguy trembling for the life of his child to go and throw himself at the feet of the Blessed Virgin, I asked this tender Mother to preserve my life at least until the day when I shall perceive Light in its very Source.

I am entirely exhausted physically; on the other hand the march of events and the spectacle of the ruins accumulated in the heart of France distress me infinitely. In your friendship alone I draw some consolation for the barbarism of our age.

Consequently your letters are always the most welcome of all.

I thank you very much for having found the *Letters of St. Catherine of Siena* for me. Could you ask the bookstore to send it to me at my uncle's, «Docteur Villard, avenue de la Gare, Avize (Marne).» I add to my letter fifteen francs to that end. I do not dare to have it sent here, for we are going to find ourselves again in conditions such that no package could reach us.

Believe, dear Sir, in my affectionate gratitude.

From Pierre Villard: *27th of June, 1918.*

Very dear Sir, In this night watch I reread with all the com-

1. [10th Company of the 26th Infantry.]

posure of which I am capable your letter received yesterday, which has caused me such a sweet and such a full joy. I would like the great breath of love which inspires it to pass into my soul without losing anything of its spontaneity, of its power and of its light.

In a few hours I shall traverse trials as difficult as those of Courcelles. These last ones were salutary for me, and so God in His goodness sends me new ones. It is necessary therefore that I feel little and miserable in my body, after having felt little and miserable in my still proud spirit, in order to compel my prayer, and to know that serene confidence, that tender abandonment into the hands of the Master of the eternal Order.

Oh! yes, open and «gaping» I am. May the All Substance pour into my heart an always growing desire for His Love and His Light.

I am more fraternally yours than ever.

From Abbé Charles Rolin: *30th of June, 1918.*

Sir, I have just fulfilled a very painful mission: one of the last wishes of your friend Pierre Villard had been that you be informed in case of accident. This sad event has just taken place. Pierre was struck mortally in the course of a relief by the fragment of a shell. His body rests now near a bit of the earth of France recently regained from the enemy by our regiment. As priest I shall tell you that this dear departed one had taken a great step towards Jesus Christ. Grace for a long time had worked his soul which was very upright and eager for moral perfection. He was incontestably of the soul of the Church, if not already of the body; and in spite of the doubts and the obscurities which still remained in him, I had judged it fitting to give him the sacrament of forgiveness which he had come to seek from the minister of Jesus Christ.

In the name of the Church I come to thank you for the spiritual charity which you had for him, for many times he spoke to me of you and told me to what degree you had been the instrument of this interior work of grace in him.

He leaves among his comrades and with his leaders many regrets, because for the latter he was the model of a conscientious soldier and for the former of a goodness which touched even the most insensitive.

What a misfortune that so many young persons, assets of the France of tomorrow, disappear in this way without having been able to do the good which one expected of them! But fortunately, thanks to the Communion of Saints, they will continue to live among us, to speak to us, to teach us, to raise us towards Heaven. I do not doubt that Pierre Villard, whom we had here on earth for friend, is for is, in Heaven, a protector.

Receive, Sir, in union of prayers and of suffering, the assurance of my devotion in Christ.

Ch. Rolin, stretcher-bearer Sergeant, 26th Infantry Regiment, 3rd Battalion, Section 126.

III

GRATITUDE TO PIERRE VILLARD

[It is astonishing to find oneself suddenly the debtor of someone whom one believed destitute of the goods of this world, and the heart is all the more full of gratitude as one was already bound to him by admiration and affection. The feelings of gratitude and the kind of astonishment which Pierre Villard's legacy to me excited in us always remained deep-rooted in our hearts. I would like our friends to continue to maintain, after us, the same sentiments towards this great soul.

A certain amount of material independence is a singularly favorable condition for devoting oneself to the works of the intellect, for trying in particular to enter into the profound life of a highly elaborated philosophical tradition, to enlarge its horizons and to transmit its message, while discerning the renewals and the recastings which it requires. Pierre Villard gave me this measure of independence. Without him it is probable that the extremely low salaries then paid at Institut Catholique would have obliged me to take on additional tasks which would have devoured my time and been an obstacle not only to study and to reflection, but also to the availability and the liberty of movement required by every real action, that is to say action of person to person, action on men and on the spirit of the time. Without the generosity of Pierre

Villard and his purpose to have a half of his fortune serve the radiance of the ideas and of the inspiration for which he did me the honor of believing me missioned, the work of my whole life – of our whole life, Raissa's, Vera's and mine – could not have been what it was. Our liking for a modest life and for «humble means» was too profound to change; Raissa and Vera detested luxury and idleness; and in France as later in America we always worked hard and lived on a small scale. But the liberty which we enjoyed at Meudon enabled us to devote ourselves entirely (entirely? to tell the truth, what had been for Léon Bloy the cross of total poverty, the cross of illness was for us) to that life of the intelligence which we have always regarded as inseparable from the spiritual life and from the love and from the service of souls.]

24th of August, 1918. – Letter from an attorney at Nancy, informing me that Pierre Villard appointed me his residuary legatee, conjointly with Maurras. Thunderstruck at the idea that he whom I took to be a poor student was the heir of a considerable fortune, deeply touched by his confidence. The will of Pierre Villard, writes Mr. Houot, bequeaths to the city of Nancy the property of Saurupt, for the Hospice des Orphelins de la Ville. The remainder is to be divided between Maurras and me.

30th of August, 1918. – I learn of two letters of Pierre Villard joined to his will. One is of the 6th of May, 1918; the other, dated the 12th of July, 1917, is addressed to Maurras, Georges Sorel and myself (when he had drafted it he was thinking of also making Sorel his residuary legatee, afterwards he had renounced this idea). He tells us his desire that the fortune of his family «contribute to safeguard what remains of the intellectual and moral patrimony of our country» – «the more I listen to the lessons of reality the more I am convinced that this patrimony cannot be saved without a return to the Christian method and without a gushing out of faith» – and that he leaves us full liberty as to the modalities of the use of his inheritance, contenting himself with designating for us its general intention. Same clause in the letter of the 12th of July, 1917.

In this letter of 1917 he addresses himself first to Maurras and to Sorel. Then he writes, in the page which concerns me: «What is the living principle which will save me at once from intellectualism and from sentimentalism? Where can I draw the spirit of submission necessary for the clear view of painful realities and the strength to surmount them?

«I opened Pascal. You know, Monsieur Maritain, what lights then appeared to me and enraptured me. But you know also the hesitations and anxieties which remain with me.

«I have not yet the happiness of leading a life of positive faith. However, it seems to me that the true Christian is only the superior expression of the conscientious and obscure worker whom, in my métier of soldier, I am striving to become. Loyalty towards oneself, towards the work to be accomplished, towards France — is it to lead me to loyalty towards a God whom I do not yet know?

«I am convinced that happiness belongs only to hearts perpetually obliged to pray, perpetually pure. I envy these limpid souls who are the living mirrors of God. I desire that through them, the Church will rise again from the profound abasement in which we see her. I do not wish to encourage mediocrity: I believe that a single holy soul would be more useful to humanity than a multitude of believers destitute of any mystical élan.»

Autumn 1918. — Examined recently the question of modalities. Consulted M. Millot, my confessor, whose advice is categorical. It is clear that he is right. Here I am charged with a responsibility which I alone can fulfill. In order to contribute to the renewal which Pierre Villard has in view weapons will have to be wielded freely. Maurras and I will each have to use them for the undertaking to which he has devoted his life. The means which Pierre Villard gives me I must employ in the service of Christian thought and of Christian spirituality: 1st through my effort in the philosophical and cultural order; 2nd through an action on souls exercised thanks to some center of spiritual radiance.

9th of January, 1920. — Maurras proposes that he and I each put 50,000 francs into the *Revue Universelle*, in this manner the twofold status of the review would be indicated; the review would be on the one hand a forum for the ideas of *Action française* in the political order, on the other hand a forum for Christian thought, and in particular Thomist thought, in the philosophical order. Massis had spoken to me of this plan of a review last September, but not emphasizing so much the part of *Action française*; the review, he said, would need the audience of *Action française* in order to start, but would be an independent organ, without express connection with them.

I hesitate, consult, and decide to accept — above all in memory of Pierre Villard, and of the manner in which he joined in his thought the work of Maurras and my own.

[Thus there was accentuated, alas, that kind of «friendly understanding» between *Action française* and me — founded on an ambiguity and owing to my political naiveté at that time as also to the influence of Father Clérissac — which I so much reproached myself for later, and which was to end at the time of the revolt of *Action française* against the Roman censures. All positive cooperation remained however limited to the undertaking of the *Revue Universelle*.

With regard to my proper field of activity, and the part attributed to it in the intentions of Pierre Villard, it was the house at Meudon, acquired in 1923, which was going to constitute the center of spiritual radiance which I envisaged. And of this house itself the center was to be its chapel (semi-public) with the Blessed Sacrament constantly present.

Casting a glance backwards now, I thank God for the way the decisions arrived at a little more than forty years ago fructified, regarding the manner in which I had to implement the intentions of Pierre Villard. However tempting it might have been in certain respects, no kind of «institutionalization» shifting my responsibilities on others, such for example as the foundation of a chair at the Institut Catholique de Paris,[1] could assure the impulse and

1. What I was nevertheless able to do in this respect was to have appointed at the Institut Catholique de Paris, as my substitute, to whom I yielded my salary for some years, a young philosopher whose intellectual value and devotion to St. Thomas I particularly appreciated. His career as philosopher was thus assured.

diffuse the waves which these intentions called for. The task to be accomplished had to be a personal adventure, risking everything for everything. I was young then; and when I think of the kind of calumnies with which certain men of *Action française* or of Vichy were to beset us later, it occurs to me to wonder if I did well to have arranged nothing which could have protected us against them, to have bet solely on the evidence of our conscience and of our reason, and the confidence in our honor on which I did others the honor of counting. Be that as it may, I took these risks. If we consider the historical moment and the awakening to which, in spite of my lacks, our attempt contributed, I am far from regretting it.

I speak of these things now with a curious feeling of objectivity, because they have now become for me something foreign, and because it is as another than myself that I see myself involved in them. For some years I have been put by Him whom I serve on the too well lit road of the knowledge of oneself and of one's misery; and since a certain day of November 1960 I scarcely live except in the manner of a phantom. I can therefore say without fear of vainglory: it is a simple truth to state that in what happened at Meudon (I think of all the souls who came there to seek an inspiration, of the baptisms which took place there, of the conversions, of the religious vocations which originated there, of the Thomist Studies Circles and of their annual retreats, of the witness borne by collections like *Roseau d'Or* and *Les Iles*, of the impulses which, born of Meudon, contributed to renewals in the spirit of the time, some of which have already passed into the common heritage) — as in the long adventure constituted by my philosophical work and by my books, and by the books of Raissa, there was the very kind of combat of spirit with which Pierre Villard desired to be united. Whatever may have been the weaknesses of the man engaged in this combat, he conducted it as best he could. And in all things Raissa, in the midst of sufferings and of illness which expiated for him and for many others, constantly and magnificently assisted him in an admirable spirit of renunciation and of fervor.]

CHAPTER FIVE

THOMIST STUDY CIRCLES AND THEIR ANNUAL RETREATS

I

THE THOMIST STUDY CIRCLES (1919-1939)

[I see in my notes, at the date of Sunday, the 8th of February 1914: «First meeting of Thomist studies at the house, with Pichet, Vaton, Barbot, Dastarac, Massis.»

To tell the truth, that was only a short-lived attempt. It was in 1919 (at the beginning of the term, in Autumn)[1] that there really began, at our house, in Versailles (rue Baillet-Reviron), regular meetings of philosophical studies attended by — at first in very small numbers — some of our personal friends and some of my students from the Institut Catholique (where I had been named professor in June 1914). This had emerged quite naturally, without any preconceived plan, from the need to examine a little more closely, in free discussions, the doctrine of St. Thomas, and to bring it face to face with the problems of our time.

Two years later, in 1921, the idea was born of more closely associating those men and women for whom the spiritual life and studies in wisdom (philosophical and theological) had a major importance and who wished to devote themselves as much as they could to pursuing them. They would form the nucleus of our monthly meetings (the latter being open to all who took any interest in

---

1. We had stayed in Vernie, in the rectory of Abbé Gouin (Raissa, Vera and their mother, since April of 1918, myself since the summer vacation of the same year) until the 24th of September 1919, the date of our return to Versailles; I had obtained a year's leave from the Institut Catholique in order to prepare my *An Introduction to Philosophy* and the outline of *Petite Logique* [translated as *Formal Logic*].

them). In this way the Thomist study circles were «formally» established, to which a minimum of organization (it was clearly necessary) was to be given the following year.

I would like to recall a few features of these study meetings, which were to expand a great deal at Meudon. First of all, those who attended them formed a most varied ensemble. There were young persons and old persons, male students and female students, and professors — laymen (in the majority), priests and religious — professional philosophers, doctors, poets, musicians, men engaged in practical life, those who were learned and those who were uneducated — Catholics (in the majority), but also unbelievers, Jews, Orthodox, Protestants. Some were already experts in St. Thomas, others were serving their apprenticeship with him, others knew nothing about him or almost nothing. They were all searching. The unity came either from a profound love, or from a more or less great interest in Thomist thought. It came also from the climate of friendship and of liberty in which all were received.

They did not go to class, they were not assembled in a classroom of a college or convent to listen to the teaching of a master or to have a seminar with him, nor were they the guests of a more or less stiff intellectual trying to offer them seats and passing out drinks and cigarettes before the exchange of ideas. They were received in the hearth of a family, they were the guests of Raissa Maritain. Such meetings and such a work in common are inconceivable without a feminine atmosphere. There were three women in the house: there was Raissa's mother — she attended the meetings more often than not, without understanding much of them, but too good a Jew, and of too serious a mind, not to take pleasure in intellectual debates. And she busied herself with the samovar, and with the dinner to be prepared for the evening. There was Vera, silent and diligent, who took care of everyone, and listened passionately to the discussions, not without secretly praying that everything would go well. And above all there was Raissa, whose gaze and smile illuminated our humble drawing room, and who received everyone in her fraternal charity, and who did not cease for many days to carry all of this work in her prayers. She was the ardent flame of these meetings, in which she took an active part, always discreetly, but with the mad, boundless love of truth which burned in her. It is very evident that without her — and without her little sister — there would have been no Thomist circles, any more than there would have been a Meudon (any more than there would have been a Jacques Maritain).

The conversation continued after tea. The friends (after a session which lasted the whole afternoon) departed just before dinner. A few remained, more or less numerous, to dine with us. And these left by the last train. At midnight we were half-dead with fatigue, but generally very happy with the day.

The other remark which I would like to make relates to the subjects treated and to our manner of working. These subjects always concerned great philosophical or theological problems, treated in all their technicality, with (at least during the first ten or twelve years)[1] readings of some texts of St. Thomas, and of long passages chosen from some *disputatio* of John of Saint Thomas — we considered this last of the Great Commentators as a kind of magical mine which, if one took enough trouble to hollow out corridors within it in order to extract the ore from the gangue (that is to say, in particular, from the interminable controversies with the classical adversaries of the Dominican school and with the lot of generally tedious and dusty contemporaries of the author) would put us in possession of the equipment most adapted to free the captive truths which we heard calling from their prisons. The fundamental idea was to bring into play at one and the same time, in the concrete problems and needs of our minds, things we knew to be diverse in essence but which we wanted to unify within us: reason and faith, philosophy and theology, metaphysics, poetry, politics, and the great rush of new knowledge and of new questions brought by modern culture.

I prepared my expositions on the eve of the meeting or on Sunday morning — hurriedly but with much care. There are still in my papers some of these notes, embellished naturally with synoptic tables and with diagrams which I sketched on large sheets to be posted on the wall. As for the subjects, here is, for example, the list of a certain number of them, according to the hazards of the

1. Afterwards, I was often relieved by younger friends, whose exposition bore upon a subject touching on their own preoccupations. Thus Olivier Lacombe spoke several times about India and about Indian philosophy. But the meeting remained always a "Thomist" meeting, by reason of the light in which all these so diverse subjects were discussed.

first ten years: Angelic knowledge; how the angels know future contingents, singulars, the secrets of hearts. — The intellect and intellectual knowledge; the agent intellect; knowledge of the singular. The vision of God and the light of glory; the desire for vision. — Speculative knowledge and practical knowledge; is sociology a science, and in what sense. The practical sciences (in the order of *factible* and in that of *agibile*); medicine; politics. Justice and friendship. — The Trinity; subsistence; person; the divine Persons. — The state of the first man; Original Sin; the sin of the angels. — The Incarnation; the motive of the Incarnation, human nature and the human faculties of Christ. — Free will; order of exercise and order of specification; the composite sense and the divided sense, the dominating indifference of the will; the last practical judgment; the analysis of the voluntary act. . . .

As Raissa remarks smilingly in *Les Grandes Amitiés*, I would never have consented — «out of respect for the queen of the sciences» — to attenuate in any way the exactitude and the barbarism of the Scholastic jargon of my masters. Hence the complaints of Charles Du Bos about my «insurmountable vocabulary, except for a very small number of us in Europe.»[1] This vocabulary however apparently did not bother anybody at Meudon. This was so, I believe, for many reasons. First, it is necessary to mention the climate of which I spoke above. Moreover, a certain appeal to experience constantly underlay our conferences, and the technical exposition was interrupted by digressions of all kinds on contemporary problems, at first sight very distant from the principal subject — the discussion also spread little by little in the most unexpected directions; and we found a particular mental stimulation in the manner in which a complete liberty of approach was fortified by a rather fierce search for intellectual rigor; Thomism all bristling with its quills was thus thrown into the bath, and it swam there with ease.
Finally and above all, it was understood instinctively that the whole carapace of words is absolutely nothing when the words are employed to facilitate some intuitive discovery. I must add that the experience of our study meetings taught me a very precious thing: namely, that discursive and demonstrative argumentation,

1. Charles Du Bos, *Journal*, IX, p. 265.

doctrinal erudition and historical erudition are assuredly necessary, but of little efficacy on human intellects such as God made them, and which first ask to *see*. In actual fact, a few fundamental intuitions, if they have one fine day sprung up in a mind, mark it for ever (they are intemporal in themselves), and they suffice, not doubtless to make a specialist in Thomist philosophy or Thomist theology, but to make a man unshakably strengthened in the love of St. Thomas and in the understanding of his wisdom. I observed this in a good number of our friends, whose example I take to be decisive.]

*

[Let us pass now to some notations, found like debris on the reefs, in scanty notebooks where gaps abound.]

1920

Sunday the 5th of December, 1920. — Afternoon, study meeting: Abbé Lallement, Roland Dalbiez, Pichet, Vaton (Vitia Rosenblum, brother of Aniouta Fumet), Mlles Bouchemousse, Denis (Noëlle Denis, eldest daughter of Maurice Denis), Clément, Marie-Emmanuele Lindenfeld. I urge them to work, telling them that minds are perfectly ready, that there is nothing in front of us, that we must charge onward such as we are, addressing ourselves especially to the lay world, and confident in God and in the power of St. Thomas to supply what is lacking in us.

Thursday the 23rd of December. — Study meeting: Dalbiez, Abbé Lallement, Noëlle Denis, Marie Clément, Mlles Bouchemousse, Wever, Moreau, Marie-Emmanuelle (who is very bored). Nothing happens. Stagnation.

1921

Sunday the 16th of January, 1921. — Study meeting. Marie Clément and Noëlle Denis have lunch with us. Everybody is there. Pichet and his sister, Dalbiez, Abbé Lallement, Vaton, Abbé Kornilowiez (passing through Paris), Mlles Leuret, Moreau and Wever, Marie-Emmanuele, Vitia, Marie-Louise (Marie-Louise Guillot, very dear friend of Vera, who had known her through Père Dehau), and even Philipon. — On angelic illumination.

Sunday the 20th of February. — Study meeting: Prince Ghika, Abbé Lallement, Dalbiez, Gouhier, Pichet, Vaton, Massignon, Noëlle Denis, Marie Clément, Mlle Moreau, Mlle Leuret, Marie-Louise, René Barthe with his wife and his son, the two Socard brothers, Juliette Pichet. — Cajetan and John of Saint Thomas on angelic illumination. St. Thomas on human magisterium.

Sunday the 3rd of April. — Study meeting: Dalbiez, Mlles Leuret, Wever, Moreau, Denis; Vaton, Abbé Richaud, Vitia, Robert Boulet, Van Vree. . . . — On angelic knowledge.

At 6 o'clock Ghéon arrives, then Rouault. Ghéon read us *Le Mort à cheval.*

Sunday the 17th of April. — Visit of Mlle Clément. The idea, proposed by Raissa and me, of a society of St. Thomas seems very good to her.

Friday the 29th of April. — Abbé Lallement, Prince Ghika, Dalbiez, Mlles Clément and Denis, Raissa and myself. Decided to establish as the basic framework of our meetings an *association of Thomist studies.* In order to aid laymen to maintain the purity of Thomism and to spread it. The members would have to declare themselves resolved to follow the guidance of St. Thomas with an entire fidelity, to read the *Summa* at least a half-hour a day, to devote at least a half-hour a day to prayer.

Sunday the 8th of May. — Study meeting: Ghika, Canon Thiéry, Dalbiez, Lallement, Pichet, Vaton, Mlles Denis, Clément, Moreau, Ernée, Leuret; Vitia, Marie-Emmanuele. . . . — The *species infusa* in the angels.

(Gap in my notebook.)

6th of August, 1921. — We have been in Switzerland, at Blonay, for six weeks. Raissa still very ill. Attended by Dr. Nebel.

Saturday the 13th of August. — Raissa tells me that Wednesday morning, during prayer, she had the clear sense that an acceptance of suffering was asked of her. And she was at the same time inclined to answer *yes*, which she in fact did. A half-hour later the crisis of these last days began.

Several times a similar thing happened to her. (At Binic, at Vernie. . . .)

Wednesday the 23rd of August. — Once again she has that countenance of a wilting violet, and those eyes of a too lively brightness and of a slightly bluish white, which tell me that she is not well. In fact she is more ill in the afternoon. And thus reduced to nothing, she weeps.

And here I am like a blockhead, unable to do anything for her, unable to act either humanly or divinely. I am going to buy some books for her at Vevey.

Thursday the 5th of September. — Vera brings home a wheel-chair from Montreux. I have great hopes of being able to take Raissa out in it and to have her breathe the pure air.

[During these weeks of suffering she talked to me a great deal about our Thomist circles and was very preoccupied with them. The sense of the distress of souls and of the immense need which they had of the light of St. Thomas, and the solicitude to do something which would help a little, did not leave her.]

Saturday the 8th of October. — Father Garrigou-Lagrange (who had already paid us a visit previously with Father Bernadot) arrives at 3:15 A.M. at Vevey, to see us. (At the end of a stay which he made in Switzerland during this vacation.)

[Did he come from Vevey to see us each day? Did he live with us? I do not remember. In any case our conversations with him were long and frequent, until his departure on the 11th. With his goodness and his simplicity which were full of playfulness, this great theologian set about relieving me to push Raissa's wheel-chair along the roads (she was benefitting greatly from these outings which I had begun in September). It was during one of these walks, Monday the 10th of October, I believe, that she made bold to say to him, while thinking that she was asking the impossible (Father Garrigou taught at Rome, at the Collegium Angelicum, and he passed his vacation preaching retreats in convents of contemplatives): «My Father, there is a great anguish and a great thirst among those who live in the world, it is necessary that they also hear you in France. If, thanks to the Thomist circles, we can bring together, as I believe, a sufficiently large number of friends anxious to hear you, would you consent to come each year, during the vacation, to preach a retreat for them, like those you preach to the contemplatives, but for those who are intellectuals in the world?» — To our great surprise and our great joy, he replied *yes* immediately. The annual retreats of the Thomist circles were founded in principle. Their organization fell on our shoulders.

But the first thing to be done was to finally settle on the organization of the Thomist circles themselves, which our friends and we had been thinking about for several months. The essential point was to assure the profound unity between the spiritual life and the work of the intelligence. To this end, was it not necessary for the members of the circles to commit themselves, before God, to live as much as possible the life of prayer? The vow of prayer — this is the soul of the work to be realized. This idea, which went much further than the mere resolution which had been discussed in April, and which put a private promise, but one relating to the regime of the counsels, a true vow, at the heart of our lay circles, came from Raissa. She spoke of it to me during the talks we endlessly pursued at Blonay, and I was immediately struck by its importance. The modalities would have to be specified later. It would naturally be a question of a private vow; and it would not bear on something material (like a minimum of time to be given to prayer), which would leave the soul free, would oblige it only as to the intention of doing its best in this respect according to its state of life and the circumstances.]

We return to Versailles on the 18th of October.

Sunday the 20th of November. — Study meeting, on the knowlege of future contingents and of the secrets of hearts. Thirty persons grouped around John of Saint Thomas, this causes us great joy.

Among the attendants: Pichet, Vaton, Abbé Lallement along with two priest friends of his (scientists), Abbé Soulairol, Robert Boulet, Ghéon, Altermann, Gouhier, René Barthe, Albert Camilleri, Robert Vallery-Radot; Noëlle Denis, Marie Clément, Mlles Moreau, Leuret, Reyre, Bouchemousse; Marie-Emmanuelle, Marie-Louise.

Jean-Pierre Altermann dines with us, as also Pichet and Camilleri.

Sunday the 11th of December. — Study meeting. Among the attendants: Ghika, Abbé Lallement and three priest friends, Abbé Soulairol, Gouhier, André Germain, Pichet, Vaton, the brother of Robert Vallery-Radot, Altermann, Ghéon; Noëlle Denis, Mlles Clément, Leuret, Moreau; Vitia, Marie-Emmanuele.

After the meeting, Ghéon reads his *Saint Maurice.*

1922

9th of February, 1922. — Abbé Lallement gives me a letter from Father Garrigou-Lagrange. He accepts the idea of the Thomist association with its vow of prayer which we submitted to him. Now we are embarked; trusting in God.

It will be necessary to see Father Louis (the Provincial of the Dominicans of the Paris province).

Abbé Lallement, Abbé Lavaud, Prince Ghika, Albert Camilleri, are already won over. Saw Dalbiez, to whom I also speak of it, and who agrees.

[We had become acquainted the preceding year with Abbé Lavaud and Abbé Péponnet, two young priests of the diocese of La Rochelle, full of fire for St. Thomas. Abbé Péponnet, whose exquisite finesse joined with a great vigor of mind charmed us, was soon to be taken from us by death. His friend, Abbé Lavaud, whose beneficent verve and good humor are a kind of infused virtue, was to become our very dear friend, Father Lavaud, O.P. — Another great friend, Abbé Maquart, of the diocese of Rheims, had come to us at approximately the same time. Abbé Richaud was also a member of our circles from the outset (although he did not often have time to attend the meetings; he was curate then, at Notre Dame

Church, if I remember rightly, and very busy on Sunday). The mutual affection which so profoundly linked all three of us to him had begun a few years after we had come to live in Versailles.[1]]

16th of February. − Cold and reserved reception by Father Louis. Father Barge is there. A certain uneasiness seems to establish itself when there is talk of Father Garrigou-Lagrange as sole director of the association. (It is a question for us of not making our group of laymen an affair haphazardly managed by the Dominicans, and of not falling under the thumb of the Provinces of the Order.)

Sunday the 19th of February. − Study meeting. Father Kremer and Mgr. Mariétan attend. − John of Saint Thomas on the agent intellect.
André de Bavier, Pichet, Altermann, Amieux, Ghika dine.

Friday the 24th of February. − Lunched at Father Louis' with Ghika and Lallement. He gives us a favorable response for the association. We can ask Father Garrigou-Lagrange to preach the annual retreat. The diplomacy of Prince Ghika greatly helped.

Friday the 10th of March. − Meeting at the house in order to draw up the statutes.

Sunday the 19th of March. − Study meeting. Question of the adequate object of the intelligence, and of the desire for vision. Altermann dines, with Pichet, Vaton, Philipon.

Sunday the 9th of April. − Worked on our statutes.

10th of April. − At Paris I consult M. Villien, professor of Canon Law at the Institut Catholique. He reads our statutes. Our affair, he says, is neither a confraternity nor a pious association

---

1. Here are, according to a list of Raissa's, the names of the first members of the Thomist circles (without mentioning Father Garrigou-Lagrange or the three of us): Abbés Lallement, Journet, Zundel, Dondaine, Lavaud, Péponnet, Richaud; Roland Dalbiez, Prince Ghika, Charles Henrion, Dr. Pichet, Henri Ghéon, Jean-Pierre Altermann, Albert Camilleri; Mme Marthe Spitzer, Mlles Denis, Clément, Leuret.

nor an ecclesiastical person; it has accordingly no need to submit its statutes to ecclesiastical authority. The only thing required is that the directors of studies (myself for Meudon, others for other eventual centers) be approved by the Ordinary, but this would not involve having to submit the statutes to him, or speaking to him of the vow of prayer, a purely private thing.

Bring out well the private character of this vow, so as to avoid all false appearance of a congregation.

Tuesday the 11th of April. — Worked with Raissa at completing the statutes.

Wednesday the 12th of April. — In the evening, when I return, Raissa presents me with a letter from Mgr. Gibier (or more exactly a request from me which he returns with a few lines in his own hand). He gladly approves and affectionately blesses our Thomist group.[1]

Thursday the 13th of April. — Raissa and I complete the statutes. At Raissa's suggestion we choose as motto: *O Sapientia.*

[The complete text of these statutes has been reproduced in an appendix. I give here a few extracts from it:]

«. . . . Because he profoundly venerated the Fathers of the Church and the holy Doctors who preceded him, St. Thomas, as Leo XIII wrote, 'in a certain way inherited the intellect of all.' He so lost himself in truth that one must say of him, with one of his great disciples: *Magis aliquid in sancto Thoma quam sanctus Thomas suscipitur et defenditur,* 'in St. Thomas it is something greater than St. Thomas that we receive and defend.' Heir of the past and treasurer of the future, he alone can teach us to become, by his example and according to the measure of our weakness, transparent to truth, docile to the Spirit who gives understanding, open to the common and century-old wisdom with which the Church is divinely instructed. An active, progressive and conquering fidelity — but absolutely pure and entire — to the principles, to the doctrine and to the spirit of St. Thomas, is therefore the means *par excellence*

---

1. This document is reproduced in an appendix.

of serving the Truth which is Christ, and it is specially required for the salvation of the intelligence threatened today on all sides.

«We believe moreover that the human intelligence is so weak by nature, and so weakened by the heritage of Original Sin, and that on the other hand the thought of St. Thomas is of such a lofty intellectuality, from the metaphysical as well as the theological point of view, that in order for this thought to be given to us, all the supernatural graces of St. Thomas were needed. The eminent sanctity and above all the unique mission of the Angelic Doctor assured him of the help of these graces. We believe that in order for his thought to live among men, a special assistance of the Holy Spirit is and will always be needed.

«In particular, in our epoch so full of errors, and especially where the discipline and the graces proper to the religious state are lacking,[1] we believe that it is impossible for Thomism to be maintained in its integrity and in its purity, without the special aid of the life of prayer.

«We know besides that this union of the spiritual life and of the life of study was not only practiced to an eminent degree by St. Thomas himself, but also by his most authoritative commentators, for example by Bannez, who was the director of St. Theresa, and by Gonet, who dedicated to the great contemplative his *Clypeus thomisticae theologiae*, and by the Salmanticenses, who remained so perfectly faithful on all points to Thomist theology, and who saw in it the foundation of the great spiritual doctrines taught by St. Theresa and by St. John of the Cross.

«. . . . It seems useful and opportune therefore to associate the souls of good will who, through love of Truth and of the Church, desire to work for the diffusion of Thomism or to draw their inspiration from it, in study circles which would help them to improve in the knowledge of St. Thomas, and to make it better known, and which would aim to perpetuate in lay circles, through a lasting institution, the living tradition of the masters of Thomism.

«But since the principal element here is, as we have seen, the spiritual and supernatural element, and since such an association

---

1. Did this interpolated clause on the religious state and fidelity to pure Thomism give evidence of a great naivete? or of a certain irony? Neither the one nor the other; but it is necessary to know how to understand it. (1962).

can only have value and effectiveness if those who compose it are dedicated as fully as possible to the action of the Holy Spirit, each of its members[1] would bind himself by a private vow to practice the life of prayer. Thus this association of secular priests and of laymen would have at the base of its activity a very intimate and very profound gift of oneself to God, and would offer to souls who desire perfection while remaining in the world a very real help, without however enroaching at all upon the liberty of each, since the vow of prayer concerns only the absolutely personal relations of God and of the soul.

«. . . . The members of these study circles bind themselves to study St. Thomas as far as possible, and they make the private vow to practice the life of prayer, as much as their way of life and their practical duties permit.

«The normal order which the members of the circles are invited to follow, with the approval of their confessor, is to carry out in practice the substance of this vow for one year before pronouncing the vow itself; then the vow is to be annual and renewed twice, and after these three years it is to give place to a perpetual vow.

«This vow, either annual or perpetual, does not bear on a materially determined exercise, which must last a precise time each day. A time so fixed could only be a minimum, and all the persons whom the study circles will bring together generally give to prayer, in actual fact, much more time than could be fixed in such a commitment. If the object of the vow is not determined in a material manner, it is in order to have it bear on the essential, the vital, not to belittle things, and also not to give occasion in certain cases to all kinds of scruples. It bears therefore solely on the *general orientation* given to life, so that only the act of *explicitly revoking* the intention to practice the life of prayer can constitute the violation of it.»

15th of April 1922. — For several weeks Raissa and I have been working at the little spiritual directory, intended for the members of the Thomist circles, which Father Garrigou asked us to write.

---

1. It is not a question here of all the persons who attended the study meetings, but, as I noted above, of those who formed the active nucleus of these meetings. (1962).

Reviewed together today the greater part of our first draft.

17th of April. — Finished the draft of our *Directory* sitting by Raissa, lying down, who works with me.

24th of April. — Mgr. Mariétan has written a very good and affectionate letter approving the study circles and especially the vow of prayer.[1]

We bring the revised statutes of the Thomist circles to Father Louis, who is very good. Thus all the steps for the study circles are now completed.

Sunday the 30th of April. — Study meeting. Question of the desire for the vision of God.

Sunday the 7th of May. — Touching letter from one of my pupils, Henri Pierre, who now attends the study meetings.

Friday the 12th of May. — Wrote to Father Garrigou-Lagrange sending him the statutes.

Tuesday the 16th of May. — Talked at length with Raissa. We have the impression that here we are the two of us, in spite of ourselves, in high seas and forced to judge by ourselves, as autonomous beings — it is just like a coming of age (I am forty! But sixteen years only since our baptism). It is necessary to be ready to receive advice, but not to *count* on it; it is necessary to have one's own point of view, the only one from which can be judged certain values referring to the place which in His providence God has assigned us. (So it is, for us, a question of what is suitable for lay life with respect to intellectuality and faith, and the spiritual life.) Immense solitude in relation to men. To act according to the spirit of Jesus. To be faithful to prayer. It is into the divine counsel, so terribly infinite and transcendent, that we are hurled.

We feel very shocked by the narrow and conventional manner in which the Benedictines judge Father de Foucauld, «that eccentric,» one of them said to us.

---

1. This letter is reproduced in an appendix.

Our lot henceforth is a greater trembling and at the same time a greater liberty and self-sufficiency.

Sunday the 21st of May. — Study meeting. On the knowledge of the singular. —Abbé Lallement is named secretary of our study circle.

At dinner: Ghéon, Pichet, Vaton, Camilleri.

1st of July. — Again in Switzerland, at Val d'Illiez. (Arrived yesterday.)

Today we finish completing our Directory.

Thursday the 20th of July. — Visit of Abbé Journet (first meeting). He is as we imagined him, humble, of an admirably lucid and generous intelligence, of an exquisite delicacy, he has humor, he is ardent for God and for truth. Fragile health, alas.

25th of July. — Sent the Directory to Fr. Garrigou-Lagrange.

5th of August. — Father Garrigou approves our little Directory. He proposes to advance the date of the retreat. The latter (the first one) will begin on the 30th of September.

30th of August. — Letter from Mère Marie-Thérèse who tells us of her «enthusiasm» for the Thomist study circles. She approves the little Directory.

2nd of September. — Sent our Directory to Mgr. Mariétan, Abbé of Saint-Maurice d'Agaune. requesting his Imprimatur.

10th of September. — Mgr. Mariétan approves the Directory.

15th of September. — Gave the manuscript of our Directory to the Saint-Augustin press.[1]

We return to Versailles on the 20th of September.

---

1. It was the first edition of the little book *De la Vie d'Oraison*, privately printed and reserved for the members of the Thomist circles. Later, and at the request of our friends, we decided to publish it in book form (chez Louis Rouart, a l'Art Catholique). [Translated as: *Prayer and Intelligence*].

THE ANNUAL RETREATS OF THE THOMIST CIRCLES (1922–1937)

1922

[The first retreat took place at Versailles. There were about thirty retreatants – male and female. How were they lodged? In religious houses? At the hotel? I do not remember. Some came from Paris each day. In spite of the efforts of Raissa and of Vera, the organization at Versailles could only be very precarious. I believe that Father Garrigou-Lagrange delivered his sermons in one of the chapels or catechism rooms of Notre-Dame Church, but I have no precise recollection on this point; we only noted the hour of the sermons (morning at 10 o'clock, afternoon at 3 o'clock). I suppose also that after having attended the instructions the retreatants returned to our house during the day.

All three of us felt with a certain anxiety, which did not prevent enthusiasm, the importance of the days when the project formed at Blonay was going to be put to the test for the first time. Raissa has noted in her journal many things concerning this first retreat; I shall give only a few brief indications.

Here is the list of the retreatants: Abbés Journet, Lallement, Lavaud, Péponnet, Dondaine, Maquart, Richaud, Canon Rageth, Brother Bruno; Mlles Denis, Clément, Leuret, Moreau, Pimor, Ressinger, Mme Lequeux; Dr. Pichet, Henri Ghéon, Jean-Pierre Altermann, Henri Croville, Yves Congar (then a student at the Institut Catholique), Albert Camilleri, René Philipon; four or five less regular attendants, and the three of us.]

29th of September. – Fr. Garrigou arrived yesterday evening. He spends the day with us.

30 September – 4 October 1922. – First retreat of the Thomist circles.

30th of September. – At 3 o'clock, instruction on «The union of the intellectual life and of the spiritual life.»

Sunday the 1st of October. — In the morning at 10 o'clock, instruction on «The ultimate End of human life.» In the afternoon at 2 o'clock, study meeting at the house. Father Garrigou speaks on the natural desire to see God. Then Ghéon reads his «Sainte Germaine de Pibrac.»

2nd of October. — At 10 o'clock, «The love of God for us and the redemptive act of Christ»; at 3 o'clock, «Mortification.»

The saintly Curé (Abbé Lamy, parish priest of La Courneuve) comes in the afternoon, brought by Pichet. They dine with us, as also Father Garrigou, Ghéon, Altermann, Canon Rageth.

3rd of October. — At 10 o'clock, «Humility», at 3 o'clock, «Prayer.»

4th of October. — At 10 o'clock, «Prayer.» Closing of the retreat. Father Garrigou leaves for Paris, and from there for Vienna. He is very happy, we likewise. The union of minds has been marvelous.

The next retreat is scheduled for the 26th of September. Father will reserve one day for private conversations; it is necessary that one be able to see him at leisure.

1923

2nd of January 1923. — Began to distribute the little Directories.

12th of March. — Vera found a house at Meudon, while she was praying to St. Joseph with an impression of sweetness and of quite special earnestness and feeling herself carried forward by a good wind. The house seems to come up to our wishes a hundred times better than all those which we have seen up to now. Excellent situation, but garden small and in bad state. Vera has her festive air, one guesses that she has the feeling of having been aided. This gives Raissa and myself much hope and a favorable inclination, because it is our little sister and high minister of Providence who has made the discovery.

I go to see this house the very next day. Raissa, very ailing, cannot accompany me. Once more it is going to be necessary to arrive at a decision which closely concerns her without her having been able to see the situation herself. It is always like this when we leave on vacation, but this time it is a question of a definitive installation, and of the place in which she will live, and of the material conditioning on which much will depend for our work and our projects.

16th of March. — Appointment for the three of us with the notary of Meudon. Today was Raissa's first opportunity to see this house of rue du Parc, and naturally with the kind of little agony she feels at the first contact with each new dwelling, always so distant from the idea which we had given her of it. She has an impression of suffocation, of humidity, of darkness (especially, I believe, because of the quite bushy narrow garden which rises in a slope behind the house as if to imprison it). It is quite different from what she was hoping for. Finally she resigns herself. We buy the small villa.

Tuesday the 5th of June. — We settle in Meudon. One of the rooms has been transformed into a chapel, in which we have the privilege of being able to keep the Blessed Sacrament. Jesus will live with us. Raissa is happy.

8th of June. — Feast of the Sacred Heart. First Mass in our house (celebrated by Abbé Sarraute, young priest friend of Gino Severini). Installation of the Blessed Sacrament.

[At Meudon Raissa was going to know some «sunny days in France,» the most happy years of our life, with those graces of recollection which were her treasure, and present close by her the three beings which her heart could not do without, and friendships, matchless joys of the spirit — and at the same time internal griefs and rendings which she succeeded in entirely hiding except from Vera and myself, and which caused her to taste the bitterness of death, leading her to that complete gift of self through which she became wholly available to souls and to the sufferings of the Cross.

Vera watched over Raissa and myself like a chargé d'affaires of Jesus sent to fortify us in our troubles. I believe that she had conversations of an extreme sweetness with Him, in a humility and an ignorance of herself that were singularly profound, but no one better sealed her secrets than this timid and adventurous (as was her father) Martha who seemed wholly occupied with exterior activities, and whose heart burned with love.

The two sisters possessed from their Jewish blood that refinement of sensibility which the habit of contemplation rendered more delicate still, and which naturally made them privileged ones of suffering.

They suffered above all from the blows I received. They never became accustomed to injustice and to calumny. With my much rougher skin I was less affected by them. I tried to hide from them the most violent attacks on me, but Raissa did not fail to find the press-clipping or the letter which I had concealed from her and which afterwards I let lie about anywhere; and there was always some well-intentioned friend to tell her with a beaming smile (was she not a Christian? she ought, should she not, to be delighted to see me insulted): «Did you see how Jacques was treated by so-and-so the day before yesterday?»

It was at Meudon, as I have already indicated, that the Thomist circles and their annual retreats received their whole development. The number of retreatants as well as of attendants at the monthly meetings increased from year to year. (In the last years two or three hundred persons took part in the retreats.) These Thomist study circles also spread abroad, in England particularly, under the presidency of Richard O'Sullivan, in Switzerland, in Belgium. . . .

When I think now of these years of Meudon, it is difficult for me to understand how we were able to bear up. In addition to the preparation of my courses at the Institut Catholique and of my books (without mentioning the conferences abroad) — in addition to the time devoted to old and new friends who were our great consolation, to unknown visitors who arrived with one knows not what vague hope and to whom it was necessary above all to listen,[1]

1. I note that we always welcomed those who desired to see us, but we never sought to make the acquaintance of anyone. This spontaneous rule was a guarantee against all risk of worldliness.

to the conversions, to the baptisms, to the religious vocations, all things which we never had the impiety to go hunting (they were not our affair, but that of grace, and sometimes of too hurried advisers, however it was necessary not to shirk) — there was not only the Thomist circles and the retreats; there was also a swarm of other meetings, particularly those called in jest «esoteric» (where a few people met to work on certain difficult questions), and inter-confessional meetings at Berdiaeff's house and at our house, and meetings (which were unsuccessful) to found a society for the philosophy of culture, and others to found a society for the phi-losophy of nature (these were successful, and the society[1] began well and published three or four books of value, before perishing miserably as a result of political conflicts between its members). There was the collection *Roseau d'Or* (later *Les Iles*), that of *Questions Disputées*, that of the *Bibliothèque Française de Philosophie*, with the whole burden of manuscripts to be read, of correspondence and of wranglings this involved; there were the *Études Carmélitaines* of Father Bruno and the congresses of Avon; there were the duties to be rendered to poetry, to music, to painting. There was the crisis of *Action Française* and the dramas of conscience caused by the civil war in Spain, there was the affair of *Vendredi*, — the founding of *Temps Présent* and the collaboration in this periodical — and all those manifestos which it was necessary to write because those given to me to sign were vitiated by partisan intentions — and in the end the rather turbulent conferences organized by André David at the Théâtre des Ambassadeurs. If peace of heart and the pursuit of wisdom were able to continue in spite of everything in the midst of such a scramble, I know a little by whom and how the check was paid.

But let us return to the annual retreats, of which I undertook to speak in this section. I would like to note first that they were above all the work of Raissa and of Vera.

They were Raissa's idea, she brought them before God in her heart. And in spite of her perpetual trials of health she helped Vera as much as she could in the work of organization (correspondence, invitations, lists to be drawn up. . . .). But it was Vera who had the heaviest burden; for weeks before each retreat is was necessary for

---

1. Its secretaries were Roland Dalbiez and Rémy Collin.

her to solve all the collective and individual problems posed by the billeting of the male and female retreatants. As a general rule, the male retreatants lodged in a vast house with a beautiful garden which the Missions Étrangères had at 87 rue de la République, and which they generously offered us for a week (the house was empty at that time of the year). The equipment was primitive, but sufficient. The eve of the opening of the retreat, I went not without emotion, — or without complicated considerations concerning the proprieties of all — to put the stickers on the doors of the rooms. The female retreatants lodged with the Soeurs de la Présentation de Tours, 18, rue de la République. But when the crowd (of the female retreatants in particular, which at one time we were obliged to check a little) became too great, we had to rack our brains to find supplementary lodgings. Our friends Pierre and Jeanne Linn helped Vera; Pierre was treasurer (charged with looking after the very small payment for board and lodging which the female retreatants had to offer to the Soeurs, and the fee which the male retreatants paid to Missions Etrangères for their meals).

While I write I see a pale image of these abolished things rise again in my thought. What trouble poor Vera gave herself! Taking care of each one, tormenting herself for the physical and moral good of each one in particular. All her life it was so. Her fraternal charity had no frontiers, she was at once daring and defenceless, very lively in temperament and feeling all things with a princely sensibility, but likewise prompt in pity and in devotion, always ready to brave anything to defend those who were dear to her or to render service to them. And now what remains of all this love dispersed everywhere we passed? A small tombstone in a small cemetery a few thousand kilometres from that France for which she had such an ingenuous and such a proud passion? All the love cast for centuries on the roads of time — is it possible that it is forever lost? To exist would be worse than absurd if there were not eternal life.

The instructions took place (one in the morrning, the other in the afternoon) in the chapel of the Présentation. They were very long, and Father Garrigou thought he had touched his audience only when he saw Ghéon weep. Sunday afternoon was devoted to a study meeting which took place in our house, when Father spoke on some doctrinal problem. Then we had a serious discussion.

What particular features did these retreats offer? I shall point out three of them. In the first place the barriers which ordinarily characterize these kinds of solemnities were abolished. Men and women, priests and laymen, young and old participated in them equally.

In the second place the barrier of silence was likewise suppressed. To be sure I believe I remember that as a rule there was reading aloud at meals (which did not prevent, at the Missions Étrangères at least, quite a lot of chatter). On the other hand, everyone took as he pleased a time of solitude which suited him for recollection and prayer. But except for the instructions and for the meals no schedule was established. And the greatest part of the time left free by the instructions was occupied by endless conversations, in which we spoke of very grave matters and laughed a great deal.

People came from different countries — principally France, England, Switzerland and Belgium — people came also from all corners of the intellectual horizon. It was a unique occasion to meet one another, to mutually share one's experiences and one's research, to prepare a multitude of projects, to compare works underway. At a certain period Dalbiez, who was preparing his thesis on Freud, would not rest until he had read some chapter to one or another of us, and he pursued Vera with his manuscript. She fled, little curious about the «dream-of-the-injection-of-Irma.» Ghéon never failed to give a reading of one of his new plays.

The conversations to which I just alluded were singularly stimulating for the intelligence. They rendered possible certain collaborations — for example, it was thanks to the friendships which were formed in them that it was possible for me to group immediately the collaborators[1] of *Pourquoi Rome à parlé*, when Pius XI asked me to prepare this book in three months. . . .

But let us leave these details. The characteristic feature I speak of at the moment (but it is a whole atmosphere which should be recreated, and I am quite incapable of it) is the spirit at one and the same time of liberty and of fervor, and the inextricable intermingling of the fires of intelligence and of those of the spiritual life, and of the quest for God through prayer, which we found in these retreats.

1. Except Father Doncoeur, who was not a frequenter of Meudon.

Finally, in the third place, it is fitting to note that to this audience composed in major part of laypersons (of whom the majority were far from having pored over the works of the great philosophers, the treatises of dogmatic theology and the treatises of mystical theology) Father Garrigou-Lagrange gave as nourishment sermons which he would have preached to cloistered contemplatives and instructions which he would have delivered before his students at the Angelicum or his colleagues at the Academy of St. Thomas. And this nourishment was received by all with joy and with a real profit. All of which proves on the one hand that one should not underestimate the powers of natural intelligence superelevated by faith, and on the other hand that what souls thirst for above all is to enter into the paths of doctrinal truth and into those of an authentic spiritual experience, and in this way to be enabled to realize within themselves the unity required by life. *O Sapientia!*

Many decisive choices were made, many rectifications were accomplished, many religious vocations and many intellectual vocations were strengthened in the course of these retreats. All the resolutions, the questions, the anguishes surged back in the conversations (it was necessary to set much room aside for them) which Father Garrigou-Lagrange had in private with all. He noted «all the good that was happening» in these few days — it is the formula he regularly used, and when he took leave of us he encouraged us to continue with this slightly hackneyed but nevertheless comforting cliché.

*

[My notebook for this year 1923 is excessively poor, and during the four following years I entirely neglected my notebooks.

As to the retreat of 1923, there are two pages on it in *Raissa's Journal*. From other documents I draw the following notes:]

26-30 September 1923. — Second retreat of the Thomist Circles. The following regularly attended this retreat:

Abbé Journet, Abbé Zundel, Dr. Saudan, M. Gauley (all four coming from Geneva);

Abbés Lallement, Maquart, Lavaud, Péponnet, Dondaine, Schmitt (curate at Rheims), Poupon, Croville, Congar, Grossin,

Ancelin, Méchain, Salaün (all three of them from the seminary of La Rochelle);

Prince Vladimir Ghika, Henri Ghéon, Jean-Pierre Altermann, Roland Dalbiez, René Kiéger, Albert Camilleri, Dr. Pénon, Robert Boulet,

Mmes Robert Boulet (Noële Denis),[1] Marthe Spitzer, François, Lequeux; Mlles Marie Clément, Simone Leuret, J. Pimor, Amélie Goichon, Fessart, Moreau, Févelat (stenographer),

and the three of us.

The retreat bore on «the two great principles of the evangelical law: love of God and love of neighbor.» Subjects treated: 1. The love of God; 2. Sin; 3. Fraternal charity; 4. The Cross; 5. The Holy Spirit and the Gifts of the Holy Spirit; 6. Zeal for the glory of God and for the salvation of souls; 7. The Eucharist.

Sunday the 30th of September, at the study meeting at our house: the diverse states of human nature.

1924

On the retreat of 1924, there are only a few lines in *Raissa's Journal*. From other documents I draw the following notes:

25-29 September 1924 — Third retreat of the Thomist Circles. Male retreatants: Abbé Altermann, Father Bibollet (of Missions Étrangères), Abbés Borel, Congar, Croville, Dondaine, Gillon, and Grossin, Heintz, Journet, Lallement, Leclef, Father Bernardot, Mgr. Paulot, Abbés Maquart, Péponnet, Schmitt, Zundel, Ancelin, and Méchain, Salaün, Guillemet (American);

Roland Dalbiez, Henri Ghéon, Charles Henrion, M. Lecoutey, Dr. Minot, Dr. Pénon, Réne Barthe, Robert Boulet.

Female retreatants: Mmes Bernadac, Boulet, Fauvel, François, Lequeux, Brétignière, Marthe Spitzer; Mlles Clément, Cohen, Esnée, Fessart, Lefebvre, Méjevaud (of Geneva), Parent, Andrée Saurin, A. M. Saurin, Vast-Vimeux; and the three of us.

---

1. Noële Maurice-Denis — my best pupil at the Institut Catholique at that time — had married the painter Robert Boulet on the 5th of January 1923, and the friendship which bound us from that time to the two of them only increased with the years.

Subjects treated. 1. The existence and nature of God, 2. His Wisdom; 3. The Will of God, its eternal act of love, 4. Creation, 5. The sin of the angel and the sin of man, 6. The mediation of Christ, 7. Mary Mediatrix.

At the study meeting at our house, Sunday the 28th of September: the increase of charity in the soul.

1925

19th of June. — The *Journal Officiel* of today announces the establishment of our Association of Thomist Study Groups (made public the 6th of June).[1]

25-29 September 1925. — Fourth retreat. Subjects treated: 1. The Incarnation; 2. The Redemption, 3. The Sacrifice of the Mass and its fruits; 4. The indwelling of the Holy Spirit in the soul; 5. Grace; 6. The universal kingship of Christ.

At the study meeting at our house. Prudence.

1926

24-28 September 1926. — Fifth retreat. Subjects treated: 1. Faith; 2. Necessity of supernatural Faith for salvation; 3. Hope; 4. Charity; 5. The virtue of Religion; 6. Union with God, the phases of the life of prayer.

---

1. The first Council of Administration was thus composed: Abbé J. P. Altermann; Abbé Beaussart, first Chaplain at Collège Stanislas; Mme Noële Denis-Boulet, M. Albert Camilleri; Mlle Marie Clément, Director of Written Exercises at the Institut Catholique de Paris; M. Roland Dalbiez, agrégé of the University, professor at the Lycée de Laval; M. Henri Ghéon; Prince Vladimir Ghika, Abbé Charles Journet, professor at the Grand Seminaire de Fribourg; Abbé Daniel Lallement, lecturer at the Institut Catholique de Paris; Mlle Simone Leuret, Mme Raissa Maritain; M. Jacques Maritain, professor at the Institut Catholique de Paris; Abbé H. Péponnet, professor at the Grand Séminaire de la Rochelle, M. Pierre Termier, member of the Institut; M. W. R. Thompson, Director of the Laboratory of Entomology of the Islands of Hyères.

(Committee: President, M. Jacques Maritain; treasurer: Abbé Lallement; secretary: M. Albert Camilleri. See the Appendix to Chapter V.)

At the study meeting at our house. What it is necessary to believe for salvation, which contains implicitly the other truths of Faith.

Maurras came one morning for an interview with Fr. Garrigou from which I had hoped a great deal, but which produces nothing because of the weakness of Father before the obstinacy of this man.

1927

23-27 September 1927. — Sixth retreat, on the Incarnation. — Subjects treated. 1. The testimony of Our Lord on His divine sonship; 2. The place of Christ in the divine plan, the motive of the Incarnation; 3. The sanctity of Christ, His plenitude of grace, 4. The human intelligence of Christ, 5. The human will and the human liberty of Christ; 6. The Heart of Jesus.

At the study meeting at our house: the passive purification of the three theological virtues.

15th of December. — Letter from Jean Daujat, giving us the address of some student friends of his who would like to attend the study meetings (René Perrin, Alexandre Quesnel, Jean de Fabrègues, Maurice de Gandillac, Merleau-Ponty, Étienne Borne). Daujat, who has a passion for St. Thomas, is a pupil at the École Normale Supérieure (Sciences Section). Olivier Lacombe is also a Normalien, but he is preparing his *agrégation* in philosophy. Our friendship with him began this year, as also with Maxine Jacob (just after his conversion) and with a pilgrim still on the way with whom we became acquainted at the end of last year (also immediately after his conversion). They came to the Thomist meetings, he and Maxime Jacob occasionally, Lacombe and Daujat very regularly.

We are right in the middle of the crisis of *Action Française,* and our relations with some of our friends are becoming very tense.

1928

27-30 September 1928. — Seventh retreat, preached by Father Bernadot (Father Garrigou was unable to attend). No notes on the subjects treated. Some names at random among the attendants. Pierre and Jeanne Linn, Jean Daujat, Albert Sandoz, Arthur Lourié, Dr. Minot, Abbé Plaquevent, Father Lajeunie, Father Delos, Maxime and Babet Jacob, Maurice Brillant, Achsa Belkind. . . . I believe I remember that Charles Du Bos came once or twice.

27th of September. — Beginning of the retreat. Mass by Father Ch. — At 5 o'clock, Abbé Journet, Father Bernadot, Jean de Menasce and Roland Dalbiez at our house. Éveline arrives from Annecy and tells of her visit to Cottolengo.

28th of September. — Mass by Abbé Leclef. — Dr. Pichet and the Briods, a woman friend of Mercédès de Gournay and Sr. Thérèse come for the retreat.

29th of September. — Mass by Abbé Journet. — At two-thirty, visit of Gonzague de Reynold. — Maximilien Vox comes in the afternoon. — In the evening Julien Lanoë dines with us.

Sunday the 30th of September. — Mass by Abbé Journet. — Abbé Lallement arrives at 10 o'clock. He comes from Rome where he saw the Pope, is to see the Nuncio at 4 o'clock. Lunches with us after the High Mass.

Dalbiez reads his study on Freud to Father Bernadot. He almost weeps if someone he would like to read it to is prevented from hearing it.

In the afternoon, at the study meeting, admirable conference of Abbé Journet on the sacraments.

He dines with us, as also Father Bernadot and Jean de Menasce. We are dead with fatigue.

1929

20th of January. — Study meeting: Jacques de Monléon, Yves Simon, Olivier Lacombe. . . .

28th of January. — Meeting at Berdiaeff's: Massignon, Fumet, Olivier, Jean-Pierre, Raissa and myself. Du Bos sick. Florovsky, Fédotoff, Wisseschlavsky, Jakubisiak, etc.

Sunday the 17th of February. — Study meeting (the love of God for creatures — free, like their very creation).

In the evening, Jean Yoshimitsu dines, together with a young German painter who is the nephew of Georgii.

Monday the 18th of February. — Berdiaeff meeting, Boulevard Montparnasse. Pastor Lecerf, Abbé Simeterre.

Tuesday the 5th of March. — Meeting at Berdiaeff's. Report of Massignon on Christine the Admirable. Discussion with Florovsky on co-redemptive suffering. It is a notion which seems strangely to escape our Orthodox friends. Raissa intervenes and makes things quite clear.

Sunday the 21st of April. — Thomist study meeting (on *scientia media*). The Severinis, the Lemaîtres, Mercédès de Gournay dine.

17th of May. — Jean Yoshimitsu has a violent hemoptysis in Paris. André Baron takes him to the doctor and brings him back in a taxi to Meudon.

18th of May. — Visit of Miss Butler who has founded a Thomist society in London. (Sent by Father MacNabb.)

Sunday the 8th of September. — First visit of Rafael Pividal (who will become our dearest and most faithful Argentine friend).

25th of September. — Father Garrigou-Lagrange arrives.

Upon my return from the Missions Étrangères where I ticketed the rooms, visit of Father Doncoeur: his Superior having learned of the approaching publication of our book (*Clairvoyance de Rome*, in which Father refused to collaborate) charges him to sign with us. It was about time! Molière wouldn't have thought of that.

26-29 September 1929. - Eighth retreat (in which there is much reference to Father Louis Chardon's beautiful book on the Cross of Jesus — the Passion, the Seven Words, Jesus dying and the Beatific vision still present in His soul but no longer radiating at all on the sensitive faculties, the union in Him of suffering and peace; the perpetuation of the Sacrifice of the Cross in the Mass, the diverse forms of sanctity.

Sunday the 29th. — End of the retreat. At 3 o'clock, study meeting at our house. Father Garrigou speaks of the problem of pure love, Richard of Saint-Victor and St. Thomas.

Raissa was able to attend all the instructions.

Father Garrigou is very happy with the retreat and even « comforted» (for he has many trials).

Sunday the 1st of December. — Thomist study meeting. I read a paper on knowledge (texts from the *De Anima*), Abbé Lallement on society and the virtue of Prudence.

Olivier, Marie-Louise Guillot, Pierre and Jeanne Linn, Paul Sabon, Robert Sebastien, René Barthe dine.

1930

Sunday 19th of January. — Thomist meeting.

At dinner Stanislas Fumet, Jean de Menasce, the Monléons, Eveline, Jean-Pierre, Yoshimitsu. After dinner Jean-Pierre reads me an article of his for *Vigile*. Just, penetrating, — a little too majestic for me.

Sunday the 23rd of February. — Olivier replaces me at the Thomist meeting, he speaks on Buddhist logic. Maxime comes with his fiancée [with whom, to our great surprise, he will break to become a Benedictine].

At dinner the Linns, Roland—Manuel, Eveline, Édouard Souberbielle.

Sunday the 30th of March. — Thomist meeting.

Termier, Brillant, Yoshimitsu, Jean-Pierre dine.

Sunday the 4th of May. — Social studies meeting (on the fecundity of money). Abbé Lallement, Borne, François Henry, Olivier, Jacques de Monléon, Pierre van der Meer.

Sunday the 11th of May. — Thomist meeting. Raissa, too tired, cannot attend. In the evening, at dinner: Ghéon, Babet, and Maxime, the Linns, the Monléons, Dr. Barthe. Robert Sebastien comes after dinner.

26-29 September 1930. — Ninth retreat. Twenty male retreatants at the Missions Étrangères. Female retreatants still more numerous.

26th of September. — Charity. — Poverty.
In the afternoon visit of Burns and O'Sullivan.
At dinner: M. and Mme Porte (of Geneva), Dr. Pénon, Abbé Journet, Father Garrigou, Nelly Ferrero. Yvan Lenain and Abbé Leclef come after dinner.

27th of September. — Chastity. — Obedience.
At dinner: O'Sullivan, Dr. Burns, Miss Borton, Father Garrigou, Abbé Leclef, Yvan Lenain, Eveline.

Sunday the 28th of September. — Instruction in the morning on docility to the Holy Spirit.
Jean Daujat asks me to be a witness at his marriage in November. Am happy to show him this mark of friendship.
Study meeting at our house. More than eighty persons. Conference of Father Garrigou on final Perseverance.
At dinner: Pierre, Christine, Anne-Marie, Tzebricov, Dalbiez, Olivier, Eveline.

Monday the 29th of September. — Instruction on the Discernment of spirits.
Chatted with dear Abbé Bréchar, Mlle Sauvanet, Dalbiez.
At dinner: Father Garrigou, Father Lavaud, Abbé Journet, Dalbiez. Charlie and René Schwob, ill, were not able to come.

7th of December. — Thomist meeting. Olivier on the Vedanta-Sara.

1931

18th of January. — Thomist meeting. Olivier on the Baghavad-Gîta.

At dinner, Olivier, Jacques de Monléon, Pierre and Jeanne Linn. Jacques Madaule comes after dinner.

20th of January. — Meeting at Berdiaeff's. After an exposition of mine on St. Thomas and philosophy «in the faith,» Berdiaeff turns towards Gilson, counting on him to contradict me and reminding him of what he wrote in his book on Thomism apropos of St. Thomas as a precursor of the philosophy of pure reason. To the great surprise of all, Gilson declares that if he spoke thus he erred, and that he is entirely in agreement with me. (He in fact considerably changed his positions in later editions of *Le Thomisme*.) Raissa and I very touched by the attitude of Gilson and by his honesty in correcting himself. From this day date our ties of friendship with him.

Sunday the 8th of March. — Social studies meeting.

Saturday the 21st of March. — Meeting of the French Society of Philosophy on Christian philosophy.

Sunday the 22nd of March. — Thomist meeting. Olivier on Nirvana.

At dinner, Willard Hill, Brillant, Ghéon, Eveline, Pierre and Jeanne Linn, René Barthe.

Sunday the 19th of April. — Social studies meeting.

25-28 September 1931. — Tenth retreat. Two women friends of Vera, attracted by the desert, Father Reeves, Abbé Bréchar, Richard O'Sullivan, the Bulloughs attend.

In Raissa's journal other names are cited: Willard Hill, Pierre and Christine van der Meer, Anne-Marie, Charles Du Bos and his wife, Abbé Journet, Abbé Lallement, Abbé Leclef, Roland Dalbiez, René Schwob, Oscar Bauhofer, Mme Jean Berchem and her father, Marek Szwarc, Cohen (who is going to be a Dominican), Jean and

Germaine Dedeken, Pierre and Jeanne Linn, Marie-Anne François, Henri Ghéon, Miss Borton, Yvan Lenain, Moureau, Eveline. . . .

There are at least one hundred and fifty retreatants — male and female. (No notes on the subject of the instructions.)

During this whole retreat Raissa suffers a great deal.

Sunday the 27th of September. — The van der Meers lunch with us. At a certain moment Raissa leaves the table. I am anxious, I go up to join her in her room, I find her in an agony of pain and anguish, as if God rejected her with an indescribable violence. She groans, she weeps. Prayed with her. After having wept much, the suffering abates. Raissa has finally enough strength to go down to attend the conference of Father Garrigou, at 3 o'clock. The hundred and fifty persons managed to stay without suffocating.

Monday the 28th of September. — At the evening service, after the last sermon, all sing the *Magnificat*.

This retreat has had an extraordinary buoyancy.

6th of December. — Thomist meeting. Jacques de Monléon on knowledge (Cajetan, on q. 14 of the *Prima Pars*). Borne on the notion of work (*Politics* of Aristotle).

Ghéon reads his new Spanish play.

At dinner: Borne, Jacques de Monléon, Olivier, Ghéon, Hill, Babet, Pierre and Christine, Eveline, Pierre and Jeanne Linn.

1932

Sunday the 10th of January. — Thomist meeting. Olivier, Borne. . . . Father Bruno brings Mme Bénard.

Sunday the 14th of February. — Thomist meeting. Jacques de Monléon on the intelligence. Borne on work.

Sunday the 13th of March. — Thomist meeting. Olivier brings Mlle Ramakrishna. Borne on work. Mounier on property.

Sunday the 10th of April. — Thomist meeting. Father Riquet on property. Excellent exposition.

Sunday the 17th of April. – Smaller meeting (chiefly for *Esprit*). Continued the discussion on property. Louis Laloy comes with his wife, like last Sunday. Berdiaeff at 5 o'clock. I speak of *factibile* and of *usus*. He says very remarkable things concerning the present state of Soviet philosophy.

In the evening the Severinis, Willard, Lourié, the Souberbielles.

Saturday the 24th to Tuesday the 27th of September 1932. – Eleventh retreat. Raissa attends almost all the instructions by courageously surmounting her physical weakness. But my heart breaks to see her transparent profile.

O'Sullivan, Woodruff, Miss Borton, Dalbiez, Paul de Brouwer, Bauhofer, etc.

Sunday the 20th of November. – Thomist meeting. Étienne Borne. Jacques de Monléon on the Will and Freedom.

Sunday the 4th of December. – Thomist meeting. Borne on Lagneau, Jacques on Spinoza.

1933

27-30 September 1933. – Twelfth retreat. Begins the 27th at 4 P.M. On the Redemption.

At dinner: Father Garrigou, Abbé Journet, Canon Leclef, Arthur Lourié.

Raissa has the impression that this retreat is especially good and blessed. This is also what Father Garrigou-Lagrange says to us at the end. – Raissa: «No longer knowing anything and no longer being worth anything, everything being reduced to nothing, then all is well.»

28th of September. – Last dinner with Pierre and Christine (before their departure for the religious life).

29th of September. – At dinner: Father Garrigou, Father Louis de la Trinité, Father Bruno, Abbé Pénido, Abbé Journet.

Saturday the 30th of September. — First Communion of Jean Hugo's mother (Mass by Prince Ghika). Admirable conference by Father Garrigou at the house, on Philosophy and Faith. (He says that he subscribes to everything that I wrote in my little book on Christian Philosophy.)

Sunday the 5th of November. — Thomist meeting. Olivier on Çankara.

Sunday the 19th of November. — «Esoteric» day of studies. Jacques de M., Olivier, Yves Simon. The conversation begins apropos of the speech of Mauriac to the Academy, and of the lag between the act of thought and its conceptual means, an atheist being able to believe in God without knowing it. And it continues concerning dialectics and the object. Raissa is very happy, an auspicious wind carried us, opened horizons, hinted at discoveries.

Sunday the 3rd of December. — Thomist meeting. Jacques de M. on Dionysus and Orpheus; Olivier on Hindu art, idealism, etc.

Sunday the 17th of December. — «Esoteric» meeting. Borne, who stays only an hour. Gandillac, Yves, Jacques. On love and the Holy Spirit.

1934

Sunday the 7th of January. — Thomist meeting, tiring. Jacques on the object and objectivity; Olivier on Ramanuja.

Sunday the 21st of January. — «Esoteric» meeting. Search for what constitutes the nature of love. Olivier, Gandillac, Yves, Jacques and Jacqueline de M., Borne.
In the evening Father Louis de la Trinité dines with Ghéon, Lourié, Jacques and Jacqueline, Yves.

Sunday the 4th of February. — Thomist meeting. I give the talk (Science and Wisdom). Olivier speaks about Hindu ethics. Very good discussion, excellent day.

Sunday the 18th of February. — «Esoteric» meeting. Borne, Olivier, Gandillac, Yves Simon. We are all very preoccupied by developments in France (riot of the 6th of February) and in Austria (workers have been machine-gunned, under a Catholic Government, — Chancellor Dollfuss).

We are going to try to draft a declaration.[1]

[My notebook mentions the thirteenth retreat, in September 1934, but gives no details concerning it, my time was too devoured. A single hasty note, concerning a conversation with Father Garrigou:] Father G.-L., whom Raissa told what she endures in prayer, tells me that it is the greatest grace that we have received. Everything, there, comes from God, it is a work of redemption which is realized in her and through her, true life. You should envy her for having entered into the states of Our Lord.

1935

Sunday the 10th of March, 1935. — Thomist meeting. Borne speaks about Blondel, Olivier about Hindu ethics.

Good evening with Duveau, Ghéon, Eveline, Willard Hill.

Sunday the 31st of March. — In the afternoon, meeting organized in order to have Abbé Albert de Lapparent (grandson of the scientist) meet with some philosophers. Dalbiez, Yves, Sandoz, Jacques, Olivier, Borne, Louis Laloy. Very good meeting. We decide to revive the Society for the Philosophy of Nature.

In the evening Dalbiez, Ghéon, the Linns, the Simons, the Seuphors, Labergerie dine. Violent conversation of Dalbiez on Freud, marriage, the books of Father Lavaud, etc. What one does hear! But so much the better.

Thursday the 11th of April. — Meeting of a group for the philosophy of culture: Gandillac, Borne, Olivier, Yves.

1. The latter appeared as a booklet, published by Desclée De Brouwer, under the title *Pour Le Bien Commun*. It inaugurated the period of collective manifestos.

Some time ago, Father Gagnebet spoke to me about the thesis which he is preparing on theological knowledge, and whose leading ideas are so important.

Thursday the 26th to Sunday the 29th of September, 1935. — Fourteenth retreat.

Sunday the 29th of September. — Father Garrigou gives a very beautiful conference at our house. Leaves at six-thirty.

At dinner: Arthur, Ghéon, René Schwob, Maurice Brillant, Georges Cattaui, Labergerie. Admirable evening. Ghéon and René Schwob speak of their enthusiasm for Raissa's poems (*La Vie Donnée* has just appeared).

Notebook interrupted. — No retreat in 1936 because of our trip to Argentina.

1937

Saturday the 30th of January. — Thomist meeting. John of Saint-Thomas on free future events. Jacques de Monléon, Olivier, Yves, Albert Sandoz, a Canadian Abbé, etc.

Saturday the 27th of February. — Thomist meeting (John of Saint-Thomas). Olivier, Jacques, Sandoz. . . .

Friday the 24th of September. — Father Garrigou-Lagrange arrives in the evening; dines at our house with Charles Journet.

[Father Garrigou was a man of the right; he had suffered a great deal from the crisis of *Action Française*, although in a spirit of obedience to the Church, and therefore without bearing me too much of a grudge for my attitude; but my positions on the war in Spain were decidedly too much for him, as later were to be my positions on the regime of Vichy. I transcribe my notes of 1937 without attenuating anything in them, I insist only on remarking that our differences in political matters never diminished the affection and the gratitude which Raissa and I had for him. (And he for his part, even when he found fault with me, did what he could to defend me.) This great theologian, who was little versed in the things of the world, had an admirably candid heart, which God finally purified by a long and very painful physical trial, a cross of complete annihilation, which, according to the testimony of the faithful friend who assisted him in his last days,[1] he had expected and which he had accepted in advance. I pray to him now[2] with the saints of Heaven.]

Father is very worked-up against me; goes so far as to reproach me, a convert, with wanting to give lessons in the Christian spirit to «us who have been Catholics for three hundred years.» (And why not since the Crusades? He forgets that he also was a convert, through the reading of Ernest Hello.) It seems that Raissa and Vera are being implicated as dragging me along by their influence. (Russian Jewesses, are they not? They who detest these political quarrels, and who would have been so glad if I could have remained isolated from them, if I had not seen there a testimony to be rendered to truth.) This puts me in a black rage, which I do not hide. The retreat begins under a very sad sign. Father Garrigou would like to prohibit me from speaking on the philosophy of history, and from judging events, and from acting on young people in these matters. (He is not the only one in Rome to think like this, I know very well, and to be terrified of the «political Maritain.») Metaphysics only! But he himself does not hesitate to pronounce in favor of Franco and to approve the civil war in Spain.

25-28 September 1937. — Fifteenth retreat. (Last retreat preached by Father Garrigou-Lagrange.)

Saturday the 25th of September. — First sermon of the retreat.
At dinner: O'Sullivan, Father Hughes, M. Alexander, Miss Butler, Dalbiez, Arthur, Eveline.

---

1. Those who, like myself, owe so much to Father Garrigou-Lagrange are profoundly grateful to Father M. R. Gagnebet for the lecture on the work of Father Garrigou which he delivered to the Roman Academy of St. Thomas, the 27th of May 1964.
2. Father Garrigou-Lagrange died in Rome on the 15th of February 1964.

Sunday the 26th of September. — Mass celebrated by Abbé Maquart. In the afternoon, I go to Paris, for a meeting concerning the crisis of the Dominican weekly *Sept.*

Monday the 27th of September. — Mass by André Baron. Finally Father Garrigou loosens up a little. Up to now he has confined himself to platitudes.

Arthur, the young Borgeaud, remarked that there was something, a hidden tragedy, which hindered everything. Father was obsessed by Spain.

Tuesday the 28th of September. — Mass by Father Garrigou. He says it for the intentions of the three of us. Impression of relaxation and of peace. He leaves at 10 o'clock.

(The retreatants were more numerous than ever: 250 to 300. Clouded by grave political disagreements and by the *twilight of* Western *civilization,* this retreat retained nevertheless the power, proper to all our retreats, of establishing a profound communion of spirit between all the participants. And, in spite of all the anguish, hope — supernatural hope — kept watch in our hearts.)

1938

Sunday the 29th of May. — Mass by Father Bruckberger.
We have the idea of transforming the next retreat (Father Garrigou-Lagrange accepted an invitation to go to Brazil in September) into study days bringing together a very small number of workers.

End of September 1938. — The Czechoslovakian tragedy and the threat of war. We pack our trunks for America (Raissa and Vera are to accompany me if we make the trip), at the same time as other trunks for Avoise (papers and letters sent to Abbé Gouin's house to be preserved from eventual bombings and fires), thinking all the while that war is going to break out and that we shall not leave.

Mobilization.

Right in the midst of these days of mobilization, meeting of our friends for private Thomist days (replacing the retreat). These hours spent together in metaphysics and Theology at such a moment give us all a feeling of astonishing spiritual gaiety and an extraordinary calm.

Abbé Journet, Abbé Maquart (mobilized), Father Lavaud, Father Bruckberger, Father Labourdette, Father Gagnebet, Father Nicolas, Olivier Lacombe, Jeanne and Georges Delhomme, Claude and Ida Bourdet, Jean Le Louët.

Saturday the 24th and Sunday the 25th of September. — I speak on divine foreknowledge and premotion (according to my course at the Institut Catholique). Abbé Journet speaks on the Church, on the crusades and on the medieval regime. Father Gagnebet, on the nature of theology.

Munich. Peace. The three of us leave on the 1st of October for a stay of two or three months in the United States.

III

APROPOS OF THE VOW OF PRAYER

The Thomist circles of Meudon were killed by the war. Perhaps some day they will come to life again under a new form. If I have dwelt on them at length, it is because I am persuaded that such study groups, with the characteristic features which I have mentioned, are required by the times in which we live. The annual retreats likewise represented a quite new type of retreat, particularly free and airy, and particularly appropriate, I believe, to the needs of many minds.

I would like to insist a little on one of the most typical characteristics of our Thomist circles, namely, that close union of the intellectual life and of the spiritual life of which the guarantee was the vow of prayer. «Thus,» as it was said in our statutes, «this association of secular priests and of laymen» had «at the base of its activity a very intimate and very profound gift of oneself to God,» and offered «to souls who desire perfection while remaining in the world a very real help, without however enroaching at all upon the liberty of each, since the vow of prayer concerns only the absolutely personal relations of God and of the soul.»

Such a vow, strictly private, had nothing to do with the vows of religion and the state of life proper to religious; and, as M. Villien had explained to me, our study circles, although including this private vow, were neither a confraternity, nor a *pia unio*, nor to any degree an ecclesiastical person. They remained purely lay. This is why it was not necessary to submit our statutes to ecclesiastical authority, and the only thing required was that the directors of studies by approved by the Ordinary.

But if the vow of prayer had nothing to do with the vows of religion, it had a great deal to do with the desire, which exists in a greater number of laymen than is sometimes believed, to give themselves entirely to Christ and to make the search for Christian perfection take precedence over all their activities, even though they remain engaged in the world. Is not to tend to the perfection of charity prescribed to all? And through their baptism are not laymen members of the Church as well as clerics and religious, all of which means that if on special grounds they are *in* the world, they too nevertheless, to the extent that they are faithful to their Christian vocation and to the promises of their baptism, are not *of* the world?

It seems to me that there is matter here for practical reflection. I mean that one can ask oneself if in the present state of the world it is not especially desirable to see develop groups of laymen which while pursuing such or such particular goals (studies and progress in the intellectual life, professional improvement, works of mercy, social action, aid to underdeveloped countries, etc., etc.), and while fully keeping their lay character, would have at their base a free gift to God whose seal and guarantee would be private vows bearing on certain requirements of Christian life and of the advance towards perfection?

There is no question here of the three vows of chastity, of obedience and of poverty, which even in the absence of community life make the one who pronounces them a religious or at least a rough-draft religious. I have nothing against associations in which persons, who while continuing to have all the appearances of lay life, pronounce these three vows and enter to this extent into the *status perfectionis acquirendae* which St. Thomas regarded as proper to religious. I note only in passing that nature shows us that amphibious species are perfectly possible, and sometimes present very beautiful types of organisms, but that they always have something exceptional and a little singular. (I note also that without a religious community life the three vows of perfection find themselves deprived of the environmental conditions which up to now, and not without good reasons, had been considered as normally required for their good practice.)

Unlike the three vows of perfection, the private vows of which I speak would in absolutely no way cause those who pronounce them to leave their condition as laymen. And indeed is not the crucial desire that one notes today in the faithful the desire of many souls to advance towards the perfection of human life without renouncing in any way the lay state, its obligations and its varied characteristics? Is not the problem consequently to aid these souls to satisfy such a desire in their lay life itself? And if it is true that the *normal* condition of lay life is marriage, is it not fitting to address oneself to married persons as well as to celibates?

Foremost among the private vows of which I speak would come the vow of prayer. For fidelity to prayer is for each a kind of spiritual equivalent of the cloister for the contemplative religious, and it is, according to all great spiritual teachers, the foundation of progress towards the perfection of love. And this fidelity, taking into account the practical possibilities of each, can be assured in lay life as well as in religious life — even if, in certain cases, it is only a quarter of an hour devoted to the silence of recollection,[1] as St. Theresa said.

But other private vows of the same kind could also be conceived. Why not, for example, a vow of compassion or of fraternal friendship by which one would put oneself under an obligation never to let an instance of human distress pass near without trying to help in some manner, even if only by prayer when every other

1. As a general rule, each must therefore strive at all cost to reserve for silent prayer, however arid it may be, a minimum of time, however short. Without forgetting for all that this still more fundamental truth: *"To love. To abandon oneself.* Nothing else is necessary to sanctification. No, nothing, not even silence with God, if that is rendered impossible by real obstacles, interior or exterior. The soul can be sanctified without, so to speak, realizing it, and find itself at last united to God without having had the leisure to practice what it would have thought most necessary for this." (*Raissa's Journal*, pp. 125-126.)

means is excluded?[1] Why not a vow of dedication to truth, by which one would put oneself under an obligation — always in the measure of each individual's possibilities — to apply one's intelligence to theological knowledge and to the other forms of knowledge adapted to bring it nearer to the Truth which is Christ?

I will be pardoned for these hypothetical views. I would like only to remark that given their establishment in the laity as such, the groups which I imagine at this moment, which would require private vows such as those of which I have just spoken, would not require any vow of obedience, and would include, as I have already noted, married members as well as celibates of both sexes. These groups of laymen, issuing from the initiative of their own members, would have for leaders laymen approved by the Ordinary; they would clearly have need of the directions, counsels and instructions which only priests or religious are able to dispense, and it is probable that in many cases they would call upon the assistance of a given religious Order. However, they would neither be a particular branch nor a proper work of the Order in question, nor would they be an «ecclesiastical person» or a work issuing from the clergy, nor an organization of auxiliaries of the clergy (these latter, which respond to an evident necessity, depend on institutions apart, specifically different from what it is a question of here). The relations of the groups of which I am speaking with the ecclesiastical hierarchy would only be an application, in given circumstances, of the general laws concerning the relations of the faithful with the hierarchy. In short, these groups would be the most appropriate equipment that a laity come (at least in certain of its most dynamic sectors) to the consciousness of its vocation to implement the spirit of the Gospel and to advance towards the perfection of charity, would give itself, for its activities in the world, and of course with all the docility which faith requires to the magisterium of the teaching Church.

*

There is so much talk today about the laity that one will

---

1. In the Middle Age the Brothers of Charity of St. Lazaurs of Jerusalem made, at the same time as other vows, a "vow of charity — to receive and to serve the poor." Cf. Michel Riquet, *La charité du Christ en action*, Paris, Fayard, 1961, p. 111.

doubtless permit me to propose in my turn, in closing this chapter, a few modest reflections on the subject. As brief as I was able, moreover.

1.   There are cases in which certain groups of laymen must be considered as extentions, so to speak, of the ecclesiastical hierarchy. The clergy, indeed, has need of auxiliaries (catechists for example) aiding it to accomplish its proper work. This work itself, on the other hand, requires it to found and to direct (parish clergy or regular clergy) groups having for their object the religious education and the liturgical formation of the faithful. Finally, the diverse branches of Catholic Action all have this essential character in common: the participation of the faithful in the apostolate of the hierarchy. In all the cases which I have just mentioned, it is to the clergy, this is very clear, that it normally belongs to orgainze the groups in question or the associations of laymen.

But however important they may be from the point of view of the clergy itself, the groups in question concern, in comparison with the whole of the laity, only a comparatively very limited number of the faithful. The faithful in their entirety — with, at their head, the little band of those who truly wish to give themselves to Jesus — remain next to these groups, a people full of needs, of anxieties and of difficulties, of frustrations and of desires, who are assigned, by the structure of the Church, their own proper function in the Mystical Body (and which, as has been finally noticed, does not consist only in sinning and going to confession). If it is a question of the faithful thus considered, engaged as they are in the turmoils and the vicissitudes of the world — and nevertheless called by divine commandment to tend, each human person according to his condition and his possibilities, to the perfection of Christian life and love — it is required of the clergy to be ready to instruct them, to enlighten them, to assist them; it is not required of the clergy to *organize* them. Priests are ministers of Heaven among men, they are not organizers in competition on earth with the leaders of the workers movement or the propagandists of a Party. And it is certainly not desirable that the Christian laity run the risk of finding itself some day divided into first-rate faithful duly organized and enrolled, and second-rate faithful, unfortunate sub-laity without a badge in their buttonhole.

2. Moreover the first and principal need of the faithful, as an essential part of the Mystical Body, is not at all to be organized, but to open themselves to the dwelling of the Divine Persons in the soul and to the springing up of eternal life already begun here on earth. This is not to say that all are conscious of it, far from it, or that souls are not often distracted from it by being prematurely thrown into action. The fact remains that in order to respond to this primary need it is first necsssary for the faithful to be instructed, enlightened and assisted.

The people are by definition the great and fruitful reserve of collective vitality. The reserve of spontaneity, of liberty of movement, of adaptability to the ebb and flow of time, of inventiveness, and of prophetic initiative, this reserve, which exists in a potential and undetermined state among the baptized, must be maintained intact, and respected as sacred.

3. It goes without saying that temporal activities and everything having to do with the common good of the earthly city, and the various efforts through which human liberty employs itself to bend in one direction or another the gallop of history's determinisms — all of this is especially the affair of laymen. To take up again a distinction which I proposed in the past,[1] let us say that Christian laymen must perform these things AS *Christians*. But it is on their own responsibility (on condition that their conscience is suitably enlightened) that they have to perform them, and PRECISELY INSOFAR AS THEY ARE MEMBERS *of a civilization and engaged in the world*, in no way insofar as they would be like the secular arm of the Church.

The ecclesiastical hierarchy — this is one of the great achievements of our age — has definitely given up using a secular arm, or, more exactly, it has freed itself from the too dearly paid for services of such an arm, which only asked (prince, State, or political party) to lie heavy on it and on the liberty of souls.[2]

1. *Integral Humanism*, Appendix, pp. 294-299.
2. The renunciation of the Pope of his temporal power is an eminent sign of such a change. As Paul VI said on the 14th of January 1964, in his address to the Roman nobility, "the Pope, even if he sees in his sovereignty over the State of the Vatican the sign of his independence with regard to all authority of this world, neither wishes to nor should he henceforth exercise any other power than that of his spiritual keys."

4. But how is it with Christian laymen PRECISELY INSOFAR AS THEY ARE A PART, I no longer say of a temporal civilization, I say *of the Mystical Body of Christ?* Insofar as they constitute an essential part of the Mystical Body they are «fellow-citizens of the saints» and «members of the house of God,»[1] and of His kingdom. In other words, they are called to live more and more fully with the life of grace, called to the sanctity and the freedom of the sons of God. «Be perfect as your heavenly Father is perfect,» no one in the Mystical Body escapes this commandment of Jesus.

It is a pity that for too long a time, and especially during the last four centuries, the Christian laity has believed itself doomed to imperfection, and even to a life of sin redeemed in the end, if possible, by a «good death,» and has cheerfully accepted the dichotomy which was the crime of the baroque age: all the joys of the earth through science and reason, and through the providence of the Prince, during the life of here-below; and afterwards the joys of Heaven for the small lot of the predestined. If among all the tasks which impose themselves these days on the clergy there is one which takes precedence over everything, it is to aid the faithful to escape from the infernal despair in which with the progress of time the dichotomy of which I speak finally imprisoned human history — in other words, it is to aid the faithful to become conscious of their vocation to participate in the sanctity of Jesus, and in His redemptive work, and to «fill up» through the cross and through love «that which is lacking» (as to the application, not as to the merits) «in the passion of the Savior.»[2]

We can be sure that in the measure in which through such a growth-in-awareness lay Christians will have freed their soul from the mirage which kept them separated from Jesus, in the same measure they will not only strive to live the Gospel, however poorly human weakness is capable of it, they will also strive to spread this life among their brothers. And it is then that by a natural consequence they will be led to form among themselves certain groups, where the element of «organization» — according to a particular style which I shall try to say a word of presently — will take its place, a secondary place, certainly, but a necessary one. There is

1. St. Paul, Ephes., 2, 19.
2. St. Paul, Col. 1, 24.

no doubt that this involves a difficult process of trial and error, and that the advice of a clergy which is itself well prepared, will be needed so that lay initiatives can avoid too unfortunate experiences.

5. A serious error, I note in passing, to which laymen of good will, but still badly cleansed of parasitical survivals, could run the risk of inadvertently yielding, would be to undertake to constitute a kind of secret army having for its object *power*, in other words, aiming above all to conquer and to exercise, for the service of Jesus Christ, the greatest possible empire in the structures of the temporal community: men who would «bore from within» in order to succeed in surreptitiously putting their hand on such and such levers of command. This would be, in comparison with the tasks which are incumbent on the Church today, a sure means to lose everything. It is important that the disciples of Christ know well of what spirit they are, which is not the case when they think: *power first,* or invoke the fire of Heaven or civil war on those whom they consider to be the enemies of God.

It is fitting here to pause for a moment on the mysterious and formidable notion of power, which a kind of reserve often seems to make political theorists hesitant to elucidate.[1] It is indeed true that there is on earth no effective liberty except when it is sheathed in some power, and that thus the search for power in the ordinary sense of this word has a truly primary role: but where then? − In the social-temporal order.

In the spiritual order, which is that of the Church, it is not the same. Or rather it is necessary to say that another power, but transcendent, has the primordial role in this order: the power of love. Love founded on truth is itself the only *absolutely incorruptible* power. And it is it alone which, when it is there, permits power considered in the ordinary sense of the word, the power of constraint (even if it is, as it should be, just and founded on a right) to escape corruption. Thus love and power in the ordinary sense of the word are in the same relation as the soul and the body.

1. Cf. the book (of exceptional importance, in spite of its gaps) of Charles E. Silberman on the racial problem in the United States, *Crisis in Black and White* (New York, Random House, 1964), with its frequent references to the work and to the ideas of Saul Alinsky.

This is why it is fitting that the Church, being on earth, have in her own hands — by reason of an accessory and secondary necessity — certain powers of the human order, for example, the power entailed by the right of ownership, or of the right to vote exercised by Catholic electors (not the least of these powers of the human order exercised by the Church being that of influencing by the prestige of her moral authority that world opinion for which the most cynical heads of State have such a burning concern). And this is why, inversely, the very prosperity of the social-temporal community requires that in her love vivify power.

That Christians propose to themselves as a principal end certain powers to be gained and to be exercised, this is perfectly normal, I mean *according as they defend such and such a temporal cause, and insofar as they are members of a civilization and engaged in the activities of the world.*[1]

But that Christians propose to themselves as a principal end certain powers (social-temporal) to be gained and to be exercised, I mean this time *according as they wish to serve the Gospel and insofar precisely as they are members of the Mystical Body of Christ, engaged in the spiritual order of grace and of charity,* this is unnatural.

6. Can one imagine a Pascal — and even, for a given epoch, a Chateaubriand or a Joseph de Maistre — can one imagine a Dostoevsky, a Léon Bloy, a Péguy, a Bernanos *organized* in community work teams? It is certainly difficult to conceive. Let us not forget however that these unorganized, and unorganizable, laymen did more for the Christian faith, in souls and in culture, than many pious associations and battalions of «shock Christianity.» It seems that certain poets and certain great writers are like the voices through which the world is made aware of the kind of prophetic sense at work in the faithful, and of which a Berdiaeff was so profoundly conscious.

---

1. Moreover, it is necessary that in this very effort charity be present, whether the "force of truth and of love" furnish itself, according to the methods established by Gandhi, a spiritual means with a view to attaining a temporal end, or whether one employs only (or *also*) carnal means, which after all one cannot dispense with in the temporal order, but which are dead and bear death if love does not animate them.

I believe that it is necessary to recognize here — thoroughly mingled with poetic knowledge, and with a kind of natural prophecy which depends on a sensibility connaturalized with the secret gestations of history — the influence also of a prophetic instinct due to a true charism obscurely at work. There are in the world many more graces — and many more contaminations of Hell — than we think (because of our distraction and of our futility, and of the conventional ideas which we fashion for ourselves from books, and because all these things are themselves masked).

If it is a question of *graces "gratis datae,"* we know moreover that they do not necessarily imply the life of grace and of charity in the soul. The prophetic instinct of which I speak at this moment does not always inhabit good Christians. Was Chateaubriand a good Christian? And Baudelaire, and Rimbaud, and Verlaine, and Lautréamont, and Nietzsche, and so many others, in whom this instinct also passed?

7.   In the penultimate chapter of this book there are some rather long reflections on Christian marriage. I shall limit myself here to remarking that married persons also cannot be *organized* in teams in which they learn to better resolve the problems proper to their state of life. I am told that attempts in this direction are not lacking. Even if happy effects have resulted in certain given circumstances (and thanks to the devotion of the one who animates them), we must recognize that in itself the idea from which they proceed squares badly with the structures of reality.

Certainly each of the spouses can join, either for his or her own spiritual progress, or for any other activity, all the groups or organizations he or she wishes. But if one has in view the conjugal family itself, it is precisely this which is the «organization,» the essential and irreducibly autonomous structure required and created by marriage, and this, unlike any other «organization,» by virtue of a primary exigency of nature itself and of its Author, and through the grace of a sacrament. A Christian family is in itself a community consecrated to God in the lay order just as an abbey or a Carmelite convent is in the religious order. And not only — if it is a question of a really Christian marriage — in order to beget and to raise offspring and in order that the two spouses may be the complement and the support of each other in this earthly life, but also in order that they may advance together towards eternal life and the perfection of charity, with the hope of being able, through all human failures, to emerge in the end into Heaven.

It is the affair of the clergy to instruct Christian spouses in a manner true enough and profound enough for them to become conscious of their complete vocation. It is not its affair to enlist them in any organization of human manufacture dressing up couples whom God Himself has united so that they may each constitute an autonomous community — nor to make their burden heavier by imposing on them additional duties and cares, and by grouping them, not according to their spontaneous affinities, but artificially, through the effect of the functioning of a charitable endeavor.

The truth, (not easily recognized, no doubt, as long as one does not have a sufficiently comprehensive idea of the proper resources of the laity, and as long as one hesitates to trust in them), is that it belongs to the spouses themselves, in a long and patient novitiate, to discover — at the same time as the sacred secrets, hidden in the recesses of the person, which each entrusts to the care of the other — the path which must be theirs in order to progress towards God. Absolutely nothing can replace such an effort of discovery and such an experience.

Does it follow that they would have to pursue their search without any human assistance? This is not my thought at all. The first help they need is that of a priest who is near enough to them to deserve being called their spiritual father. I know well that spiritual direction was not always reserved to the clergy, but in actual fact it became so, and this was normal. The paradox is that for this most important function there is today a scarcity of candidates, as if the aiding of individual souls in their ascent to God was henceforth too trifling a matter for a priestly vocation. To analyze the reasons for this phenomenon would lead us too far, I merely note that if one seeks efficacy before all else one can have the satisfaction of more or less controlling the results obtained when it is a question of visible things, like a mass organization formed on earth, but how control the efficacy of what concerns the things of Heaven and the invisible progress of grace in a soul? The fact remains that it is very certain that the primacy of efficacy will never impose itself in the Church, for the day when a concern for efficacy would take precedence over the concern for truth, then the gates of Hell would have prevailed against her. . . .

And another help is also normally required, this one issuing from the laity itself: I think of the aid received from friendships spontaneously formed under the action of «elective affinities» and of the Providence of God. Two things appear here as particularly appropriate to the element of risk and of adventure essential to the life of the Christian in the world: in relations with men, to recognize the central importance of *friendship*, in relations with God, to venerate the «sacrament of the present moment,» and to expect a great deal from the manner in which divine Providence, in the mysterious configuration of the destiny of each, arranges *the chance meetings themselves* that have cropped up all along the roads of the world.

While the conditions created by modern civilization test the life of the family community more and more severely (and purify it to the same extent, when it resists them), there are good reasons to think that the day approaches when, if not in the great mass of the laity, at least in those «prophetic minorities» on which all great historical change has always depended, Christian marriage will finally assume all its dimensions, which are spiritual also: so that the two spouses, while facing the continuous harassment of the turmoils of the world and of the malice of time, can be at the same time refreshed by the dew of God and experience a little of its sweetness; and that they themselves (with their children also, whom grace introduces into a certain equality with them, and asks them to treat as far as possible, there where it is a question of the things of God, as having access by anticipation to the universe of grown-ups) may help one another, by dint of attentive love and thanks to a constant opening of the heart, to each make his or her unique and secret way with Jesus.

8.   There exist in the laity, even among those baptized, vast desert zones where the laity would deserve less to be called «the faithful» than «the unfaithful,» and in which faith, supposing it is nevertheless present, remains miserably infantile. It is not in these regions of the laity, it is in zones in which it is truly «the faithful» that problems concerning the Christian life actually arise. And to the extent that such is the case, they need (and not only in order to be evangelized, but in order to practice the Gospel as best they can) to be instructed, enlightened and aided by the clergy.

To what end, however, when the problems which engage their solicitude for the good of souls *are proper to lay life as such?* In order (for the faithful of the Church are not infantile, but persons of full age)[1] for them *to be able to resolve these problems by themselves,* not to receive prefabricated solutions and means of action dispensed by the paternalism of a *social service* from on high. I have already noted, at the outset of these reflections, that apart from the particular case of formations specifically destined to be auxiliaries of the clergy or to participate in the apostolate of the hierarchy, it is from the Christian laity itself that there should normally[2] arise the diverse forms of «organization» for which their solicitude for their own problems and for the good of souls, in the midst of the misery of the world, can cause them to feel the need.

To tell the truth, the forms in question ask to be so little institutionalized that the very word «organization» seems quite heavy with respect to them. As a matter of fact it seems to me that ordinarily it is a question here of better assuring the progress of some initiative previously taken by such and such an individual or by such and such a family, and grouping about this initiative a spontaneous *friendship.* For just as an individual or a family need to be aided to find their path by the friendships which come to them, so likewise it is normally through the friendships which have come to them that one sees them (and will see them more and more, I hope) begin to assist in a collective undertaking those who have in common with them such and such a desire to act or such and such specific aspirations. It is natural that these groups of lay initiative enjoy a particular suppleness of adaptation to the needs of a cultural moment or of a given generation. And it is natural also that they have to pay for this privilege by being destined to a particularly ephemeral existence. As I wrote elsewhere,[3] «the Holy Spirit is not at work only in the durable institutions which go on for centuries, He is also at work in ventures which vanish overnight and must always be started afresh.»

1. "Vos autem genus electum, regale sacerdotium, gens sancta, populus acquisitionis. . . ." I Peter, 2, 9.
2. I say *normally*, I do not say *always* ꞏ
3. "Foreword" of *Raissa's Journal*, pp. 14-15.

9.   There have always been, there will never be enough centers of peace and of radiance in which men find a little silence to listen to God, and to join their energies with a view to what He can eventually inspire them to undertake, and which are like portals through which the angels of Heaven steal invisibly in among us. For centuries it was the monasteries and the religious houses which above all fulfilled this office, and they will not cease to fulfill it; and everything new that is tried will always need to come there to be reinvigorated. My conjecture is that with the growth in awareness effected these days by the Christian laity, which marks a decisive turning-point in the history of the Church, it is in the bosom of the lay world itself, at least in certain of its «prophetic minorities,» that the function in question will also be exercised. May God grant that there will multiply — for how many years have we awaited them under the most diverse names, ashrams, houses of wisdom, etc. — centers of spiritual radiance which, dispersed in the great night of common human misery, will be like new constellations of faith and of love on this poor earth.

If it is a question of the great mass of the lay world, we know well enough with what violence it is carried along towads practical atheism by the movement of a materialist and technocratic civilization. It is above all to the teaching Church and to the hierarchy, and to those, clerics or laymen, who are missioned to participate in its apostolate, that there belongs the immense task of announcing to this mass the word of God and of trying to open for it the ways of grace. To say nothing of those, clerics or laymen, religious or seculars, who, leaving all other work but the gift of oneself to contemplation and to fraternal charity, have as their office only to cause *to be present* among men that Love which is «the true face of God.»

In the future as I conceive it, what would belong above all to the Christian laity, whenever it wishes to be truly the disciple of the Savior, is, it seems to me, and if what I have advanced in these pages is correct, the radiance produced, by reason of the mysterious solidarity of souls, starting from the new constellations of which I have just spoken, not only under the influence of the specific activities of the various centers of energy which compose them, but also through the power, on which Bergson insisted so much, of heroic example, and through that of prayer, and of suffering united with the Passion of Christ.

To suppose the best, these dispersed centers of spiritual radiance would some day become, if human liberty does not give way too much, the yeast which will cause the whole dough to rise.

To suppose the worst, they would become a more or less persecuted diaspora thanks to which the presence of Jesus and of His love will remain, in spite of all, in an apostate world.

CHAPTER SIX

OUR SISTER VERA

I said a few words about Vera in the preceding chapter. I would like to speak of her more, and to make the present chapter a kind of memorial dedicated to her. Shall I succeed in doing so? Will she permit it? She always kept her treasures carefully hidden, but I have a duty of justice regarding her. And then I suppose that in the eternal light, while knowing well that, according to the saying of Mélanie, «the eyes of men are thieves,» one no longer fears having these hapless eyes see what on earth one kept for God alone.

When Vera was born, her parents no longer lived in Rostov-on-the-Don, but in another city of southern Russia, Marioupol (which is now called Djanovgrad), on the shore of the sea of Azov. She was born in 1886, the 20th of June in the Russian calendar — which, in the Latin calendar, corresponded to the 2nd of July, on which the Catholic Church celebrates the Visitation. Raissa was also born on a day of the Blessed Virgin, the 12th of September, feast of the Holy Name of Mary (in the Russian calendar, the 31st of August 1883). In *Les Grandes Amitiés* Raissa speaks of their childhood infinitely better than I can do. This childhood, this garden of an unforgettable fragrance, in which they had made so many marvelous discoveries, always haunted their hearts, and I relived it with them, I did not tire of questioning them about it, nor they of replying to me. I had my entries into the world of Pifo and of Mimo. «My little sister was growing up. From the time she knew how to speak we talked together a great deal. And we had our own special game, a game which lasted throughout our entire childhood. We imagined that she was my little mother, that I was her little boy and that we lived in a world entirely different from that inhabited by man. It was a world where no one cried or was sick, where flowers and fruits grew all the year round, where children played with birds and could fly like them, where ages are fixed and never change. Mothers never grew old and children were always the same age as they were when they were found in the well, that is, they were always the age at which they were 'born.' Thus I was always two years old. We lived in this world all our playtime hours, and after a fashion, it grew as we grew. When we were big enough to have an idea of good and evil, the very idea of evil had to be shut out of our world. We also had to watch ourselves so as not even to mention words which indicated evil, wickedness — even words which by contrast might make one think of evil. Thus we must not say 'well' in order not to have to think of 'ill,' nor good' in order not to think of 'bad.' It was an extraordinary exercise for the little minds of children, and we often made mistakes, but we would catch ourselves and would try to correct our way of speaking and thinking.

«There was nevertheless a sort of permissible imperfection — joking, teasing, playing tricks. It was the imagination's revenge, in which all kinds of absurdities and nonsense were permitted. For example, Pifo — that was my name in this game — would perch upon a growing cherry (we thought that the pit grew first and then the fruit) and the cherry would grow all about the child and hide him from the eye of his mother who was looking for him. But Pifo would eat the cherry and fall into the arms of his mother, Mimo. This game we played endlessly. We were still playing it when my sister was eight years old and I was nearly eleven.»[1] To tell the truth, this game, in which refinement and ardor of spirit had such a part, had a fundamental importance for the two sisters; in it they revealed themselves to one another, and it foreshadowed what they were to be for one another all through life, the vital depth of their mutual attachment. The tenderness of Vera with regard to Raissa always preserved something maternal. And Raissa always felt herself surrounded by this tenderness and protected by it. Raissa forged ahead; her initiatives, infinitely more serious than those of the little Pifo, were those of a humility which braves the perils of the unknown by a mad, boundless love for justice and for truth, she took

---

1. *Les Grandes Amitiés*, pp. 20-21 (Eng. trans.: *We Have Been Friends Together*, pp. 6-7).

her risks, she risked everything when it was necessary. The humility of Vera inclined her to efface herself, but in reality it was not so much this humility which caused her to keep withdrawn, it was rather an admirable virtue of *discretion*, the discretion of a mother proud of her child who keeps herself quite close to him, but a little behind and always on the alert, always ready to assist him and to defend him. And by a high grace from God, I also, her brother, was admitted into the strength and the goodness of this maternal protection. It was necessary for Raissa and myself to face the world. The first task of Vera was to watch over us. And blessed be her great heart, in it she found her joy: «I would like to learn the language of birds, in order to sing the happiness of having a ewe and a lamb.»[1]

Outside of the game of which I have just spoken, I have little to say concerning the very young Vera in Russia, except (as I was told) that she showed herself, at those moments when children feel hurt by some injustice or some offence, more carried away than her elder sister. Outraged and indignant, Raissa retreated without raising her eyes; Vera stamped her foot. She flared up so quickly that people liked to call her «little match» (*spitchka*).

At Marioupol she attended the classes of the elementary school, but not, like Raissa, those of the high-school (Raissa was admitted there at the age of seven, and Vera was this age when the family, having left Russia forever, established itself in Paris). Younger and less well prepared, the school years in Paris were more difficult for her. Without a shadow of jealousy (nothing was more foreign to her nature) she admired Raissa all the more; moreover it was on Raissa that the mind of their parents concentrated for that ascent into the world of science which is the great ambition of Jewish families. But it was not only because she experienced little attraction for the Sorbonne, it was above all out of necessity, because of her failing health, that after several years of secondary schooling Vera gave up regular studies, without giving up for all that her curiosity of mind, her love of books, her passion for everything which ennobles humanity. The doctors had detected an attack of pulmonary tuberculosis, which however was cured in a few years. She was sixteen or seventeen, I believe, when she spent a winter in Pau, where she

---

1. Fragment of a draft of a letter, undated.

boarded with the family of another doctor. She was a quite romantic young girl (the poems of Éphraïm Mikhaël delighted her), of an extraordinarily delicate charm, and of an extreme gentleness from which sparks did not fail to fly. Independent and proud of her independence, she had repulsed with a flick of the wrist the timid apostolic advances of two old ladies whom she often visited and who tried to interest this unbeliever in the Catholic religion. Protestantism had no more luck one or two years later (my chronology is very uncertain), when she sojourned in Switzerland where Raissa came to join her for the vacation, and where both met the future minister Paul Vergara, whom they introduced to me afterwards and who remained our friend.

When a year after our marriage Raissa and I came to know the Bloys, in 1905, we naturally immediately spoke of them to Vera. She went to see them with us, read like us the books of Léon Bloy and those of the spirituals whom he recommended to us. And certainly she had her own problems, she loved beauty too much to be able to satisfy herself with the human condition. But of what passed within her, never a word; our mutual confidence had no need of words. When the two of us had finally reached the decision to ask for baptism, Raissa informed her of it, and she replied simply, as a thing which was a matter of course: I am ready. She was baptized at the same time as we were, the 11th of June, 1906 — with many tears. On that day she gave herself to God forever, even making to Him, in imitation of her godfather, some of those unreasonable requests which He is only too ready to grant; — Raissa, who dreaded everything which seemed exaggerated, merely asked Him for «something»;[1] full measure was given to both of them, by way of suffering and love.

*

It is easy to picture to oneself Raissa as a Mary devoted to contemplation, and Vera as a Martha devoted to the active life, a Sister of charity par excellence. In reality, Raissa was as active as Vera, although on another plane; goodness, tenderness, devotion

---

1. Cf. *Raissa's Journal*, p. 76 (3rd of August, 1918).

to neighbor were likewise ardent in her. And like Raissa, Vera lived by prayer; she also knew that it was necessary *to give everything* to Jesus, *everything, absolutely everything;*[1] she also had made unity in herself under the peace which God gives. (It was certainly moreover the case of Martha and Mary themselves; the diversity between them was exaggerated by the function principally assigned to each — diversity of lighting which made appear deep-seated a contrast wholly secondary to tell the truth.)

If it is a question afterwards of character, of temperament, of natural dispositions, the contrast between the two sisters was very great. Raissa took more after her mother, Vera after her father. Raissa herself had a taste for wisdom, Vera for temerity. Raissa scarcely liked to go outside, «the humble kingdom of her house» mattered to her first; appropriateness in the arrangement of things, the very simple harmony of her room was the repose of her eyes; she had a passion for order, undertook projects for arranging things which she rarely had the strength to carry through (it was an annoyance for her, and we did not help her enough), she had a respect for the humblest objects which she knew was required by the spirit of poverty, kept the same clothes in perfect condition for an improbable number of years. It displeased her if a woman made herself ugly or neglected herself, she liked pretty dresses — ready-made dresses of the most moderate price, which one «adjusted» at home (it was on this occasion that at Princeton she came to know a black woman of great heart, a seamstress by profession, who quickly became a very dear friend, and who assisted us in the most difficult moments until the end; in hearing Jane Somerville speak to us of her father, who as an adolescent had been a fugitive slave, the tragedy of the South, the suffering and the courage of a whole race became suddenly tangible).

Vera, who was also a woman, and did not detest being pretty, was however naturally inclined not to care a bit about her clothes, and it took a long time before she one day thanked her sister for having taught her to become «a little stylish.» She let things lie about anywhere, forgot them, preferred her dreams. Her room was precious to her also, above all her little room in Princeton in which

1. From the sole notebook (1912-1913) that Vera forgot to destroy (16th of April, 1913).

she found a peace near to her heart (she said that there she was in the house of St. Joseph), it was our consolation to feel her happy there. But still she had an instinctive horror of everything having to do with ordering, arrangement, rules of organization, and left to her native dispositions she would have lived in the midst of a disorder cheerfully increased or renewed each day (which never happened because she did not wish to displease her sister; and even, in the last years, she had almost been converted to the advantages of «order»). She liked the nickname of «Barbed Cat»; her taste for extremes and for a certain irrationality caused us to call her the surrealist of the house. However disarmed she was, for she was in a holy ignorance of the century's sharp practices, she had no fear of facing the external world, of protecting me against invaders and of showing so much inflexibility to friends who asked for me on the telephone that she drew the resentment of many, of discussing with tradesmen and of imposing her authority on the maids, before whom Raissa and I trembled miserably. During our stays in the United States, Raissa, who knew English much better then she, and who read it easily, never wished to speak it — because she feared pronouncing it badly, and above all because she waited obstinately, and in vain, to «know the irregular verbs» to perfection (the time that she would have liked to devote to English lessons she gave to *Les Grandes Amitiés*). Vera, on the contrary, shamelessly spoke an imaginary English thanks to which furthermore she made herself understood as much as she wished, and won, first in New York, in the quarter of the «village» where we lived, then in Princeton, the esteem and the friendship of managers of drugstores, grocery stores and stationery stores, not to mention the supermarkets where she gaily pushed about the small shopping cart in which she stacked her purchases.

Raissa's sleep was of an astonishing tranquility; one could hardly hear her breathe, she hardly budged the whole night, did not make a crease in her sheets. Vera threw everything into disorder while she was sleeping; in the morning her covers were on the floor.

Striking at first, all these differences between the two sisters were only differences of temperament, which covered a fundamental likeness of a much greater importance.

They had the same voice, or very nearly — astonishingly pure, gentle and clear; Massignon, when he telephoned us, complained of not knowing which of them he was speaking to.

They had that same quickness of mind, that same delicacy of sensibility, of almost airy perceptiveness, that same sense of humor in tears which stems in the children of Israel not from blood nor from the flesh, nor from racial heredity, but from the kind of refinement or of sharpening of nature which since Abraham and Moses grace has effected in this people and in its culture. Such a quality, which is also a particular aptitude for suffering, can become exacerbated in certain persons, but in others it is the seal of a kind of royal dignity (Raissa's voice and that of Vera made me dream of the harp of David). Our friend Dr. William Welch, who tended them in their illnesses in Princeton over a long period, called them regal. (Shall I tell, but so much the worse for the Gentiles, that he added that his other patients were «horses»?) The true words which it would be necessary to use for them have nothing to do with the stateliness of pomp, one would have to say «humble grandeur.»

They had the same purity and uprightness of heart, the same candor, the same horror of all falseness. The only lie that Vera committed was not a lie, but a slip dictated by the unconscious and which amused the three of us very much. She was on good terms, at Versailles, with the Mère Supérieure des Auxiliatrices du Purgatoire, a very distinguished and somewhat solemn person. In the course of a visit which Vera paid to her, this good Mother questioned her concerning her godfather and asked her the title of his books. Vera, in recounting the conversation to us, told us quite calmly that when she came to the Journal of Léon Bloy she had enumerated its different volumes, *le Mendiant Ingrat, l'Invendable, Quatre ans de captivité à Châlons-sur-Marne. . . .* And it was only after our surprise that she realized, bursting out laughing, that without noticing it she had translated for the sake of a Mère Auxiliatrice too well brought up to endure a swear-word, the title of this last book, which is, as one knows, *Quatre ans de captivité à Cochons-sur-Marne* (Cochons-sur-Marne is Lagny).

The two sisters had the same love of truth and of beauty, the same simplicity, the same humility, the same liberty of spirit, the same indifference to worldly conventions. Their Christianity had the same evangelical quality, the same tenderness for souls which was but one with the love of Jesus, the same spirit of poverty, which with the years was going to cause both of them to enter, without any noise betraying their steps, into the narrow path of interior destitution and of the complete divesting of self. Speaking of the imprudent generosities of her father and of the terrors which resulted at the end of the month, Raissa writes in *Les Grandes Amitiés*: «In this fashion I learned what the acquisition of a little money can cost in effort, what suffering the lack of a little money can occasion. And when several years later I saw Léon Bloy in the grip of poverty and misery, it was easy for me to understand and to sympathize. This won for me the very high privilege of being welcomed and considered by him as belonging to his own sorrowful world, the world of those who do not look at poverty from the outside.»[1] As to Vera, her spirit of poverty was such that she never thought of the fact that she depended on her sister and on me for everything and had nothing of her own, except her clothes, her books, her identity card, and that famous *private law*, signed by President Truman, which we had obtained with some difficulty and which permitted her to reside *hors quota* in the United States.[2]

The silence which she generally observed at the meetings in Meudon signified neither timidity nor indifference, and did not prevent her from expressing her own judgment about people, sometimes more severe than ours. She detested pretension, affectation, and sentimentality. It was by reason of the intensity of her own interior ardor that she exposed herself so little.

Served by the vivacity of her character, she could moreover display a flawless boldness as soon as the cause of justice was at stake. At the time of Meudon and of the battles which I then fought, she could publicly refuse her hand to a male friend whom she judged had betrayed me; and I myself, when she related this adventure to me on her return home, was so stupid and so fatuous as to criticize her for this as a breach of charity. I still have regrets for having made her weep that day.

Her compassion was not greater than Raissa's, but it was of a little different quality, because of the maternal nuance it contained. Her pity for human beings was so profound that, paradoxically, she, so strict with herself, sometimes seemed, when it was a question of sinners, to look upon sin as not much, as a paltry accident of the

1. *Les Grandes Amitiés*, p. 44 (Eng. Trans.: Vol I, *We Have Been Friends Together*, p. 30).
2. "Private Law 357, 82nd Congress, approved October 25, 1951."

human condition. I mean that she regarded with a kind of immediately pardoning indulgence, not, to be sure, the proud and the cruel, but those whom the weakness of the flesh, or the work of our poor passions, or misery leads astray.

A particularly beloved book for her, in the last years, was *Requiem for a Nun*, which she read in the excellent translation of Coindreau. For very different reasons she also placed very high (less high however than the great book of Faulkner) *The Sea*, of Conrad, and above all *Le Lotissement du ciel*, of Blaise Cendrars, whose resplendent baroque pleased her in the extreme. She loved Saint-Exupéry; and, more profoundly, Baudelaire, and Apollinaire, and Reverdy. There was also, of course, *Union With God* of Albert the Great, the opusculum on *The Divine Ways* attributed to St. Thomas and which Raissa had translated, *The Dialogue* of St. Catherine of Siena, Grignion de Montfort, Caussade, *L'Abrégé de la Doctrine spirituelle de saint Jean de la Croix* done by Charles Henrion, the writings (or rather stenographed copies of retreats) belatedly published by Father Dehau. And, a treasure entirely apart, the books of Raissa, and her poems, as also the volume on *The Living Thoughts of Saint Paul* which I had published. Although she had received no philosophical formation she also read my other books, and she understood them very well, if not technically, at least through the heart.

If intelligence was the native land of Raissa, the proper climate of Vera was the quickness and the exactness of sensibility. She amused herself, though without attaching any importance to it, by pencilling sketches, birds, boats, exaggerated silhouettes and then writing satirical captions under them («A father-in-law, here is my daughter», «A sad lady on a visit»; «An acid lady». . . .) On her sickbed she still drew them with her trembling hand, was happy as a child with the sketch-books and the colored pencils we brought her. She wrote stories for children in which all the animals of the earth figured, short fanciful poems which could have been very good if she had wished and which Raissa begged her to work on, but which she left as seedlings. From a small number which I have found I extract and regroup these few lines.

The ox escorting the tortoise
thinks of the lost paradise.

Do you hear the carillon of the Antilles,
the swarms of the withered flowers?
Along the ponds unicorns sing
the story of the ewes.
All the stones of the universe are moved to pity
and tears flow all along craters.
O my friends these are songs
of love and of agony.[1]

And a small poem for *C.J.:*

Lamb with blue eyes — impossible dust, luminous diamonds —
hard head, serried like truth, gentleness of angels, implacable
tenderness, drop of water which hollows out rocks, impregnable,
peaceful, tranquil.[2]

She had a passion for the sea, our crossings of the Atlantic put her
entirely at ease, and the more the boat tossed the happier she was.
The voyage to South America on the *Florida* was her great joy,
nothing pleased her so much as her little cabin which was however
not very comfortable, and in walking about on the bridge in the
storm she felt more secure than on the streets of Paris.

But let us speak of things which matter more. If Raissa and
Vera both welcomed the slightest joy with tenderness and gratitude,

Protect your happiness by thanksgivings
Surround it with a hedge of roses,[3]

it was Raissa, though so grave, who had the most humor and the
most playfulness, and the most need of a certain light gaiety. By
her natural instinct she would have asked only to be overjoyed at
the beauty of the world. In looking at her one thought, sick at heart,
of these lines of Baudelaire on the poet:

And the Spirit which follows him in his pilgrimage
Weeps to see him gay like a bird of the forests.

1. Rome, 1946; Princeton, 1950.
2. Rome, Christmas 1945.
3. 'Aime le don de Dieu," in *Au Creux du Rocher.*

And it was she who had to bear the heaviest burden, entered farther into the thickness of the Cross. All of which does not mean that the cross of Vera was light, for she also had entirely sacrificed herself — patiently, silently, all the time, in a kind of luminous darkness, without anything, except our mutual love, coming to give her any human encouragement, but with the consolations of Jesus.

She did not have the extraordinarily broad culture and the genius of her senior, and was not at all humiliated by them: for she loved her Creator enough to be happy with what He had made her, and she possessed in any case enough exquisite natural gifts not to have to complain about her lot. In a general way I shall say that along with an astonishing spiritual relationship and a similar attitude before life, Raissa, in all things, whether it is a question of human experience or of spiritual experience, and of intuition, and of suffering, advanced farther and deeper. But nothing was more beautiful and more moving than to see the two sisters move thus through life, Raissa first, Vera second, inseparable, and this so simple and so generous acceptance of the role of second, and of the function of assisting, conferred on Vera a similar and eminent dignity. For it was an equally great love which caused both of them to act, fraternal love for one another, love of God, love of neighbor.

I have said that there was something adventurous and rash in Vera. But it was Raissa who, at sixteen, had declared that she wanted a life «which would not be quotidian.» She often reminded us of this remark, which amused all three of us, for we had indeed been served. Vera would certainly have been able to say the same thing, the meaning however would have been a little different. Raissa knew too much of it to love adventure for itself, even if only in imagination; it was on life and death that she was engaging herself.

*

Here I would like to include a parenthesis concerning Raissa. Because of the firmness of her will Maurice Sachs, in *Le Sabbat*, said of her, if I remember rightly, that she was «a woman of steel.» Such an expression is suitable for what they call in America «metallic women»; applied to Raissa it is a flagrant absurdity. Raissa had nothing of feminine ruses and of feminine swoons — she had all the grace, the ardor and the fragility of femininity. Airy delicacy, light sweetness of the little hands of Raissa! Vera also had hands of an admirable sweetness, but larger, less fairy-like. Raissa's incomparable spirit of childhood must also be spoken of, a spirit which she kept intact until the end. This innocence, which one attributes to children — she truly had it. Her simple attitude in the presence of things and of persons, the way she carried her head, that way of standing up straight without the slightest stiffness and of looking people in the eye without the slightest arrogance, or apprehension, or precaution, that presence which consisted simply in *being there* without deceit, that welcome without premeditation — it was enough for me to see it to be overwhelmed by the feeling of this innocence — innocence exposed to all blows. In Raissa there was no steel, but an ardent flame. Or, if one holds to the idea of steel, one must say that the blade was enclosed in an incredibly vulnerable and tender sheath. She was very quick at repartee, but she was totally *defenseless*. I always reproached her for being «without a shell,» and for not wanting a shell or a shield. «She reminds me of a lily of the valley which too heavy a ray of sunshine would bend on its stem. In this charming and so frail creature there lives a soul capable of making oaks kneel,»[1] Léon Bloy, from the first meeting, had divined his beloved goddaughter. As I said in the Foreword of *Raissa's Journal*, «In no one (and certainly not in myself) have I known such strength and such unflinching courage of will, nor such lucidity.» Well, nothing had more need of being protected than this strength, because, even already as mere gift of nature, it was not of this world, in the sense in which poetry is not of this world either. It was enough to enable her to triumph, at any cost, over fear and over anguish, it was not enough to spare her from them. Through the blessing of a complementarity which love alone can produce, the admirable courage of Vera before the chicaneries, perfidies, calumnies and cowardices which one rubs up against as soon as one acts, protected the strength which made oaks kneel by protecting the lily of the valley, the too vulnerable envelope, the heart of Raissa open to all suffering as well as to all beauty.

1. *L'Invendable*, p. 301.

Before finishing this parenthesis, I note also that one would be completely mistaken if because of the long agony of soul which is spoken of in the *Journal*, and of the trials of all kinds which Raissa had to endure, one saw in her only struggle and austerity. I have insisted above, as also in the Foreword which precedes the *Journal*, on the gaiety and the playfulness which were in her a need of nature and which she was always able to preserve, as well as on her untiring interest in the works of men and the movement of life. In writing these lines I think of a photograph of her at sixteen, wholly radiant with the ardor of living. With what passion she willed happiness — and first Truth — happiness in Truth, without knowing then at what a bloody price such a happiness is bought. When she began to know it, she never drew back. As a friend who had known her well, the eldest daughter of Pierre Termier, wrote to me, after having read the *Journal*, «her gifts, truly exceptional from all points of view, seemed to promise her an easy life, a life filled up to the brim; and one sees her in these pages at grips with heart-rending difficulties, traversing months of anguish and of agony, because she chose the highest possible life, the desolation of the great altitudes.»[1] In order to face this desolation, as well as to sympathize with all the sadness of which she was the confidante without wasting away with sorrow, she needed the never changing freshness of her native gaiety. She could amuse herself with a trifle. She loved — much more than Vera — play and dance. Very young, as she related in *Les Grandes Amitiés*, she used to go dancing — in her everyday dress — at the balls of the Russian students; Isadora Duncan had delighted her; and if afterwards there was no longer ever any talk of dance for her, it was much less for reasons of moral severity than because in fact our kind of life included no occasion for worldliness. As for the dance of David or of the Hassidim, she found them again in Chagall and in her own poetry. In her last illness she made gentle fun of the doctors who tended her, and whose powerlessness she knew. One day, in the course of one of those absurd and distressing examinations which a great specialist in neurology made her periodically undergo («Madame, what is this? » he asked her while unexpectedly presenting his watch or tie, or his wedding ring — as if the memory could be jogged without the help of an associated train of thought) he asked her: «Madame, what would you like to do at

1. Letter of Mme Jeanne Boussac, 7th of January, 1964.

this moment?» «Doctor, I would like to dance,» she replied, raising her beautiful laughing eyes to this man with whom, immobilized in her bed, she had found a means of playing because she knew him to be superlatively intelligent (but did he deserve the favor of such a game at such a moment, I doubt it very much).

To tell the truth, when she was not taken up by prayer, poetry, or suffering, her relations with things and with people were a kind of game which she kept up by instinct, and which were a great help to her in enduring the perpetual emotions and the harassment of the life of Meudon. The game in which she delighted most (and which was much more than a game) was that of conversation with her friends. At Princeton another game, it also much more than a game, consisted in selecting and cutting out among the multitude of photographs of children which one found at that time in American periodicals, the pictures of those whom she called *beings*. It is natural that very often the child, in his devouring eagerness to see and to touch, exercises only the most common vitality, but at other moments certain children, especially certain little children, seem — and with what almost unbearable gravity, in comparison with which the countenance of adults is ridiculous and affected — solely and mysteriously occupied with existing, turned towards the act of being and absorbed in it. Abolition of appearance! These latter were beings.

Being astonishes in the eyes of the child
and refuses to see the world[1] . . .

Still another game enchanted Raissa — it was a game of reflections. Are windows in America made with thicker glass than in Europe? At any rate it behaves more, at certain moments, like a mirror. When twilight came, the windows of our rooms began to reflect the objects and the lights inside our house with brilliant vividness; and since at the same time they continued to show the things on the outside, there resulted fantastic pictures; one saw the dining room table suspended in the midst of a tree, a bed on

1. "L'Echelle," in *Poèmes inédits* of Raissa Maritain, *Nova et Vetera*, No. 3, 1963, p. 161. [Cf. Raissa Maritain, *Poèmes et Essais*, Paris, Desclée De Brouwer, 1968, p. 175. — Tr.]

the lawn of the garden, one of us seated on a chair in the clouds, our lamps or the books on our shelves straddling the door or the wall of the neighboring house. Raissa always called Vera and me to come share the pleasures of this spectacle, which we could vary in all sorts of ways simply by changing our position.

We laughed a great deal in our house. On certain evenings, when Raissa was sick, I went to her bedside to read to her, imitating the accent of Marseilles, and thanks to this very simple stratagem there were crystalline bursts of laughter in which Vera joined. We detested both bohemianism and bourgeois conventions. I was (I am still) very foul-mouthed. This displeased Raissa very much, but what to do about it? At Meudon an agreement was finally established between her and myself (at my expense), once a month I had the right to employ a certain forbidden word which relieved my bitterness, but only after twenty-nine days of constraint.

What chatter! After everything that I have just told you, do you think that I am intelligent enough to enable you to understand Raissa and Vera? Myself, I admired them and loved them with all my heart, and I knew them well indeed. But was I capable of understanding them? One never understands a soul.

Among the friends whom Raissa and Vera saw most frequently at Meudon, I shall name three particularly dear children of Israel, who had devoted themselves to Jesus with all their heart; Jeanne Linn, the very sweet and very faithful Jeanne Linn (she and her husband Pierre also lived in Meudon); — Achsa Belkind, who had been sent to us from Palestine (as was formerly, at the time of Bures, the noble and ardent Absalom Feinberg; he did not become a Christian and returned home where, during the First World War, he sided with the Allies in order to better serve the cause of Zionism; and was put to death by the Germans); Achsa is also from a family of Zionist pioneers, but the courses of Guignebert at the Sorbonne, with their anti-Christian bias, caused her to reflect so well that she became the goddaughter of René Schwob and of Raissa; — and Babet Jacob, so radiant with intelligence and with life, who during the second war, in the so-called free zone, was to be handed over to the Gestapo by the Vichy police, together with her old mother of eighty years and her brother Emmanuel, my godson; these Christian Jews, who had put too much confidence in France (they loved her to the point of almost being militarists) were deported to Germany,

Babet and her mother thrown into the gas-chamber of Buchenwald, Manu assassinated one knows not where, their death darkened our hearts forever.

In general our friendships were common to all three of us. Vera however had also her private friendships; in the first place Marie-Louise Guillot, her great confidante (she was a cousin of Father Garrigou-Lagrange, we had known her through Father Dehau; one saw in this tall, chaste young woman an unforgettable light and an unforgettable courage, an unforgettable gaiety, an unforgettable piety; she died at the age of seventy-two, the 21st of September 1962).

It was also to Father Dehau, I believe, that Vera owed another friend to whom she was very attached, Mme Aline Masurel, who lived in the North of France and who came from time to time to Paris. Vera saw her each time, in Paris or in Meudon.

There was besides — chronologically I should have begun with her, for it is a question of very early times — the Mother Superior (Mother Rosalie) of a Community of which I have forgotten the name, which took care of the poor and the sick, somewhere in the vicinity of the Gare du Nord. Vera admired her very much, and she always returned happy from the visits she went to pay her (sometimes bringing back some penitential instrument which she procured for herself at the gate-lodge of the convent).

There was above all (many years later, at the height of the Meudon period) Mother Madeleine, that Dominican nun of an incomparable generosity and an incomparable liberty of spirit, who, very much in advance of her time, saw in manual work[1] and in a perfect availability to the requests of compassion for one's neighbor the privileged soil of an authentic contemplative life. With the aid of Father Bernadot she had founded a Third Order Regular («of St. Catherine de Ricci»); and this wholly evangelical small community which Mother Madeleine still animates and which resides now in Crépieux, lived then in Meudon. They were very close to the heart of all three of us; but it was Vera who, more free to come and go than Raissa and I, saw Mother Madeleine most frequently.

And there was, for a certain time, Gwen John, a difficult

---

1. At the outset, embroideries of liturgical vestments; afterwards, and definitely, weaving, learned from the last artisans of Lyons, and done by the Sisters in the community.

friend whom it was a question of aiding in her anxieties and her
torments. An excellently endowed painter, she lived in Meudon
as a recluse buried in her art and in her reverie. She went to Mass
every morning, and it was there that she had seen us, before in a
moment of great moral anguish it occurred to her to approach us.[1]
From that time she confided in Vera, whom she saw after Mass, on
Mondays especially. Vera did all she could for her, and the burden
was heavy. In the end it became clear to her that it was better to
break off. But she always kept Gwen John in her prayers.

*

Since she had come to join us in Heidelberg, in December of
1906, Vera always lived with Raissa and myself. We served our
apprenticeship together as converts, each using a total frankness
towards the other two, and trying to aid each other while aiding
oneself. At that distant time she was still very touchy, and often
felt offended by trifles; she quickly cured herself of this natural
susceptibility, and I believe that in not sparing her from our jokes
we did her a service. It was from that time that the three of us
formed a closely united little community in which, while employing
at first, at the very beginning, some idiotic practices of piety (such
as the daily reckoning of faults and of «victories» over oneself) −
this did not last long − and some illusory means of mortification
suggested by the Lives of the saints which we devoured without
discernment but with delight (belts equipped with nails, hair shirts,
bitter power discreetly thrown onto the plate, and what not),[2] −
this also passed quickly enough − then, without great profit, the
reading and private meditation on the *Exercises* of St. Ignatius −
and a little later (this finally was reasonable) certain practices borrowed from monastic life such as the regular «chapters» (one would
say today, in the discount vocabulary with which people feel com-

1. See the Appendix to the present chapter, "Apropos of Gwendoline and
Augustus John."
2. Raissa disapproved of these practices; for her part she was content − and
this was much better, but scarcely wiser − with ruining her health a little more
by going to Mass at all costs every morning, which was then very much beyond
her strength.

fortable, the «revisions of life»), we took our first steps towards a Milky Way which recedes in proportion as one advances.

Our life in Heidelberg was discussed in a preceding chapter. Afterwards it was Paris (rue des Feuillantines), than Versailles (rue de l'Orangerie, then rue Neuve, named later rue Baillet-Reviron). In February 1909, Vera, in spite of her shaky health, decided that she would be a nurse, and began to serve her apprenticeship at Hôpital de la Pitié, one of the most dilapidated and squalid hospitals of Paris, but with which she was delighted. We still lived on rue des Feuillantines; but in October of the same year we were going to move to Versailles, and it was from there that at the cost of great fatigue, soon complicated by pulmonary troubles, Vera continued to go regularly through her course at the hospital. She had entered the surgical department of Dr. Walter, and always kept a vivid gratitude for this man who was as good as he was learned, who had quickly become attached to her. During these hours spent at Pitié she saw from close up human suffering and human misery, sometimes human hideousness, and her compassion for the poor of Jesus Christ grew not only in extent, but in strength and determination. At the end of a little more than a year it was necessary for her to withdraw, Dr. Walter having intimated to her that the work for which she believed herself cut out was absolutely incompatible with the weakness of her health. It was a very hard blow for her. But to have been a nurse always pleased her magnanimity, and she always considered herself to be such (not only was she a very good judge in all departments of first aid, she also enforced over us the inescapable symbols of antisepsis: absorbent cotton, alcohol, the obligatory passing of the least instrument in flame or in boiling water). More truly and in a more profound sense, she was all her life a Nurse par excellence.

I suppose that she had like everybody a period of hesitation concerning the paths in which she would direct her life, not being attracted by marriage and wondering what God wished of her. Everything became clear when (at what moment, I cannot say; perhaps when we became oblates of St. Benedict at Oosterhout, she under the name of Agnes, Raissa under the name of Gertrude; myself, by antiphrasis apparently, under that of Placidus) the three of us decidedly understood that our little lay community formed a unity apart, was something in the midst of the world which was not of the world, without having need for all that to belong to any secular imitation of the religious state, or to any pious organization. It is true that at the outset we regarded ourselves a little as lay monks and lay cloistered nuns, and that not without some bravado and much naiveté I carefully inscribed a Benedictine *pax* at the head of letters which most often had nothing pacific in them. But these illusions soon vanished. We were laymen, engaged unreservedly in the state of lay life; and the more the years passed, the more we felt ourselves simple laymen, laymen of the common run of the people. But this little flock of three belonged to Jesus Christ.

It was in this spirit, and with a perfect clearness, that Vera became conscious of her destiny. If she chose to remain with Raissa and me, it was for no kind of temporal reason, be it for love for her sister, it was by reason of her personal vocation and of her free gift, and of a call which she knew came from the depth of eternity.

The vocation of which I have just spoken is the supernatural root of the sublime devotion which she had for us. It explains also why she felt herself at no moment a sister and a sister-in-law a little isolated in the presence of the couple Raissa and Jacques. There was between the three of us a profound and tranquil unity, a radical unity which we always considered to be an immense grace from God. The number three is a particularly holy number and one which signifies the most complete plenitude — this is the idea or the impression which our hearts never ceased to experience. When Vera departed for the other life, what inconceivable solitude suddenly pounced upon two beings even though united by such a great love! Raissa could not survive it; Vera had prepared a place for her. And now, for my part, I survive the two of them. But the truth is that I also survive *myself.*

However profound and however total the human affection was which united the three of us, we knew very well that more profoundly and more totally still it was another love, come from on high, which united us also. We knew likewise, scarcely without formulating it to ourselves, for in itself it was rather inexpressible, that we were engaged together in a certain work for which it was necessary to follow as one blind a hand which guided our steps. Raissa and Vera knew it better than I, but I knew it also, in my own manner, in the manner of an apprentice-philosopher engaged to explore caverns in search of captive truths — all of which presupposed, at the same time as a certain amount of temerity, the disquieting, sometimes distressing help of those *gratis datae* motions which are not given for the sanctification of the one who receives them. (The she-donkey of Balaam was a good example of this truth, and I thought, not without reason, that the best image of the Christian philosopher is that young donkey for which St. Augustine has a gentle word; *asinus es*, he says to it, *sed Christus portas*.) [You are a donkey, but you carry Christ.] Well, the three of whom I speak were surrounded and aided all their life by very precious friendships, true gifts of Heaven. Furthermore I must say that they followed a wholly solitary path. Whether it is a question of what we did at Meudon, or what we did in America, or of the poetry of Raissa or of my philosophy, we took our risks and our initiatives all alone, without maneuvering with any group or playing the game of any party.

But let us leave this digression, and return to what concerns Vera in particular. Everywhere and always she was for Raissa and me a great helping Angel, I refer to the angels intentionally, she seemed on such good terms with them. (There are insignificant things which pass by us in time, but like a sign which one seizes on the wing and whose memory imprints itself on the soul. One day, in New York, while I was giving a lecture I know not where, and Vera had suddenly fallen gravely ill — Raissa saved her by changing doctors — our friend «Maou» — Marguerite Baudains — who claimed to be a strong spirit and rejected any belief, exclaimed in entering her room: «But there is nothing to fear, she has a crowd of angels around her bed. . . .»)
Naturally the aid which Vera gave us manifested itself first on the plane of visible things. Let it not be thought that Raissa shifted the responsibility for the whole care of the house on her, Raissa took most attentive care of all the details of the house; but Vera *aided* her considerably in the affairs of the household — especially of the kitchen (when their mother was no longer there to take charge of them) — and in «external relations»; just as she aided me on all occasions; she prepared with me the orthographical Dictionary in the *Tout en Un* [*Everything in One*] of Hachette, she was my secretary, the manuscripts of all the books written at Versailles and at Meudon were typed by her. She not only aided us, she *defended* us, as I noted above, and this first of all in all the little difficulties of life. She had assumed this function of defence and protection with joy, and I believe that she drew from it a kind

of humble pride. She would have liked, but Raissa prevented her,[1] to take for herself all that was less good. She was always available and always enterprising. It was she who after many vain searches found the house at Meudon. (Raissa, betrayed by her physical strength, was depressed at not being able to look with her for such things. It was intended that she be so disappropriated as never to be able to examine beforehand, in order to consider its merits, the place where we were going to live, whether it was our different successive dwellings or merely vacation places; it was Vera and I who made the choice; and almost always — in the case of Meudon in particular — the first contact was a rude shock for Raissa, what she saw not corresponding at all to the idea she had formed from our descriptions. She never chose her abode — and neither, my goodness, her last abode — here on earth.)

We could have said about Vera what the weeping St. Bernard said of his brother Gerard: «The eyes of Gerard preceded all my steps, my cares were more known to his heart than to mine, he was more preoccupied with them, felt their urgency better.» And that whole long lamentation, that immense sorrow which St. Bernard emits in the 26th sermon on the *Song of Songs*, because his beloved brother is no more, I recall how much Raissa was touched by it, and how she blessed the saint for it when the visible presence of Vera was taken from her.

I have said that Vera aided us and defended us first on the plane of visible things, and in all the little difficulties of everyday life. It is necessary now to go much further, to try to speak of the spiritual assistance which she constantly gave us, and of the fortitude of this defenceless one whose support never failed us. Here, I am afraid to speak of things too mysterious and too pure for me. I noted above that Raissa's exceptional strength of soul, and the invincible will which attached her to the absolute, because they inhabited a fragile body and a defenceless sensibility, made her more painfully vulnerable to all the cruelty, stupidity, treachery and meanness that there is in the world; far from dispensing from anguish they were, like the «giant's wings» of which Baudelaire

---

1.   This propensity of Vera drove Raissa frantic, she could not stand Vera "wanting to sacrifice herself": these were the only times that Raissa got angry with her, then Vera went to cry in her room, returned, promising not to do it again, and the two sisters kissed, laughing and weeping at the same time.

speaks, an inconvenience on the paths of the earth, and in this sense, they themselves had need of being protected. It was to protect them that Vera employed her own strength, more at ease in the confusion of the here-below. And thus the weaker supported and protected the stronger.

But the words which I use scarcely satisfy me, and could lead to error. For if Vera's strength of soul did not have the extraordinary intensity of her sister's, how much even so I would have liked to have Vera's strength, not so much before men and human grandeurs, which have never impressed me much, but in the face of long and cruel physical sufferings endured without lament, and in the face of trials of the spirit, I say before the threat of the most serious, and at certain moments, it seemed, the most hopeless, external events, I say in the total confidence in God and the total abandonment to His will, and the hoping against all hope! The strength of soul of our little sister aided the least strong among us as it aided the strongest.

Of this blessed aid it seems that Heaven wished to give us a particular sign. Here I touch on one of the secrets of Vera; and I know well that aside from an exception of which I am going to speak presently, she did not want to confide anything of these things — she destroyed all her notebooks (except one which escaped her by chance, lost among other papers).[1] However since I am trying here to sketch her portrait, how can I not say a word about her prayer, which was the life of her life? I believe that unlike Raissa she received many sensible graces, and that she was fortified by their sweetness, as well as by the sweetness of tears — she wept with tenderness and with amazement much more often than with sadness. (At Rome, when I presented the two of them to Pius XII, Vera never left off streaming with tears the whole time that this audience lasted. I teased her a lot afterwards. . . .)

She needed to talk to Father Dehau longer than Raissa, in order to submit to him, as her spiritual guide, the details of her secrets with God. Concerning these secrets silence reigned for years. And then, one day, fraternal charity made her divulge something of them to Raissa and to myself, when in September 1939 she saw us overwhelmed by the horror of the war which had just been declared and which we knew well would be monstrous. Then she decided to confess to Raissa that Jesus often spoke to her (in the depth of her heart,

1. See above, p. 190, note 1.

without any material sound) and that now He allowed her to transmit messages of His mercy. «I told you,» Raissa wrote to Henry
Bars (19th of January, 1969), «that her spiritual life was wholly
secret. We suspected that God spoke to her often. And in an altogether particular case, when it was a question of strengthening us
during our exile and the anguish of war, she made an exception.
She communicated to us the words which she heard from time to
time, above all during Mass, and which transfigured her with joy,
and which always told us to have confidence, to fear nothing, to
know that God watched over us.»

All three of us knew very well that «extraordinary graces»
in the mystical life are only an entirely secondary accessory;[1] they
are often liable to illusion, and it is a classical rule not to take one's
stand on them, but on faith and reason, for the acts which one has
to do (although under the New Law they are given, according to the
teaching of the theologians, only *ad directionem actuum human-
orum*: which signifies that they are given, not in order for themselves
to direct action, but only in order to aid, like flares, the virtue which
directs action, and whose name, although degraded by centuries of
philistinism, is Prudence). However everything in Vera was too clear,
too pure and too simple, her whole conduct too balanced, and the
so-to-speak substantial peace, the recollection, the joy, the light
which emanated from her when she brought to Raissa, sometimes to
me, the few lines cast by her on a scrap of paper, bore a too evident
witness for us to imagine the slightest illusion in her. She herself
never doubted that what was said to her came from Jesus.

As to the danger of regulating our actions according to these
brief messages, it would have been very difficult to detect, for in
actual fact no indication concerning something to be done was ever
contained in them, they were only testimonies of love and mercy,
and a constant exhortation to fear nothing. Sometimes, in certain
difficult circumstances, it was said that, whatever it was, the deci-

1. In the past, edifying literature attached too much importance to these kinds
of graces, and to the formidable rhetoric in which the communications often
abound, even when they are authentic (it is indeed clear that for these communications the divine action uses, as instrument, the material of images, of ideas
and of stylistic forms habitual to the subject). I am inclined to believe that
today, by reaction, we mistrust them in a too systematic manner; for finally
there is the liberty of the Holy Spirit, and there is also human weakness with its
need of being aided.

sion that we would come to would be blessed; this decision to be made was always left to our free will.[1]

Raissa kept all her sister's messages like treasures, she and I copied them in our notebooks. They were for her and for me a help and a blessing from Heaven. Moreover, as much as we felt moved, encouraged and strengthened in receiving them, we reproached ourselves afterwards for not thinking of them more; what they brought us was a kind of habitual climate, or rather a kind of support as secret as the movement of life.

In the letter to Henry Bars which I cited above, «we spoke to nobody,» wrote Raissa, «of these messages received by Vera, and given to us by her. It must be noted that she gave all of them to us without keeping anything for herself, she no longer had to re-read these papers, what they transmitted was in her. Several months ago she asked us to destroy everything which concerned her correspondence with Father Dahau and Father Charles Henrion, which she kept in two packets. But she added: *As to the messages which I gave to you, they belong to you.*» I have no desire to infringe the laws of discretion with respect to them; it is better however to cite a very small number of them, in order that one can have some idea of their simplicity and their sweetness.

«Fear not. Do not be afraid, my little children. I shall guard you.» (Fontgombaud, 5th of September 1939.)

«The sufferings of your little sister are transformed into graces and blessings. . . . Tell her that she has received the dew of fire — but let her not lose her composure, I am in her and with her. . . . Spiritually she is stronger than you, it is necessary that I aid you in a more sensible manner. She is a true little ewe of Israel. I shall guard you, I shall protect you, my children.» (29th of July 1945, they were both on the point of leaving New York to join me in Rome.)

«. . . I ask much of her, but I have few friends from whom I can ask so much. Let her fear nothing, never. Let her know that she is to participate in My joy and in My glory some day.» (Princeton, 10th of April 1949.)

«Yes, I shall be merciful to you, to you, to your little sister,

---

1. One example: "Whatever decision your brother arrives at you can consider as mine; and let him be in peace, and let my peace dwell in him." (New York, 11th of January 1945. I was then in great anguish concerning the mission to Rome which I was being asked to undertake and which I tried in vain to escape.)

to your brother, to all those who are here and who will come here. Tell your little sister that her sufferings are precious to me, that I have *need* of them for the salvation of souls. I keep her in my heart (I understood: like a little bird in its nest). Be sure to tell her that her sufferings are precious to me, it is I who send them. Let her be confident of my tenderness. As regards yourself, my little daughter, he who has not given everything has given nothing.» (Kolbsheim, 17th of July 1949.)

«Your little sister suffers for the salvation of the world. I Myself take into account each second of her sufferings. Let her fear nothing, let her be wholly confident in Me. The sweetness of My Heart will come into her heart. You also (I understood: Jacques and myself), be confident, My love watches over you. *Fear nothing* (this was emphasized). You are My little people. My love watches over you.» (Princeton, 1st of January 1953.)

Halt, poor Jacques! Too pure a memory is not bearable. One thing however which it is important to note also, is the manner in which Vera was treated with regard to the sensible aids which she received. She was severely deprived of them at the most difficult times, in which it would have seemed that she had the most need of them. And she bore this privation without ever bending or complaining. She had been strengthened; it belonged to her to conduct the combat. Consoled, long consoled; but in order to become capable of facing desolation.

There was first the time of war. When the latter broke out, the assurance that France would be saved was given to her immediately (5th of September 1939) and several times renewed. At the moment of the disaster it was said to her: «France will be saved. Your hope will be your cross, but after the cross there is the resurrection.» (New York, 14th of June 1940.) Four months later: «The darker your night will be, the more your confidence must be unshakable. I ask for your confidence as an act of faith in my love.» (27th of October 1940.) And it was then that came the three terrible years, during which misfortune did not cease to persevere, and despair to strike at the windows. And during these three long years 1941, 1942, 1943, total silence and total night for her who had confided her secrets to us. She was harshly led, the little Vera. She experienced interior distress, she aroused pity — her certitude remained absolutely unshaken. If, in spite of the anguish renewed each day by the events, all three of us were able, as we were often told, to contribute to maintain among our compatriots in exile an atmosphere of firm hope, Raissa and I were immensely indebted in this to the aid which we received from Vera and from her obstinate confidence, seemingly absurd at certain moments, in the final victory of France. It was only in the first months of 1944 that the grace of the interior words returned for her.

But I am thinking above all of the time of her last illness, and of the long twilight of suffering in which she advanced towards death. On the 15th of May 1958, Holy Thursday, it was said to her at Mass, a little before the Elevation: «Your sacrifices are like a dew for me, tell this to your little sister and to your brother. You are my little flock. I am always with you and I shall be always with you, fear nothing. I guard you and shall guard you.» It was the last message which Vera gave us,[1] the last words of Jesus which she heard. From that time, nothing and nothing but dryness, until her death, a year and a half later. «I abandon myself entirely to the Blessed Virgin,» she had said to Raissa.

She quickly understood that it was over for her with guarding by her daily zeal the two beings whom she had been missioned (this also had been said to her) to protect as her children. It belonged to Raissa and to myself, now, to watch over her and to torment ourselves for her. A total renunciation was required of her. She accomplished this sacrifice in her own silent, elegant and gentle manner. Do you suppose that she said a word to us about it? A glance sufficed. It was as if she kissed the hands of Him Whom she loved, and to Whom she gave back everything. Thus we saw consummate itself, in the pure and naked grace of the three theological virtues, a life full of abandonment to God and of disappropriation.

She was in bed in her little room, surrounded with her familiar objects, tended as well as possible by Raissa and a little by myself with the aid of a day nurse and a night nurse. These «practical nurses» (non-certificated nurses) were not dragons like many French nurses. They let us look after Vera, give her her medicines, talk with her as we wished. But we could not remain constantly with her. In order for her to feel at peace, it was necessary that the pace of our life continue, or have the appearance of continuing. During the hours of solitude in which she did not sleep under the influence

---

1. Raissa always kept in on her; it is still in the purse which she carried in her hand, and which is now in Kolbsheim.

of sedatives, she read (a great deal during the first months, less and less when fatigue gained the ascendancy), drew in sketch-books on her little bed-table, prayed above all, said rosary upon rosary. And in proportion as the illness advanced, and the suffering, it became more difficult for her to concentrate; sometimes a word which she sought escaped her, like the word «dying» which she asked me for one day while she was praying for the dying (which she did very often). Then, in spite of the sufferings (in the bones) which ravaged her arm, she began to write endlessly prayer after prayer (there are pages of them), thus she held at least for an instant, by dint of will, the fugitive expressions of what she wished to say to God. Sensible graces were remote. It is a heart-rending thing to see these poor scribbled lines of a hand which could scarcely hold the pencil, with these words unceasingly taken up again and repeated, in which passes the supreme appeal of a generous and humble soul.

Lord, give me patience and peace. Courage, help me. My Lord and my God, I love You, have pity on me. The cicadas sing in the summer, in the winter they can only suffer. The birds of Paradise do not come here. Whence comes courage? Sent by God. Patience is a virtue given by God.

. . . It is necessary still to hope for a little from all of this. I cannot write anything but I wish (phrase interrupted).

It is necessary to have imagination, it is necessary to have patience, it is necessary to have hope. Who says patience says hope. What to do. What do do. Nothing. It is not very much.

My God, I love you more than I can say. Lord my God, have pity on me. I am weak and without strength, give me will, peace, courage, patience and perseverance.

The weather is mild but the flowers have gone. The birds are hidden in their nests. The caravan for Heaven slowly gets organized. Peace will come some day. But when.

*

I would like, in order to conclude, to note a few more memories concerning the last illness of Vera.

Vera, I note first of all, was always frail and suffered physically in one manner or another (like Raissa) and like Raissa she surmounted everything by her courage.

She had long suffered from pains in the stomach. An admirable old doctor in New York, a doctor like the kind they don't make any more (Dr. Roy Upham), whose waiting-room was filled with patients who sang his praises, apparently not bothered by the small rubber tube, extremity of a stomach-probe, issuing from their nostrils, had finally, in 1949, I believe, by a series of examinations and of x-ray photographs, discovered the cause of these disorders: a congenital malformation of the stomach, which caused a hernia through the diaphragm and compressed the heart and the lungs. And in proportion as she advanced in years the troubles thus caused tormented her more.

In 1956 she had a heart attack, no doubt caused in part by the shock she experienced one day, during the preceding summer vacation, in Paris, when Raissa, who was beside her, had been knocked over by a motorcycle which had suddenly emerged from a street-corner (Vera thought that she had been killed instantly — she did not have a fracture, but had to remain in bed several weeks).

At the end of 1956 the great anguishes began, the threat of cancer. Dr. Welch thought her still too weak to be operated on; a little later, having left Princeton to install himself in New York, and having consulted a surgeon in whom he had particular confidence, he settled on the operation — removal of a breast. Vera was taken to Doctor's Hospital in New York, where a marvellous American friend, Doris Dana, who had been the guardian angel of Gabriela Mistral, shared her room, unravelling all the practical problems and serving as interpreter with the nurses. Raissa and I had put up at a hotel in New York; Raissa could scarcely stand, but we went to see Vera twice a day. The operation — very long — took place on the 28th of May 1957. Doctor and surgeon were radiant with optimism, they had dug to the very deepest of the tissues, the cancer was checked.

In the summer of 1957, at East Hampton, in spite of fatigue and sufferings which without being grave symptons almost never ceased (the scar did not stop being painful), Vera resumed her activity (less briskly, alas!), somewhat directed again the affairs of the house; each visit to the surgeon confirmed the hopes of complete recovery. Raissa and I were then able to write *Liturgy and Contemplation*.

The respite lasted a little less than eighteen months. And then towards the end of Autumn of 1958 pains in the joints appeared.

The doctor in Princeton who had succeeded Dr. Welch thought at first that the lumbago from which she suffered was going to disappear of itself. Indeed she felt better, was able to attend Mass on Christmas Day (and it was the last time that she was able to go to Church). But immediately after Christmas the pains began again.

On the 23rd of January 1959 a strange incident took place. On that day they had taken[1] an x-ray photograph. In the evening, the doctor telephones, delighted to announce good news; the photograph is excellent, no suspicious shadow, it is a question surely of a mere arthritis. What joy for the three of us! We are happy, completely reassured. — The next morning the doctor rings at the door and asks to see me; he announces the catastrophe to me: he had been too quick to telephone us, after having examined the still wet photographs. The dry photos reveal without any possible doubt that the cancer has passed into the bones.

In agreement with the doctor I kept the news to myself, the intensive radiotherapeutic treatment which was necessary being the same as in the case of a grave arthritis. I even tried for some time to hide from Raissa what, I knew, would be a mortal blow for her; but one day she said to me: «Jacques, it is serious, isn't it?» There was no question of lying to her, I myself sank the dagger. From that time her strength of soul did not flag for an instant, but all that remained to her of physical defence was destroyed little by little. As to Vera, the incident of which I have just spoken allowed us to leave her in ignorance. To tell the truth she had so given up everything to God that the name itself of her illness no longer mattered to her. We had a presentiment of this mystery, and wished to respect it. We knew that she was ready; and we knew also, the Curé of Courneuve had often repeated it to us, that man must always take care not to add on his own initiative a supplementary weight to the one with which a soul is burdened. With what love and what passionate attention Raissa saw to it that nothing occurred to trouble the last steps, more and more light, in the midst of a transparent but each day more profound darkness, which on this poor earth Vera took toward her God.

The x-ray treatment was a kind of torture. Each day, from the

---

1. In order to avoid all confusion, I note that the examination mentioned in *Raissa's Journal* (p. 329) is another examination, very much earlier, which took place on the 21st of November 1956.

26th of January to the 9th of February, Vera descended the stairs, at the cost of what sufferings, so that we might take her to the hospital and bring her back from it by taxi. To accept the suffering of those whom one loves is the most difficult thing in the world. One day when I was saying the rosary for her recovery, beseeching God, in a total dryness of spirit, I heard a few words (it is not my custom); words hard as stone: «You must not deprive her of her glory.»

The radiotherapeutic treatment succeeded in removing the sufferings of the back, but completely exhausted her. She was almost prostrated, not eating or scarcely so, for two months, with incessant nauseas. A complementary treatment, with a base of hormones, had had no effect and had had to be discontinued. We then consulted a doctor of great renown, Dr. Irving Ehrenfeld, of Passaic (a city not very far from Princeton). This man, whose intelligent goodness I will never forget, did not tire of telling the invalid that she should be optimistic, and will to be cured (to which she applied herself, the poor child, with all her heart); nor did he tire of explaining to us, Raissa and me, that this will to be cured has a fundamental biological importance, even, alas, in incurables. He and our doctor at Princeton henceforth formed a team. A new medicine was prescribed, with a base of cortisone, which restored Vera's appetite and momentarily succeeded.

But before they had begun to give this medicine, Vera told us one day: «I had a marvelous dream last night — was it a dream? At any rate it is very important, I must tell it to you. I saw Papa radiant with youth and with light, he approached me, I said to him: Papa, are you coming to take me? And three times he replied to me: *No, not yet.*» She herself was radiant. It was the 10th of April.

Since the month of March she had begun to suffer, from «migratory pains» which scarcely ceasing in one place appeared in another; perpetual pains but all the same nearly tolerable, which tablets of an ordinary sedative sufficed to alleviate after a certain delay, then she slept for some time (but it was necessary to increase the dosage little by little). She struggled against the illness with a great courage, surprising the doctor by progress of which she was proud (leaving her bed to spend a few hours in an armchair, taking a few steps in her room, then even going, with the aid of the nurse and wholly bent in two, from one room to the other). She thought of all her friends, worried about each, offered her pains for them — and for the unknown persons for whom the Blessed Virgin was solicitous.

She was able to see — very rarely — a few friends in her room; at one moment, about October, we believed there was a real impovement. Then the «migratory pains» moved to the legs, putting a stop to her progress in getting about. She received Holy Communion when she could. The last time was two days before Christmas. Everything seemed to continue as usual, the doctors said that the illness, while worsening little by little, would last several years. And the day after Christmas the pains suddenly (a new metastasis in the bones of the hip had occurred) became atrocious — entirely intolerable as soon as one moved her ever so little; she did not utter a cry but wept with grief. It was necessary to have recourse to drugs. Dr. Ehrenfeld then put Raissa and me to the rack by insisting that she be taken to the hospital, which alone was well equipped (from this point of view he was right) for such grave cases; he did not understand that this was impossible, she would have felt abandoned and in frightful distress, no longer physical but moral, our presence was her whole human support; moreover our doctor in Princeton affirmed that she could not be transferred, nor above all placed on the metal table employed for the radiotherapeutic treatment. Ehrenfeld was to come to Princeton on the 4th of January for a decision which in one way or another could only be abominable.

On Thursday the 31st of December, Vera fell asleep after an injection of morphine at 10:30 in the morning. Then, instead of awakening at the end of four hours, she continued to sleep. We thought at first that it was a good sign. But the sleep or half-sleep continued, interrupted by a little delirium, incomprehensible words, except the word papa, papa, which she said several times. We became anxious, telephoned to the doctor. He replied that there was no reason to be alarmed, that her general state excluded all idea of an imminent danger; it was entirely unnecessary that he come, we had only to gently awaken her gradually. We tried to awaken her, she seemed to hear us but could not open her eyes, the breathing was difficult; she took two spoonfuls of tea.

And at 7:30 in the evening she turned her head a little, breathed twice deeply, her face became white as snow, she was dead. Dead, under our eyes, of a death so gentle that it seemed to have shattered nothing. The doctor arrived upon our call, could only establish the death, saying: «It's a blessing, it's a blessing.» The parish priest immediately informed gave her the Anointing of the Sick.

The next day the 1st of January, her body was in our home in the open coffin, her face of an astonishing beauty, without a trace of suffering. Friends prayed near her with us; in the evening, according to the local custom, the parish priest recited the rosary before her. The funeral Mass took place on the 2nd of January (1960). The grave of our sister is in the little cemetery adjoining the Catholic Church in Princeton.

At the end of a long letter which Raissa and I, by turns, wrote to Henry Bars on the 19th of January, and which I have already cited, Raissa said: «When we were converted, and when I announced to Vera that we wished to ask for Baptism, she immediately replied: 'I too, I am ready.' I did not question her then, I knew that God acted in her; but a few weeks ago I asked her how things had taken place. 'I was in the country,' Vera said, 'in the house of peasants. I was reading a book of Bloy, *La Femme Pauvre*, I believe. Suddenly I threw myself on the floor, and I said: I believe.'

«She was an extremely pure and ardent soul, very secret also, of a very lively sensibility, of an unshakable firmness. Limitless devotion, humility, concern to efface herself did not at all prevent a perfect liberty of judgment and of decision, and a sort of poetic liberty in her behavior. . . .

«You know that during the fifty-two years that she lived with us she had assumed the role of Martha, yes, but it was a way of hiding a life of prayer and of union with God which she hardly spoke of, but which we knew to be very profound. She was a very loved spiritual daughter of Father Dehau, who, until his retirement at Bouvines and our departure for America was director for the three of us (and whom the character «Theonas» reflects, while veiling a lot of things, for the great concern of this extraordinary friend of God was to remain absolutely hidden). Vera loved very much some young girls who left the world to form a small contemplative community. They then invited her to join them. Vera refused. At the time we knew nothing of this incident, she spoke of it to me only much later. I mention it because it shows an important aspect of herself. If she preferred to remain with us, it was certainly not only because of the love which bound us to each other, it was first and above all because she believed that this was her own religious vocation, and her manner of consecrating herself to God.»

I cite another passage written by Raissa, at the outset of this same letter to Henry Bars: «The spiritual strength of Vera, her love, her union with God, were a pillar of our life. Now it is necessary to proceed alone. She is not separated from us, that is impossible, how could such a union break asunder? Vera will aid us. But the physical absence, the void which has taken her place — how to endure this!

«It seems to me that to confide to you certain things which better reveal Vera, her greatness of soul, her sufferings also, is a duty towards her.»

It was for the same reason that I wrote this chapter, while the memory of so much beauty which it was given to me to see, and of so much suffering, silently enveloped a solitary old man.

CHAPTER SEVEN

LOVE AND FRIENDSHIP

(A MARGINAL NOTE TO "RAISSA'S JOURNAL")

[Friends whom I specially trust advised me to replace one of my footnotes, in the private edition of the Journal de Raissa *printed in 1962, by a much longer and much more detailed note which they wished to see placed as an Appendix to this* Journal, *in the trade edition of the latter. I allowed myself to be persuaded, but I did not wish to place my new note as an Appendix to the* Journal de Raissa, *— it is quite out of the question to weigh down with my explanations, my commentaries and my ideas such a pure text, whose value as direct and living testimony must be respected above all. The long note in question has perhaps some interest in itself. I publish it therefore as a chapter of these* Notebooks. *If it contains something good, it is right to attribute it to what, in the* Journal de Raissa, *nourished my reflection. If it contains anything controvertible, and even (I would be very sorry about that) erroneous, it must be attributed to me alone.]*

In the following pages a first part has for its aim to comment on and to develop certain things which Raissa has said very clearly but very briefly. In a second and a third part I would like to propose my own views on some problems which today preoccupy many minds.

I am speaking here, let it be well understood, neither as a philosopher (which I am), nor as a theologian (which I am not). I am merely proposing some reflections drawn from the experience of an old man who has seen many things, and who remembers what Aristotle said of old men whose judgments it is fitting to take into consideration, even if they cannot give the reasons for them (or if

219

they give them wrongly). Raissa had the wisdom of the Holy Spirit. I hope that some of the privileges of the wisdom of great age will be granted to the thoughts expressed here. I have naturally tried to put my reflections into a certain logical order, but this is only an old habit which should not take anyone in. It belongs to others to treat these questions in a systematic form and in the appropriate technical terms.

I. LOVE AND FRIENDSHIP

A necessary distinction within disinterested love[1]

I am referring here above all to page 149 of the *Journal*[2] (20th of April 1924), I am referring also to other connected passages in which one finds a more or less marked echo of what is said on this page.

Raissa distinguishes within disinterested love, or love-for-the-good-itself-of-the-beloved (which St. Thomas calls *amor amicitiae*[3] as opposed to *amor concupiscentiae*, that is to say, to love-for-the-good-of-the-subject, or love of covetousness), two kinds of love, which she calls, in following quite simply the common and obvious acceptation of current language, *love* and *friendship*; but she gives to this common acceptation of current language a rigor and a depth which go beyond current language. «The essence of love is in the communication of oneself, with fulness of joy and delight in the possession of the beloved. The essence of friendship is in desire for the good of one's friend, strong enough to sacrifice oneself for him. God loves us with friendship by providing for all our necessities and

1. The French words are *l'amour de dilection*, and translate literally as "the love of dilection." Since this is not a common English term the phrase *l'amour de dilection* has been translated, according to its meaning, as "disinterested love." (ed.)

2. Paris, Desclée de Brouwer, 1963; Eng. transl.: *Raissa's Journal*, Albany, N.Y., Magi Books, Inc., 1974, pp. 162-163.

3. *Amor amicitiae* is *amor benevolentiae* or disinterested love (love for the good of the beloved) that is mutual (*Sum. theol.*, II-II, q. 23, a. 1). In the perspective in which we are placed it is this *mutua benevolentia* that we have to consider in our discussion; the expression *love of friendship* is therefore the one which is fitting here.

by dying for us on the Cross.[1] God loves us with love by making us participate in His nature by grace — by making the sanctified soul His dwelling.»

The words which are the richest in meaning for human life are always difficult to encompass; they run the risk either of lessening or of surpassing thought. Let us try therefore to enter into a few precisions, be it at the price of a bit of heaviness. All disinterested love is gift of self. But this itself is understood in two typically different manners; there is on the one hand the love of benevolence or of devotion, in which the lover gives himself to the beloved by giving to the beloved his goods or that which he *has* — and this more or less completely up to that perfect love of devotion in which one gives all that one has, all one's goods, and one's life itself. This is *friendship;* and in this friendship the friend, in giving that which he has, no doubt also gives, *in a certain manner*, at the same stroke that which he is, his own person or subjectivity itself (since what he is has need of what he has, and since he can go as far as to give his life itself) — he no doubt gives himself, and really, but *covertly and indirectly, through something else*, in other words through the means and the intermediary of the gifts which hide his gift of himself under signs and more or less parcel it out, and which permit him to more or less reserve his own self as long as he has not given absolutely all that he has.

In *love* on the contrary, love of truly human dimensions, in which the spirit is engaged — I say in love envisaged under its extreme and entirely absolute form (for under its ordinary form the process of which I am speaking is indeed there, but only sketched) — the person or subjectivity gives himself *directly, openly or nakedly*, without hiding himself under the forms of any other gift less absolutely total, he gives himself wholly from the very first in giving or communicating to the beloved, in ecstasizing in him that which he *is*. It is the very person of the lover which is the Gift, simple, unique and without any possible reserve, made to the beloved. This is why love, especially in the extreme sense in which we are taking it here, is gift-of-self *absolutely and pre-eminently.*

The difference between love and friendship is not necessarily a difference in the *intensity* or the greatness of disinterested love.

1. Cf. John 15:13. "There is no greater love than this: to lay down one's life *for one's friends."*

Such or such friendship can be as intense as, or more intense than, such or such love. The difference between love and friendship is a difference in the *intrinsic quality* of disinterested love or the *ontological level* at which it constitutes itself in the soul, in other words, in the power which it has of alienating the soul from itself.

In God *friendship* and *love* are only two aspects of one and the same infinitely perfect disinterested love, which is the transcendent God Himself — two aspects which we distinguish according to our human mode of conceiving and by analogy with that which appears in human disinterested love, all of whose qualities and perfections are supereminently contained in their uncreated Exemplar.

In the creature (and to consider things in the natural order) *friendship* and *love* between two human beings are two different kinds of disinterested love (and, in *love* — because on this wholly human plane where the differences of the sexes enter into play, the flesh is also interested — the love of covetousness is joined to disinterested love).

The various kinds of human love

I specified a moment ago that in speaking of love I was speaking of love in which the spirit is engaged, love on a level with man and human dignity — and that I was speaking of it under its extreme and entirely absolute form.

For the fact is that, taking the word in the common acceptation of current language, according as it distinguishes love and friendship, there is in man a kind of love which is of a merely animal and not properly human order — the love of which it is a question in many masculine conversations and in erotic literature, love exclusively carnal or connoting exclusively the pleasure of the senses. This kind of love relates *solely* to the love of covetousness, and has nothing to do with disinterested love. We shall not consider it here.

Love of the properly human order begins when to the attraction of the senses there is joined, at least in outline, that gift of the person himself, direct and open, of which we were speaking above, and which proceeds from disinterested love. One can say that the moment this threshold is crossed, and from the very fact of the gift through which the lover gives himself to the beloved, the meaning of the word «to exist» splits into two: the beloved alone exists fully and absolutely for the lover, the existence of all the rest being struck with a kind of invalidity.

This love of the properly human order includes in itself many different forms, which there is no reason to analyze here. Let us be content with three typical cases.

There is first that which can be called love-passion, which can also be called, in its most sublimated form, romantic love. This love plays a central role in human life, it is a mirage in which a nostalgia inherent in the human being is going to be caught, it has its initials intertwined on all the trees of the world. It lives on a lie and an illusion; it is the mirage or the semblance of *entirely true* love («*amour fou*» — «mad, boundless love»). It believes itself eternal and it is ephemeral. The lover gives himself to his beloved (and she gives herself to him), true enough, but in imagination or in dream more than in reality; it is the love of covetousness or of carnal desire which occupies here (often without one knowing it) the essential and preponderant place; the total gift of oneself that with the utmost sincerity one imagines oneself to have made is not real but dreamed, and as a matter of fact a disguise by which our spirit covers with a royal adornment the desire of the senses, and which the species uses for its own ends in deceiving the individual. It is good for the human being to pass through this exultation, which evokes the nuptial songs and the nuptial dances of the birds — provided one does not claim to remain in it, for a man is not a bird.

There is in the second place authentic love, into which it is rare (though not impossible) to emerge at once. Man ordinarily attains to it only after a certain maturation in the experience of life and in suffering. It is the love in which one really gives to the other, not only what he has, but what he is (his person itself). Under the ordinary form of this authentic love (let us call it quite simply *bel amour*) such a gift is no doubt made, but as begun or outlined (always in outline, at all degrees of more and less), not as made to the very end.

Finally, when such a gift is made to the very end, one has, in the third place, authentic love under its extreme or entirely absolute form. This love in which the very person of each gives itself to the other in all truth and reality is, in the order of the ontological perfections of nature, the summit of love between Man and Woman. Then the lover truly gives himself to his beloved, and she truly gives herself to him, *as to his or her Whole*, in other words, ecstasizes in her or in him, makes himself or herself — although remaining ontologically a person — a part which no longer exists except through and in this Whole which is his or her Whole. This extreme love is *amour fou* (mad, boundless love); and such a name properly befits it, because it accomplishes (in the special order or, if you will, in the magic and spiritual «superexistence» of love) precisely that which is in itself impossible and insane in the order of mere existence or simply of being, in which each person continues to be a whole and cannot become mere part of another whole. This is the proper paradox of love: it requires on the one hand the onto-logically indestructible duality of persons, and on the other hand it demands, and *in its own way* accomplishes the unbroken unity, the actually consummated unity of these same persons («in a single spirit and love,» St. John of the Cross will say apropos of supernatural mystical union, but this is already true, on an altogether different plane and in an analogical sense, of the natural union between man and woman[1] in mad, boundless love). On the plane which we are considering just now, and which is the earthly plane, mad, bound-less love (human), unlike mad, boundless love for God, relates to the merely natural order; moreover, in this order itself, it is, as I noted above, an *ontological* perfection of nature — available from the moral point of view to the best and to the worst. Hence its splendor and its ambiguity. Its object is a created object. He who loves with mad, boundless love gives himself totally; the *object* of his love is a lim-ited, fragile, and mortal creature. It would be to ignore the grandeurs of our nature to believe that this creature loved with mad, boundless love *necessarily* becomes an idol for the lover, and is *necessarily* loved by him more than God. But it would be to ignore the miseries of our nature to believe that she *cannot* be loved more than God by him who loves her with mad, boundless love, and *cannot* become an idol for him. Human mad, boundless love can radiate within a life morally upright and submissive to the order of charity.[2] It can likewise radiate (and not only outside marriage, but in the state of marriage also) within a life of sin.

1.   "In a single spirit," — I say *spirit*, I do not say temperament, character, tastes. etc.
2. Cf. further on, page 246, note 1, and pages 249-251.

Three remarks now: 1) Mad, boundless love always implies and presupposes (not necessarily as prior in time, but as necessarily prior in being) the love of devotion or friendship, while going far beyond it. — 2) It goes beyond friendship because it constitutes itself at a more profound — absolutely radical — level in the soul, from the very fact that it is the direct, open, naked, gift of the person himself in his entirety, making himself *one in spirit* with the other. But by virtue of the very nature of the human being, who is flesh and spirit, it implies in itself[1] union *in the flesh* also, at least in desire, along with carnal joy, the pre-eminent pleasure of the senses, which is linked with it. A human person can give himself to another, or ecstasize in another, to the point of making of the latter his Whole, only if he gives to the other or is ready to give to the other his body while giving to her his soul. — 3) Nevertheless mad, boundless love is infinitely more than the desire of the senses. It is by essence, primordially and principally, disinterested love; the love of covetousness (for the advantage or the joy of the loving subject himself, not of the thing loved) is secondary in it, entirely subordinated to disinterested love. The person is above all and principally spirit, and it is therefore as spirit that he gives himself above all and principally in giving himself in his entirety. In the same way as the spirit is elevated above the flesh, mad, boundless love, authentic love under its extreme form, is elevated above love-passion.

The love of charity and uncreated Love

In distinguishing *love* and *friendship*, it was above all of mad, boundless love, of love under its extreme form, that Raissa was thinking in the notes of what I have called her *Journal*. And, further-

---

1. All of which does not mean to say that through an act of his free will a man cannot — just as he can, if he wishes, mutilate his body — do violence to nature and disjoin carnal desire from his mad, boundless love, either for a spiritual motive and by renouncing the flesh if she whom he loved, indeed would still love with mad, boundless love, asks it of him, or if both feel themselves called to it by God (one has seen engaged couples separate thus to enter into religion, or spouses make thus a vow of continence) or for some other motive (if for example the woman whom he loves with mad, boundless love is married to another; actually in this case it is more probably in an altogether opposite direction that he will effect the disjunction — by indulging in debauchery).

more, it was in an analogical and transcendent sense that she took this word, for she was thinking above all not of the human mad, boundless love on which I have just insisted, but of the love of God for man (uncreated Love) and of the love of man for God (love of charity).

In the love of charity, whose *object* is the Spirit subsisting through Himself in His transcendent infinity, the inscrutable deity itself, the three uncreated Persons[1] — and which is a gift of grace and belongs to the supernatural order — friendship and love (mad, boundless love) are clearly not two distinct species, they are two different degrees (not necessarily in intensity, but as to the power of alienating the soul from itself) — and, at least in a certain sense, inseparable — of one and the same disinterested love. Does not mad, boundless love still imply here, though in an analogical sense, a certain love of covetousness, this time of the wholly spiritual order, the desire of possessing the Beloved and of becoming intoxicated with Him, and of feeling oneself loved by Him? Yes, doubtless: this love requires in itself «fulness of joy and delight in the possession of the beloved.» But then not only is the desire, having God for its object, absolutely pure of any carnal element; and not only is it subordinated to disinterested love; but further, it has ceased and must completely cease to have for its justification (as in the love of covetousness properly so called) the good of the subject himself; it is not for itself, it is *for* God first loved that the soul wishes God *to* itself or desires to possess Him, and the more this is so the more this desire is bewildered. And here on earth it cannot be completely accomplished. And it will have to traverse perhaps terrifying nights, and instead of joy and of delight it is perhaps agony and death which will be offered to it, precisely because disinterested love requires total and absolute sovereignty, and relentlessly breaks one after another all the roots which the desire to possess the beloved can have in the lover insofar as he naturally loves himself.

As to the love of God for man, I have already remarked that in God friendship and love are only two aspects, distinguished accord-

---

1. This is why the love of charity itself is known by our intellect only by an analogical knowledge, as the superior *analogate*, in us, of a reality first attained in the human world.

On the notion of love such as I have just tried to analyze it, see the synoptic table No. 1, in the Appendix to Chapter VII.

ing to our human mode of understanding, of a single love, perfectly one, which is God Himself. The notes which characterize in us what I call mad, boundless love are found again in God in a supereminent manner, infinitely purified and analogically transposed according to what is compatible with divine transcendence.

In God there is absolutely no love of covetousness, because God has absolutely no need of anything. There is only disinterested love: friendship certainly, and infinitely generous, but also mad, boundless love, in which He gives Himself to a whole (the created person) other than Himself, whom He has rendered through His grace capable of receiving Him, and of loving Him in return – so that the created person, in this free boundless gift by which he gives himself entirely in return, can become a single spirit and love with the Love by which God eternally loves Himself, and thus reverberate to Him, so to speak, the Joy by which He eternally exults in Himself.

And if God requests our love in return for His love, it is purely by virtue of disinterested love itself: not because He had need of being loved by us, but because He loves us. It is for us, not for Himself, says St. Thomas Aquinas, that God seeks His glory.[1] It is for us, not for Himself, that He asks that we give Him our heart. *Praebe mihi cor tuum* [Give me your heart].[2] «It astonishes me to think of the value the Lord attaches to our poor love. One would really think that possessing our hearts is the end He proposed to Himself in creating us; and He seriously pursues what He has proposed to attain: 'It's no laughing matter that I have loved thee!' Is there not in this, as it were, a metaphysical necessity? Uncreated love, in pouring itself out on creatures, remains love and consequently is not satisfied unless another expansion responds to its expansion and makes union possible.»[3]

Human mad, boundless love and mad, boundless love for God

Let us return now to human love. We have said that in us mad, boundless love is there, like Venus emerging from the sea,

1. "Deus suam gloriam non quaerit propter se, sed propter nos" [God does not seek His glory for His own sake, but for ours] . *Sum. theol.*, II-II, 132, 1, ad 1.
2. Proverbs 23:26.
3. *Raissa's Journal*, pp. 75-76.

when the person gives himself, openly or nakedly, in his entirety to another person as to his Whole, in which he ecstasizes and of which he makes himself a part. The *Journal* of Raissa brings to light in this connection a central truth on which I must insist, in the language which I am using here. A warning however, which I indicate once and for all: a condition is presupposed in the following remarks, namely, that we are considering in the human being not what can spring up in him momentarily from time to time – or, if this is lasting, suffers obstacles and contradictions – but what is for him a habitual state, a way of life in which he can constantly progress.

Well, account being taken of what I have just mentioned, it is necessary to say that it is possible for a man or a woman who has for her or him whom he or she loves a perfect and complete *friendship* (love of devotion), and an authentic *love* in its ordinary form, to have at the same time mad, boundless love for God; but that a human being cannot give himself at one and the same time to the very end, in an absolute manner, to two objects as each constituting his Whole; in other words if a soul has entered into mad, boundless love for God, then it is necessary for it to renounce human mad, boundless love – whether, as in the religious state, it completely renounces the flesh – or, whether, remaining in the bonds of marriage it does not renounce this unique and sacred love in which man and woman are two in a single flesh, but renounces that which, in the order of the ontological perfections of nature, is the summit and the perfection of conjugal love, namely, mad, boundless love. Because disinterested love of such a kind that the Beloved is truly and really given *the Whole* of the Lover, has to be unique in the soul, and if such a love (mad, boundless love) is given to God, it has to be given only to Him.[1]

The human soul can have only a single Bridegroom, if we understand this word of the supreme nuptials in which mad, boundless love reigns as master. This is why, if it is God who is this Bridegroom, His love is jealous. It is necessary that God, it is necessary that Jesus be the *Only Beloved*, the Only One loved with mad, boundless love.

«How can I prove my love to Him? – By giving myself to Him from the bottom of my heart, in such a way that no other *love* ever

1. Cf. further on, pp. 249-251.

dwells in it. . . . . God is jealous of that particular gift of the heart which is love, and which is total and exclusive in its nature.»[1]

II. THE MYSTICAL STATE

Love and friendship in charity

I said above that in the love of charity, friendship and love (mad, boundless love) are two different degrees (not necessarily in intensity, but as to the power of alienating the soul from itself) — and, at least in a certain sense, inseparable — of one and the same disinterested love. Let us try to explain our thought on this point. By charity you love God «with all your heart, with all your soul, with all your strength, and with all your mind.»[2] It is evident that such a love does not only comprise friendship, in which, as I said at the outset, friend gives himself to friend, really but covertly and indirectly, through something else, in other words through the means and the intermediary of the goods which he gives and which hide his gift of himself under signs and more or less parcel it out as long as he has not given absolutely all that he has; love of charity also comprises mad, boundless love, in which the lover gives his person itself and his subjectivity in its entirety, the very depth of his being, directly, openly or nakedly, without any possible reserve, while ecstasizing in the beloved as in his Whole. Mad, boundless love in which God is loved not only as Friend, but as Bridegroom.

However, here an important distinction must be made. With regard to God there is not possible, as there is with human beings, any mere friendship which would exclude mad, boundless love. But it is possible for a love to exist with regard to God which *appears more as friendship than as mad, boundless love*, a friendship in which mad, boundless love is also present, but buried in it, and not manifested except at times. More precisely it is possible that *as to the*

---

1. *Raissa's Journal*, p. 163 (20th of April 1924). — The renouncement (of mad, boundless love) of which there is question here is what in another passage Raissa admirably refers to as "what must be suppressed, or rather surpassed, is the limits of the heart" (*Raissa's Journal*, p. 239).

2. Luke 10:27. (Cf. Matt. 22:37; Mark 12:28). - "You shall love the Lord, your God, with all your heart, and with all your soul, and with all your strength." Deuter. 6:5.

ordinary regime of life charity may exist in a soul *especially* to the degree of friendship — then the degree of mad, boundless love will also exist in it, either in such a way that, perhaps by reason of a kind of reverential fear, it is not or is scarcely conscious, or in such a way that it reveals itself, so to speak, by flashes only at certain moments, even if at the last instant of life. In this case, in order to simplify language, we shall say that this soul lives under the predominant regime of friendship (implicitly including mad, boundless love). It is under this regime *at least* that every authentically Christian soul, every soul which has received and which keeps charity, finds itself.

And it is possible for charity to exist in a soul, as to the regime of life of the latter, *especially* to the degree (which presupposes that of friendship) of mad, boundless love itself taking possession of the human being and ruling his action in a habitual and permanent manner. In this case, in order to simplify language, we shall say that this soul lives under the predominant regime of mad, boundless love (implying and presupposing friendship).

The regime of mad, boundless love and the regime of friendship

These things being granted, it immediately appears that a definition of what is called the mystical state[1] — equivalent to the one which describes it as a life under the habitual regime of the gifts of the Holy Spirit, but less technical and more accessible to current language — is possible: one will say that a soul passes to the mystical state when it passes under the regime of mad, boundless love for God.

And it is of the very nature of charity that it thus tends to pass from the regime of friendship to the regime of mad, boundless love. This is why one can say that *de jure* [by right] every human soul,

---

1. The word *mystical* is the accepted word. In a sense it is an unfortunate word (like many of our words), because it frightens many poorly informed persons. In reality it does not relate to any extraordinary privilege (graces *gratis datae*), but designates only a state in which human life and human conduct are ordinarily aided by the invisible and very secret *inspiration* of God (a state which in itself, and if everything did not go wrong in the human being since original sin, should be normal in those in whom the three divine Persons dwell through sanctifying grace).

being called to charity, is called at the same stroke to the mystical life, in a proximate manner or in a remote manner.

But this is a wholly theoretical truth, in which only the internal exigencies of charity taken in itself are considered. If one considers on the contrary the concrete state in which such or such a given soul finds itself, then it is necessary to say that those are called *de facto* to the mystical life who can find their reason for living only in mad, boundless love for God; those are not called *de facto* to the mystical life who can find their reason for living either outside of God, or, if they have charity, in a love for God in which mad, boundless love remains buried in friendship.

The perfection of human life or the perfection of charity considered in the pure and simple sense, or under all relations, clearly presupposes the passage to the predominant regime of mad, boundless love for God, or to the mystical life; then the love of charity expands fully and freely in the soul, as well with regard to its power of alienating the soul from itself (it is openly, nakedly, directly, that the person or subjectivity itself is given to God) as with regard to its intensity.

But we remarked above that in the love of charity the degree of friendship and the degree of love do not necessarily differ as to intensity. We must therefore say now that if it has remained under the predominant regime of friendship, in which it has not crossed the threshold of the mystical life, the soul can still attain here on earth a certain perfection of human life and of charity (perfection under a certain relation) — then the love of charity expands without obstacle in the soul, as to intensity[1] but not as to the power of alienating the soul from itself. And it is in Heaven that such a soul will know the perfection of charity in the absolute sense of the word.

1. Let us understand that then the intensity of charity is great enough for the latter to fan out without obstacle in the soul, *on condition* that too crushing a trial is not imposed on it. In the concrete perspective in which we are placed, it is necessary indeed to take into account the trials that God permits, and the measure which He assigns to them. God tempers the wind to the shorn lamb.

It is clear that under the regime of mad, boundless love a soul, in the course of its progress, can reach a perfection of charity, in intensity as well as in depth of gift of self, *greater* than under the regime of friendship. (Let us not forget that the perfection of charity which man can reach here on earth is not an indivisible point, it is a greatness which continues to develop and entails various degrees.)

Let us not forget moreover that when it lives under the regime of friendship with its God the soul has already, like every soul in the state of grace, a mad, boundless love for God, although buried in the unconscious and revealing itself only through flashes, from time to time. This soul does not live in the mystical state or under the regime of mad, boundless love, but it receives in its life touches of mystical inspiration and of mad, boundless love for God. Does not St. Thomas teach that the gifts of the Holy Spirit are necessary for salvation? So much the more are they necessary for the perfection, even if only in one respect, of charity.

The instant of death

Now, what about the preparation or disposition of the soul with regard to the instant of death?

A soul which, after having entered into the mystical life or the regime of mad, boundless love for God, has gone to the very end of its road and has attained, as much as it is possible here on earth, the perfection of charity, purely and simply or under all relations, is ready or disposed not only to be saved in perhaps passing through Purgatory, but to rejoin Jesus in Paradise at the very instant in which it will leave its body. If therefore it perseveres in this disposition and crosses the threshold of death in a perfect act of mad, boundless love for God, it enters directly into Heaven.

A soul which, having remained under the regime of friendship, and not having entered into the mystical state, has gone to the very end of its road and has attained here on earth the perfection of charity under a certain relation (under the relation of intensity, not as to the power of alienating the soul from itself) is ready or disposed not only to be saved in perhaps passing through Purgatory, but to rejoin Jesus at the very instant in which it will leave its body. If it perseveres in this disposition the instant of death will be also the instant in which mad, boundless love will proclaim in it its empire and its sovereignty, it is in a perfect act of mad, boundless love for God that it will cross the threshold of death, and it will enter directly into Heaven.

A soul which has charity but has not reached here on earth the perfection of charity (neither absolutely speaking, nor under a certain relation) is prepared or disposed to be saved in perhaps passing through Purgatory, but not to rejoin Jesus at the very instant in which it will leave its body. We know however that it can rejoin Him at that instant. If it crosses the threshold of death in a perfect act of charity (which can then be only an act of mad, boundless love for God), it will enter directly into Heaven.

A soul, finally, which does not have charity and which lives in evil is prepared or disposed neither to be saved nor to rejoin Jesus at the very instant in which it will leave its body. We know nevertheless that in a supreme leap of charity it can be saved at this last instant, nay more, that it can immediately rejoin Jesus. *Hodie mecum eris in paradiso.* [Today you will be with me in paradise].

Open contemplation and masked contemplation

Now, what of infused contemplation with regard to the perfection of charity? I know that the subject is much debated — but this itself gives everyone more liberty to propose the opinion that he thinks is true.

I would like to remark first that the expression «mystical life» and the expression «contemplative life» are not synonymous. The first is broader than the second. There is mystical life when the soul has passed under the regime of mad, boundless love for God: but men who devote themselves to the active life can pass under this regime as well as men dedicated to the contemplative life. In other words, there is mystical life when a soul has passed under the habitual regime of the gifts of the Holy Spirit. But among the seven gifts it is to the two highest — to the two first ones — the gift of Wisdom and the gift of Understanding (and also, as to the knowledge of creatures tasted in union with God, to the gift of Knowledge), that the contemplative life relates above all. The other gifts have more or less to do with the active life; it is to them principally that this life relates if it has passed under the habitual regime of the gifts of the Spirit, in other words if it is dependent upon the mystical state and mystical inspiration.

But at the same time it is necessary to immediately remark that the gifts of the Holy Spirit are connected among themselves, and that the gift of Counsel or of Fear, for example, cannot exercise themselves without the gifts of Wisdom and of Understanding being also at work. The difference will be due to the manner in which the exercise of such or such a gift will appear or will manifest itself more, at once in the soul and in behavior. In the man engaged in the active life the inspirations concerning the decisions to be reached will have a central role, those concerning the taste of divine things a perhaps merely marginal role as to the field of visibility, the exercise of the gift of Wisdom and of the gift of Understanding will remain more or less occult or unapparent.

It follows from this that in those who have passed the threshold of the spirit, or of the mystical life, the grace of contemplation, of the loving and felt entry into the states of Jesus, will ordinarily operate in a very different manner according as they will be contemplatives or actives. For there is, as I once noted, a *masked* infused contemplation, of an atypical, mitigated or discontinuous mode (with which the «actives» will very often have to be content), as there is an *open*, typical or manifest, infused contemplation (more proper to «contemplatives»). Among souls delivered to the liberty of the Spirit of God, those «whose style of life is active will have the grace of contemplation, but most often of a masked and unapparent contemplation; perhaps they will be capable only of saying rosaries, and mental prayer will bring them only headaches or sleep. Mysterious contemplation will not be in their way of praying, but in their sweet-minded hands perhaps or in their way of walking, or in their way of looking at a poor man or at suffering.»[1]

Let us conclude from these considerations that to say that a man is devoted to contemplation or that he leads the contemplative life, and to say that he is nourished, even though unconsciously, by a more or less masked infused contemplation (and that he spreads about him, without knowing it, the fragrance or sweetness of this contemplation) are very different things. But in the two cases the man in question will have entered under the regime of the mystical life or of mad, boundless love for God, and he will tend to the perfection of charity considered absolutely speaking and under all relations; and contemplation, on one ground or on another, even though secretly, will have a habitual directing role in his life.

---

1. "Action et Contemplation," in my book *Questions de Conscience*, 1938, pp. 145-146. — Thus all souls which have crossed the threshold of the mystical life share at the same stroke "a *typical or atypical, manifest or masked* contemplation, which is the multiform exercise of the gift of Wisdom, free and unseizable, and transcending all our categories, and capable of all disguises and of all surprises." (*Ibid.*, p. 146.)

One thus understands that, as Raissa and I wrote in *Liturgy and Contemplation*, «what seems to follow from experience is, in the first place, that higher infused contemplation seems to be always linked to a high perfection; but, in the second place, that high perfection does not seem to be always linked to higher infused contemplation, in the sense of the typical forms expounded by the masters.»[1] In advancing towards the perfection of charity considered absolutely speaking and under all relations (under the relation of the power of alienating the soul from itself as also under the relation of intensity), one goes his way in one manner (contemplative life in which the gifts of Wisdom and of Understanding exercise themselves in a predominant manner and in which a more complete testimony, the only absolutely necessary one, is rendered to the supreme source of all perfection among us: the mad, boundless love of God for men and His desire that the soul become a single spirit and love with Him) — another goes his way in another manner (active life in which the exercise of the other gifts is predominant but in which those of Wisdom and of Understanding are indeed there, although often more or less hidden, and in which more complete testimony is rendered, let us not say to fraternal love, let us say to the service of one's neighbor, with respect to the soul and with respect to the body, which is a *consequence* of this love, and to which this love wishes that some will devote themselves).

Contemplative life and active life
in the regime of mad, boundless love

As to the mission of contemplatives, both in what concerns their role of witnesses among men, above all by their example, but also, when they have received the grace for it, by their word, I would be very presumptuous to say anything after what Raissa has said about it. To this mission all the rest is suspended.

As for the actives, it indeed seems that the greatest are those who, better enlightened about the secret springs of their own life, and paying more reverent attention to the inspirations from above which pass in them, are raised, in the very midst of the requirements

1. *Liturgy and Contemplation*, p. 45.

of fraternal devotion or of the apostolate, to a contemplation not only masked, but open and typical[1] and, just like the pure contemplatives, put in a particularly vivid light the major observation stated by Father Lallement: «Without contemplation we will never advance far toward virtue . . . we will never break free of our weaknesses and our imperfections. We will always be attached to the earth, and will never raise ourselves much above the sentiments of nature. We will never be able to offer a perfect service to God. But with contemplation we will do more in a month, for ourselves and for others, than we would have been able to do without it in ten years. It produces . . . acts of sublime love for God such as one can hardly ever accomplish without this gift . . . and finally, it perfects faith and all the virtues. . . .»[2]

It's the honest truth. And it is true also, however, that for a great number of those whom the Spirit leads, this blessed contemplation remains, as was remarked above, more or less unapparent and hidden. And it is possible also that, dedicated, by the state which it has chosen, to the contemplative life or to the active life, a soul often believes (because contemplation can be *entirely* masked, and because love, even mad, boundless love — this is already true in the merely human order — is not necessarily conscious) that it has not crossed the threshold of the mystical state or of the regime of mad, boundless love, whereas it has for a long time crossed this threshold. It does not much matter; what appears or not to consciousness is in such a case very secondary. The fact remains that for all those who in reality have crossed the threshold in question there is but a single road, but one goes there in one manner, another in another (*alius sic, alius sic ibat*, as St. Augustine said). And on this road towards the perfection of love considered absolutely or under all relations, finally action, in one way or another,[3] superabounds from contemplation — open contemplation or masked contemplation, whose sapiential savor passes secretly through inspirations which

1. This is the proper ideal of those who lead the so-called "mixed" life, (in which action demands in itself to superabound from contemplation), such as an Albert the Great, a Tauler, a Henri Suso. . . .

2. *La Doctrine spirituelle*, pp. 429-430.

3. Whether *de jure* and by virtue of a requirement of its *nature* itself (as in the case of the preaching of the Gospel or of the teaching of *sacra doctrina*), or (in the case of any other activity) by virtue of the *mode* according to which it *de facto* proceeds under the regime of mad, boundless love.

concern more especially the active life, and through the exercise
of the corresponding gifts; finally, whether it leads an active life
or a contemplative life, and whether in one state of life as in the
other it has the grace of an open contemplation, the soul raised to
the mystical state *habitually* participates in a contemplative influx,
it refreshes itself in one manner or another in the sources of contemplation, whether it drinks there long draughts or whether the living
water reaches it drop by drop and through intermediaries. It is the
road of mad, boundless love.

The regime of friendship

In actual fact however, we have seen (it is a *de facto* question,
not a *de jure* one), there is another family — and doubtless much
more numerous — of authentically Christian souls who also advance
here on earth towards the perfection of charity, but this time considered under a certain relation only. In their relations with God
these souls are not under the regime of mad, boundless love, but
under the regime of friendship. It is on the road of friendship[1] that
they progress here on earth towards the perfection of love considered
under the relation of intensity, not under its power of alienating the
soul from itself; and in following this road they can open, in the
evening of their life here on earth, directly on to Heaven — but it
is at this instant only, then all through their eternity, that they will
have passed in a total and complete manner under the empire of
mad, boundless love. In their life here on earth they do not enter
under the habitual regime of the gifts, they do not cross the threshold of the mystical life. In the concrete situation or circumstances
in which their existence is placed, they are not called, in actual fact,

1. The two roads — the road of friendship, and the road of mad, boundless
love — of which I speak here have nothing to do with the theory of the *two ways*
proposed by certain authors, which they maintain as *de jure* distinct and as leading to a *same term*, holiness or high perfection. It is only *de facto* that the road
of friendship is contra-distinguished from that of mad, boundless love. And it
should open onto the road of mad, boundless love, and the perfection to which
it leads is *less high* than that to which the road of mad, boundless love leads.
And if in the evening of this life a soul which has lived under the predominant
regime of friendship with God can enter straight into Heaven, it is because in
this case it has made at its last instant a perfect act of *mad, boundless love.*

to infused contemplation; they do not drink at the sources of contemplation.[1]

However, we have also seen that these souls, which have mad, boundless love, though more or less buried in the unconscious and revealing itself only by flashes, from time to time, receive in the course of their life *touches* of mystical inspiration or of mad, boundless love for God. For if the higher inspiration of the Spirit did not come, be it only at certain particularly decisive moments, perhaps very rare (but there is always, in any case, the instant of the first act of liberty, in which a man opts for his last end, and the last instant of life, in which he throws himself or not into the eternal Mercy), to elevate our action above the powers of our reason even enlightened by faith, there would be no salvation for us — all the more reason to progress towards the perfection of charity.

Consequently it is necessary to say that the persons of whom we are speaking receive at the same stroke more or less profound fugitive *touches* of the gift of wisdom, and therefore more or less profound fugitive *touches* of contemplation. All of which does not signify certainly that they should make desperate efforts to strive to attain to contemplation, but does signify that it is necessary for them to be faithful to vocal prayer, and, if they have the time for it, to meditation, and to keep themselves available to any moment of passive recollection which some day could be given to them. For who knows if some day contemplation will not come without their knowledge to hide itself in their vocal prayer, in order habitually to spread its influence on their life? Who knows if some day mad, boundless love for God will not surge up from the depth of their

---

1. Owing to the very fact that love for God and love for one's neighbor are two faces of one and the same charity, the distinction between the predominant regime of friendship (in which the active life has not crossed the threshold of the mystical state) and the predominant regime of mad, boundless love (in which contemplation is *open* in the "contemplatives" — and *masked* in the "actives") should be met with again in the attitude of the soul towards its neighbor. How so? One can say, it seems to me, that under the predominant regime of friendship with God it is in trying *to love our neighbor as Jesus loved him* that we love our brothers; and that under the predominant regime of mad, boundless love for God it is ALSO (and first) *in seeing Jesus in our neighbor* that we love the latter ("For I was hungry and you gave me food, I was thirsty and you gave me drink·' Matt. 25:35).

On the pursuit of the perfection of charity, and the different distinctions which one must bear in mind when one seeks to form for oneself a sufficiently comprehensive idea of it, see the synoptic table No. 2, in the Appendix to Chapter VII.

soul with an irresistible force to take control of how they govern themselves, so that they find themselves brought from the regime of friendship to the regime of mad, boundless love? Everything depends in these things on the liberty of the Spirit of God, which is an *absolute* liberty — and which can cause anyone, whatever his state of life may be, to pass under the regime of the gifts, perhaps by modifying (perhaps by over-throwing) such or such elements of the situation or such or such concrete circumstances which are an obstacle in actual fact, for such or such a given soul, to the proximate or remote call to which by right, and theoretically speaking, every human soul, and especially every soul vivified by charity, is subject with regard to the mystical life and to contemplation (open or masked).

The fact remains that the obstacle which I have just mentioned comes into play for multitudes of souls, even of authentically Christian souls; the given situations and the concrete circumstances to which such obstacle is due can sometimes spring from the negligence of the soul, but as a general rule they depend on the human condition itself, which is to say that divine Providence accepts responsibility for them. And the fact remains that all the souls for which the Spirit of God has not removed the obstacle in question can — and should — advance towards the perfection of love to be attained here on earth, be it only under the relation of intensity and while proceeding only under the predominant regime of friendship.

And if many show themselves incapable of even this, and are too weak to practice the law of God in all its precepts, at least they know or they should know that love is *the true face of God*, and that this love never ceases to have pity on them and to ask them for their love, and to wait for the time when they will turn towards Mercy.

On the word "contemplation"

One will find perhaps that in the whole preceding discussion the word «contemplation» has been employed in a somewhat too elastic manner. I shall reply that this elasticity was objectively necessary. Why? Because the word «contemplation» is a word which it is indeed necessary to use, for want of a better one, but which itself is not good. There is no word to express something which takes place

in man and which nevertheless transcends every human concept —
that *passio divinorum*, that knowledge of God which is more experience than knowledge and yet supreme knowledge, and which comes
about through love and the union of love, and which is miles from
the *theoria* of the Greeks and from philosophical speculation or
contemplation. The word «contemplation» was kept by Christian
tradition because at least it saved the characteristic of supreme
knowledge proper to the experience in question. But to tell the
truth it survived only because it let itself be conquered by a meaning
too heavy to carry, and because by virtue of an *unconditional
surrender* it consented to become ambiguous, with a fortunate
ambiguity moreover, and fruitful, and profitable to minds, except
for those which do not know how to dominate the signs which
they use.

Exemplary saints and unapparent saints

There are doubtless in Heaven many more, immensely more
saints than we can imagine.

This is true first of saints in the ordinary sense of this word,
I mean of *exemplary* saints, of the heroes of the moral and spiritual
life whose practice and example (be it in the final period of their
existence here on earth, as in the case of certain martyrs who before
bearing the witness of blood may have committed serious faults,
or in the case of the Good Thief, who made his great act of love just
before breathing his last) passed beyond the ordinary life of men and
are fit to exercise on humanity that sovereign *attraction* of which
Bergson spoke. These exemplary saints do not live like everybody,
in this sense, that even sometimes in their external behavior the
measure of their action, being that of the gifts of the Spirit, surpasses
that of the acquired or infused moral virtues; they surprise us, always
baffle us in some manner; their heroism, however secret its sources
may be, cannot not manifest itself in some way. They are canonizable saints. A certain number have been canonized. Others, who
form an incomparable greater multitude, will never be canonized.
All passed, at a certain moment of their life, under the regime of
mad, boundless love, and consequently advanced towards the perfection of charity considered absolutely or under all relations. All
at the same stroke, be it in the final period of their existence, passed
the threshold of the mystical state and received the manna of infused

contemplation (open or masked); all were co-redeemers with Christ, because they were already united with Him here on earth, not only by their belonging to the Mystical Body, but also in an immediate relation or immediate mutual donation of person to person — as to the Bridegroom of their soul.

In saying that in Heaven there are immensely more saints than we can imagine, I am thinking also of the saints whom one could call *unapparent*, because, except as regards the secret of hearts, they led among us a life like everyone else. If there is heroism in their life, and there is without any doubt, it is a perfectly hidden heroism. The name of saints befits them however, in this sense, that from this earthly life they passed directly into Heaven,[1] having proceeded with perseverance on the road of friendship with God as far as to attain here on earth the perfection of charity (under the relation of intensity). Then, as I have already noted, their last instant was an instant of triumph of mad, boundless love, which will continue for eternity. These saints (who are not canonizable) form, I do not doubt it, a still much greater multitude than the canonizable saints who will never be canonized. And for them also, for them especially, the Church celebrates each year All Saints' day. It is the immense mass of the poor and the little people of God that we must first think of here, I am speaking of all those among them who practiced to the very end self-abnegation, devotion to others and firmness in the virtues. There were for centuries (this is only one example among others) peasant families in which work was sanctified by the sacraments, common prayer and the daily reading of the lives of the saints, and in which the fear of God, the virtue of religion and a certain strictness of manners served as a sanctuary or as a tabernacle for the theological virtues: such families must have produced a substantial percentage of saints who, after having «lived like everyone else,» passed directly into Heaven. Père Lamy, whom we used to call «the holy Curé,» did not fail to insist in this point. The saints of whom I am speaking here had doubtless, for the most part, neither crossed the threshold of the mystical state nor experienced contemplation, even diffuse or masked (except through the fugitive *touches*, more or less rare, and generally unnoticed by them, which I mentioned above). They, too, had however — not doubtless with the full liberty and the

1. One will grant me this definition, although in a more general sense the name of saints clearly befits all those who are in Heaven, even if they had to suffer first the purifications of Purgatory.

supreme sacrifices of mad, boundless love which are the privilege of canonizable saints, but like them in carrying their cross with Jesus, and as members and parts of that unimaginably great human-divine Whole which is the Mystical Body of Christ — satisfied for their part, like every Christian who has charity, the co-redemptive vocation which baptism imprints on souls.

Is it true to say that in proportion as evening descends and as the old Christendoms come apart it becomes more difficult for the mass of men to keep charity and to remain faithful to the very end under the mere regime of friendship with the Lord, and to populate Heaven with saints who have «lived like everyone else»; whereas at the same time, in order to compensate and supercompensate for the losses, there is growth, whether in quantity or in quality, on the side of souls who live under the regime of mad, boundless love, and whose role in the economy of salvation increases in importance, because (and this is especially true, however small their number may be in comparison, of those in whom infused contemplation freely expands) their lived intimacy with Jesus, their renunciation and their self-abasements are more and more necessary to pay for the salvation of many, and to render present among the unfortunate, and accessible to their eyes, the depths of the goodness, of the innocence and of the love of God?

I would readily think so. I wrote a long time ago that a day would come when the world would no longer be habitable except by beasts or by saints — great saints.

III. ON CHRISTIAN MARRIAGE

Marriage, friendship and love

I have already proposed elsewhere[1] some more or less random reflections on marriage. I permit myself to take up some of them again here, as a beginning, while stating them a bit more accurately.

I noted first that it would be a great illusion to think that marriage must be the perfect accomplishment of love-passion or of romantic love. For love-passion and romantic love, being nothing other in reality than animal desire disguised as pure love by the

---

1. Cf. *Reflections on America*, pp. 137-141; *Moral Philosophy*, pp. 356-357.

imagination, are in themselves impermanent and perishable, apt to pass from one object to another, and therefore unfaithful, in short, intrinsically torn between love for the other, which they have awakened, and their own essentially egoistic nature.

No doubt love as desire and passion, and romantic love — or, at least something of it — should be present as much as possible in marriage as an initial stimulant and starting point. But far from having as its essential aim «to bring romantic love to perfect fulfillment, marriage has to perform in human hearts quite another work — an infinitely deeper and more mysterious, alchemical operation: I mean to say, it has to *transmute* romantic love, or what existed of it in the beginning, into real and indestructible *human* love, and really disinterested love»[1] which certainly does not exclude carnal passion and desire but which rises more and more above them, because in itself and by essence it is principally spiritual — a complete and irrevocable gift of one to the other, for the love of the other.

The love of which I am speaking here is above all a disinterested love. It is not necessarily mad, boundless love; but it is necessarily and primordially a love of devotion and of friendship — that entirely unique *friendship* between spouses one of whose essential ends is the spiritual companionship between the man and the woman in order to help each other to accomplish their destiny here on earth, and it is thus a *love* (I am speaking of love in its ordinary form, what I called at the beginning quite simply «bel amour»)[2] which is truly in the measure of man, and in which the soul as well as the senses are involved,[3] so that in this love, in which desire is there with all its power, disinterestedness really takes precedence over covetousness. Finally, actual carnal intercourse is also normally implied there,[4] since the other essential end of marriage is the perpetuation

1. *Reflections on America*, p. 140.
2. Gift, still *in outline form*, more or less advanced, of what the person himself *is*.
3. Such a love is *normal* in marriage, but it is not *necessary*, it is lacking in actual fact in many marriages whose motive has been above all of the social, not personal, order — obedience to parents, social conventions, to say nothing of financial advantages and of "hopes," of "status" or of family pride, etc. — in short, "marriages of convenience."
4. Even in marriages without love which are mentioned in the preceding note.

of the human species; this is why each spouse has a right over the body of the other.

In the unique and sacred friendship of which I have just spoken, together with (when it is there) the love, the *bel amour*, equally unique and sacred, which is joined to it or should normally be joined to it, consists the essence of conjugal love. It is through it that marriage «can be between man and woman a true community of love, built not on sand, but on rock, because it is built on genuinely human, not animal, and genuinely spiritual, genuinely personal love — through the hard discipline of self-sacrifice and by dint of renouncements and purifications. Then in a free and unceasing ebb and flow of emotion, feeling, and thought, each one really participates, by virtue of love, in that personal life of the other which is, by nature, the other's incommunicable possession. And then each one may become a sort of guardian Angel for the other — prepared, as guardian Angels have to be, to forgive the other a great deal,» in short, a being «really dedicated to the good and salvation of the other,» and consenting «to be entrusted with the revelation of, and the care for, all that the other *is* in his or her deepest human depths. . . .»[1]

To such a fundamentally and primarily required friendship, to such a love of entire devotion, together with the carnal intercourse implied by marriage, and with the love of the senses and of the soul, the *bel amour* which it entails or should normally entail, there can be joined mad, boundless love, in which there is brought to its extreme and absolutely complete form the direct gift, open and naked, of the person or subjectivity in its entirety — and not only in its body, but in absolutely all that it is — so that it makes itself truly part of the other as its Whole. Mad, boundless love arises in this case as surplus, but in response to a radical desire inscribed in the human being, since, as we have seen above, mad, boundless love, in which the loving male ecstasizes in the loved female, and the loved female in the loving male, and becomes flesh of her or his flesh and a single spirit with her or him, is the summit and the perfection of love between Man and Woman. It is therefore by this very fact the summit and the perfection of love between spouses.

I do not think that this summit is often attained — far from

1. *Reflections on America*, pp. 140-141, 143.

it! But when it is attained, by virtue of an extraordinary luck, which is a special and gratuitous gift, it is the glory and the heaven of the here-below, in which a dream from the depths of the ages consubstantial with human nature assumes reality, and whose nostalgia inherent in poor humanity is revealed by all the songs of marriage sung throughout the bygone centuries.

The state of marriage, the regime of friendship with God,
and the regime of mad, boundless love for God

What about the relation of marriage and conjugal love with regard to the spiritual life, and to that perfection of charity to which every Christian is prescribed to tend according to his condition and his possibilities?

It is well known that statistically speaking few institutions among men are subject to so many social servitudes varying with time and the areas of civilization, to so many accidents, hazards and miseries, to so many habits of egoism and of rudeness, nay of lie or of pretence, and exposed to so many failures as marriage. This is not surprising, since the state of marriage is the condition of the very great majority of human beings. The fact remains that there are actually many good marriages, in which human nature attains a real happiness proportionate to the here-below, and through which, in causing God to create immortal souls and new human persons to come into the world, man and woman accomplish the work of propagation commanded by Him to our race in such a manner that it is truly for them and for their children what it is in the purpose of God — the great and primordial earthly blessing.

And the fact remains that the state of marriage, as Christianity sees it, and as the grace of the sacraments makes it possible to be lived, is neither that resolutely accepted *state of imperfection* to which a pseudo-theology at work in the imagination of certain laymen seemed sometimes to want to pledge them, nor that caricature of self-styled Christian union in which a husband saw in his wife only a flesh destined for him so that he might put his concupiscence in conformity with the law of God. The state of marriage is a holy or consecrated state, in which, companions on earth in the afflictions and the joys of life, as in their mission towards their children, the two spouses are always (by the very fact of their differences, and of the accommodation they require) mutually freeing themselves from the hereditary fatalities which their departed ancestors make weigh on each, and should normally help one another to advance, against winds and tides, towards the perfection of human life and of charity: so that for the soul of each, in the measure in which it is faithful to grace, the state of marriage can finally open not only into that anti-chamber of beatitude which is the purification of Purgatory, but directly into the vision of God and blessed eternity.

If we refer now to what was indicated above about the regime of *friendship* in the relations of the soul with God, and if we remember that given the human condition this is what, in actual fact, one must expect to find most frequently in the great multitude of souls who have charity and advance in it as best they can, we must say that it is under this regime of friendship with God that no doubt in actual fact the greatest number of souls who advance towards the perfection of charity in the state of marriage find themselves. These souls do not cross the threshold of the mystical life; nor do they refresh themselves, if only by drinking there drop by drop, at the sources of contemplation, if only atypical and masked; if they do receive fugitive touches of the latter, it is in a wholly intermittent and generally wholly unnoticed manner. But they advance faithfully in love and can attain its perfection[1] here on earth, if not as to its power of alienating the soul from itself, at least as to intensity (and provided to be sure that God spares them too crushing trials). They can supply Heaven with many *unapparent saints*.

Do I mean to imply that in the state of marriage the human soul could not, in its relations with God, pass under the regime of *mad, boundless love*? Nonsense! Not only can it, but the history of the saints shows that in actual fact such has been the case for many spouses (and it speaks only of canonized saints, but there are also the non-canonized canonizable saints. . . .).

How could it be otherwise, since all are called *de jure* to the perfection of charity considered absolutely speaking, under the

1. Let us note here that when one proceeds towards perfection under the regime of friendship, one can advance very far on this road without too grave a conflict while loving a human being with mad, boundless love, precisely because under such a regime divine mad, boundless love does not manifest its exigencies to the very end.

But it is not the same when one proceeds towards perfection under the regime of mad, boundless love: then conflicts will arise on the road such that it will be necessary to renounce human mad, boundless love, willy-nilly, or betray the exigencies of divine mad, boundless love.

relation of its power of alienating the soul from itself as under the relation of intensity — and therefore to the mystical life, and therefore to contemplation, either open or masked?

There are even probably particular cases in which the state of marriage — supposing that the spouses, or one of them, are the object of a proximate call from God, and respond to it — offers to certain married persons, at the same time as greater risks owing to all the allurements of the world, more propitious moral conditions than the state of religion offers to certain religious for the passage of the soul under the habitual regime of the gifts of the Holy Spirit, given the perpetual mutual attentions and the daily sacrifices which marriage requires, and the human experience and the innumerable occasions for compassion and for fraternal help which life in the midst of men entails. And this remark can be true, when exceptional circumstances lighten somewhat the crushing material burden of the father and mother of a family, with regard to contemplative life itself, I mean in the renunciation and the simplicity of the «little way» taught by St. Theresa of Lisieux rather than with the great typical signs described by St. John of the Cross and St. Theresa of Avila.

«Indeed,» wrote Raissa in *Liturgy and Contemplation*, «contemplation is not given only to the Carthusians, the Poor Clares, the Carmelites. . . . It is frequently the treasure of persons hidden in the world, known only to some few — to their directors, to a few of their friends. Sometimes, in a certain manner this treasure is hidden from the souls themselves who possess it — souls who live by it in all simplicity, without visions, without miracles, but with such a flame of love for God and neighbor that good happens all around them without noise and without agitation.

«It is of this that our age has to become aware, and of the ways through which contemplation communicates itself through the world, under one form or the other, to the great multitude of souls who thirst for it (often without knowing it), and who are called to it at least in a remote manner. The great need of our age, in what concerns the spiritual life, is to put contemplation on the roads of the world.»[1]

One must always reach for the highest. Accordingly, it is desirable that among the young spouses who wish to devote them-

---

1. *Liturgy and Contemplation*, pp. 74-75. — The book is by the two of us, but it was Raissa who wrote this page.

selves to the Christian life with all their soul (much more numerous than, as a result of certain prejudices, it now seems to be) there be some who, without laboring under delusions concerning the roughness of the path, aspire to the highest ideal of Christian marriage, and to a common life in which the two of them, in advancing towards the perfection of charity, do not stop in their relations with God at the regime of friendship, but pass to the regime of *mad, boundless love.*

The state of a father or of a mother of a family is compatible with progress in infused contemplation and in mad, boundless love for God

Let us note here that although Christianity recognizes in the chastity of the body[1] the mark of a more exclusive consecration to God, and even sees, as I shall indicate further on, not, certainly, a necessary link, but a certain particular suitability between it and specifically Christian contemplation, carnal intercourse between spouses is not at all an obstacle to the mystical life or to contemplation, even very high, for the spouse (or for the two spouses) who has (or have) entered into the ways of the spirit. This is evident if one thinks on the one hand of the fundamental and universal importance which marriage and the fecundity of marriage had in the Old Law (and still have in Judaism), and on the other hand of the great and holy contemplatives, of the contemplatives of great caliber who lived under the Old Law, as also of the mystics who have not been lacking among the Jews in modern times, in particular among the Hassidim. The Moslem mystics (I am thinking, as for the Hassidim, of those among them who went beyond natural mysticism and knew infused contemplation) could also be called in testimony — we know that Hallaj, the most sublime and the most heroic of them, tortured and put to death on the gibbet for having taught contemplation through a union of mutual love between God and man, was married and left two sons.

Finally, examples are not lacking either among Christian con-

---

1. I mean abstention from all carnal intercourse (*opere et cogitatione*). It is clear that the virtue of chastity (part of temperance) in the use itself of the flesh ("conjugal chastity") is, like the other moral virtues, necessarily presupposed by contemplation in the state of marriage.

templatives. Their number is relatively small among the canonized saints (it is not the custom, it seems, to canonize mere laymen, with the exception of some great leaders of the people). However, some holy widows, such as St. Bridget, St. Frances of Rome, St. Jeanne de Chantal, Venerable Marie de l'Incarnation (Ursuline), clearly did not await their widowhood to enter into the ways of infused contemplation; nor did St. Nicholas of Flue await for this to leave his family and to become a hermit; all were *first* great contemplatives. Blessed Anne-Marie Taigi was the mother of a family. And the case of married persons who lived with infused contemplation without being beatified or canonized for all that, as in the sixteenth and in the seventeenth century (I cite Brémond at random), Marie de Valence and Mme Acarie, Marguerite Romanet, Mme du Houx, Mme Helyot and her husband, or in our time Lucie-Christine, Madeleine Sémer or Élizabeth Leseur, is certainly much more frequent.

Spouses who have passed under the regime of mad, boundless love for God, and more particularly under that of infused contemplation are certainly not obliged for this reason[1] to renounce giving themselves carnally to each other and engendering offspring.

Human mad, boundless love is not compatible
with progress in infused contemplation
and in mad, boundless love for God

There is however (I have already touched on this point in passing, I would like now to insist on it more) a renunciation, and a much more serious one to tell the truth, to which they are obliged. They are obliged to renounce, if ever they have known it, mad, boundless love for each other. Living under the regime of mad, boundless love for God they cannot live at the same time — at least without a contradiction and a rending which would prevent them from advancing as God wishes, and would block their path — under the regime of mad, boundless love for a created being. In mad, boundless love does not the lover give himself to the beloved as to his Whole, of which

1. That certain spouses can decide on such a renunciation by reason of a particular and entirely personal call to follow at all costs, while remaining in the world, at least one of the counsels of the perfect life — this is an altogether different question — cf. further on, pp. 252-253.

he makes himself a part? My Whole is my Unique. Already in the natural order, in human mad, boundless love, the total gift that the lover makes of himself entails and requires an absolute exclusiveness. How much more so is this the case in the supernatural order, in the mad, boundless love whose object is God! Doubtless it remains psychologically possible (because one has to do now with two different and incommensurable orders) that along with this divine mad, boundless love, and at its expense, and in what an irreconcilable conflict with it, there exists in the soul, at least for a time, a mad, boundless love for a creature. But this will be all the more dearly paid for; for it is then the Beloved Himself who, jealous of every other attachment, and all the more of another mad, boundless love in the soul which loves Him, will undertake to destroy in it what is still an obstacle to mad, boundless love for Him.

If a human person gives himself truly and absolutely to another human person as to his Unique and to his Whole, because he loves this person with mad, boundless love, he can indeed, certainly, love God more, as the order of charity requires — as to the sovereign lovability, to the sovereign perfection and to the sovereign rights which he recognizes in Him, and to the obedience which he is ready to render to Him willy-nilly — in short, he can love God with friendship, more than the human being whom he loves with mad, boundless love[1] (then, we know, he also loves God with mad, boundless love, at least with a mad, boundless love buried in friendship, and perhaps with a mad, boundless love which has already begun to freely expand); he cannot however go to the very end of what mad, boundless love for God requires as to the integrity of the gift which he makes to God, I do not say only as regards himself, I say as regards the one whom he loves more than himself.[2] There is some-

1. In this sense human mad, boundless love is then ruled by charity.
2. In this sense human mad, boundless love cannot be ruled *perfectly* by charity. One obeys doubtless, but reluctantly, nay, with rage in the heart. One is far from *perfect* obedience.
   However is it not true that when he advances towards the perfection of charity under the regime only of friendship with God, man does not have to renounce human mad, boundless love? Unquestionably, but under this regime one does not advance towards the perfection of charity considered absolutely. And the perfection of charity considered under a relation only is not such that the soul can perfectly surmount in it certain too crushing trials. We remarked above (p. 231, note 1) that God measures trials to the capacity of souls, and that under the regime of mad, boundless love the soul can reach a perfection of charity greater, in intensity as well as in depth of gift of self, than under the regime of friendship.

thing which he will give, but only up to a certain point, not as far as certain extreme instances of the divine demands, not as far as immolation:[1] him or her precisely to whom he has absolutely given himself as to his Unique and his Whole. The paternal love of Abraham was not a mad, boundless love. The maternal love of Mary for Jesus — the most tender and the most perfect maternal love which can be conceived — was not a mad, boundless love.[2] Mad, boundless love is mad, boundless. If a man loves a woman with mad, boundless love, he will not consent to give her so far as immolation, even to God. (He will struggle against God, he will be broken.) If the two spouses who pass under the regime of mad, boundless love for God know what they are doing, they know that it is necessary for them to renounce at the same stroke mad, boundless love for each other, to renounce that which in the natural order is the summit and the glory of conjugal love, but in the supernatural order is much less than the unique and perfect friendship rooted in charity and the grace of the sacraments. It can happen that a man or a woman who has made his or her Whole of another human being loved with mad, boundless love may enter into the authentic ways of contemplation. A day will come, very late perhaps, when they will understand that an internal division renders progress in these ways impossible for them. It is necessary for them to sacrifice, not, certainly, their love for this human being, but their mad, boundless love for him or her.[3]

1. Not every death is death on the cross. "Factus obediens usque ad mortem, *mortem autem crucis.*"
2. What I mean is that Mary very clearly had mad, boundless love for Jesus, God and man, but that her *maternal* love for Jesus, *man* and God, being *perfectly* ruled by charity, was not a mad, boundless love.
3. The saints make this sacrifice without delay. I think of St. Elizabeth of Hungary who loved her husband, as Mme Ancelet-Hustache has noted in her beautiful book: *L'or dans la Fournaise* (p. 44), with a profound love of body and soul. The episode in which we see her, from the first years of her marriage, pass nights in prayer, while Louis holds her hand — and so long that the two of them finally fall asleep on the rug (*ibid*. p. 45) — does not signify only that she wished for a time to do violence to her flesh. Much more profoundly still, I have no doubt, it signifies that during these nights she accomplished a definitive sacrifice, renounced for the mad, boundless love for God, however it may have been with the carnal intercourse between the spouses, the human mad, boundless love which she felt rising in her.

The author of the Song

The *Song of Songs* is not a song of profane love, a song of human marriage which one would have to plagiarize in order to apply it to divine love. Its original object, as the tradition of the Synagogue maintains, and as the best Christian exegetes maintain, was to extol the love between God and His people — and, more truly still, to extol in a prophetical light the nuptial love, the mad, boundless love, between God and His Church, and, inseparably, between God and the soul who has arrived at mystical union with Him.

But it is clear, at the same time, that the author of the Song of Songs was a man profoundly versed, much more than Dante himself,[1] in the things of profane love, the experience of human mad, boundless love, and of the carnal love which is normally linked to it. Had he, when he wrote his Song, renounced the flesh — no one, I think, can say anything on this subject. But one thing is certain, it is that at this moment, in which he extolled from experience (and from what a marvellously unitive experience, in the rapture of a total gift!) mad, boundless love between God and the creature, he had renounced human mad, boundless love.

Although Christian contemplation does not require chastity of the body it has however an affinity with it

I noted just now that if the contemplative life does not require in itself chastity of the body, the latter however (whatever many Christians of today — more or less intoxicated with bad psychology — think of it, and with whom it does not have a good press) has a certain relation of suitability or of affinity with specifically Christian contemplation, and that in any case Christianity recognizes in it the mark of a more exclusive consecration to God.

Moreover it happened formerly that spouses, at a given moment of their conjugal life,[2] not only renounced mad, boundless love for

---

1. Shelley said that Dante had understood the secrets of love better than any other poet.
2. Sometimes as early as the reception of the sacrament [of marriage], which remained valid after this vow [of chastity] was made — the vow [of chastity]

each other, but further sometimes made a vow to renounce the flesh itself in order to devote themselves more exclusively to Jesus. These were doubtless very infrequent cases, and ones due to a clearly manifested particular vocation. In actual fact, no one was astonished at it. One knew that the sacrament of marriage was only more profoundly lived by them, because one of the essential ends of marriage, the spiritual companionship between spouses in order to mutually help themselves to advance towards God, found itself strengthened and realized in a higher manner in mad, boundless love for God. As to the other essential end, procreation, it was not denied but transferred to another plane, it was a spiritual progeniture that these spouses awaited from God, and it was to it that they devoted themselves. *Centuplum accipietis* [He will be repaid a hundred times over].

And after all they had great examples — even at the heights of creation — in which humanity was brought to the confines of divinity, and in the most humble, in the most poor and in the most hidden life among men. The love which reigned between Joseph and Mary was conjugal love in the purest plenitude of its essence. However not only had the supreme *natural* perfection of the love between Man and Woman, mad, boundless love, made room, according to the law of the cross, for a supreme *supernatural* perfection incomparably higher, the mad, boundless love of the two for their God. But further, one sees there that if chastity of the body, whatever its particular suitability with regard to Christian contemplation, is not at all required in itself for contemplation, it maintains however a primary importance with regard to the *state of life* — a state of perfection not only to be acquired, but, if it is a question of Nazareth, already *acquired or possessed*, where, by a unique privilege, Joseph and Mary found themselves in the state of marriage.

The merits of chastity

Why this importance and these special merits of chastity of the body as well as of the soul?

taking place not before, but after the act of mutual consent in which each of them had given to the other full right over their body, and as an effect and a confirmation of this consent. And to tell the truth, these things did not happen only in past times — I think of two friends very dear to us who married in these conditions. Raissa and I had been the witnesses of their marriage.

I shall recall in the first place that if there can be carnal union without mad, boundless love, on the other hand there cannot be any human mad, boundless love which does not also normally entail, at least in desire, carnal union. In renouncing all carnal union, even in desire, the religious who makes a vow of chastity not only sacrifices the flesh, he also makes and at the same stroke a sacrifice which, to tell the truth, goes much further, which attains the depths of the natural aspirations of man, not only in his flesh but in his soul and his spirit. Doubtless he does not renounce (which would be a great loss for the very progress and the refinement of his moral life) all feminine friendship, however subject it should remain to a strict internal vigilance. But he sacrifices all possibility for himself of attaining and of desiring that earthly paradise of nature whose dream haunts the unconscious of our race — mad, boundless love between man and woman. It is of such a renouncement that the vow of chastity or that of virginity are above all the sign.

I shall say in the second place that in mortifying in himself the carnal instinct, man does not have to do merely with something which properly concerns or affects his person as such, as happens when to perfect himself in virtue he mortifies in himself the instinct of gluttony or of slander. He has to do with an instinct which is *first* that of his species, much more than that of his own person, and which dwells in the latter as a strange dominator, and which holds it and torments it with a violence all the more tyrannical. Chastity checks a furious force immensely more ancient than the individual through which it passes. Even in the merely natural order it is a liberation — in one sense and in a certain manner it delivers man from the servitudes of the species. It is a kind of victory, of liberation, which men, unless certain prejudices, either religious or naturalist, cause them to believe is prohibited or impossible, have a natural tendency to envy, be it from a very great distance. Is this not one of the reasons why virginity was honored by the pagans themselves? And is this not why many pagan wise men — and I am not only speaking of those of India, whose testimony on this point is so striking — thought that when a husband (nothing was said about women — they were too despised) had reached a certain age, when it was more fitting for him to devote himself to meditation by retiring into his inner freedom, it was fitting for him also to discontinue carnal relations.

In the third place, and more simply, it is clear that by the very fact that the mysteries of the Christian faith put in a particular relief the importance and the dignity of the flesh and of the body, as also the metaphysical unity of the human person, whose immortal soul is proper to a given body («individuated» by its relation to it) — it is only normal that, in the religion which teaches the Incarnation of the Word and the Assumption of the Blessed Virgin, he who wishes to consecrate himself to God consecrates to Him not only his soul, but also his body. Did not Jesus give Himself in His entirety, body and soul, to men, in order to save them? He who loves a human person with mad, boundless love gives himself to this person in his body and in his soul. He who enters into a state of life dedicated to mad, boundless love for God must give to God his body as well as his soul. His soul gives itself to Him by love, his body by chastity. And even if one does not especially consider the religious state, it is necessary to say that in general, in insisting on the human person and on his dignity, and in restoring the condition of woman, and in teaching that the redemption of humanity had depended on the consent of a little virgin of Israel, Christianity also restored chastity, under the lights of grace, in the esteem of men.

There is finally a fourth consideration, which this time concerns contemplation itself, I say *Christian* contemplation, and which furnishes in relation to the latter a certain nuance or attenuation to the statement (however valid it still remains) that the contemplative life in itself does not require chastity of the body. Christian contemplation in reality is inseparably the contemplation of the uncreated Trinity and of Jesus, God and man, the humanity of Christ — that humanity which belongs to the second divine Person, and all of whose properties are therefore also attributes of this divine Person Himself — is always present in it in a manifest or hidden manner, and cannot be detached from it. That to which the Christian contemplative has his eyes constantly attached is, at the same time as the one and triune God, a man perfectly chaste, born of the most chaste of Virgins, and who Himself is God. How would the Christian who aspires to contemplation not feel himself drawn also to a life of continence or of chastity — not, once more, as to a necessary condition (except,for some, because of the religious state), but as to something which better accords with his desires?

Moreover, there is in Christian contemplation a certain innocence of approach, a sweetness and delicacy of the hands, if I may venture to speak thus, a certain candid demeanor and a certain

matchless simplicity, and also a certain winged liberty which familiarity with the Holy Spirit gives, and that intimacy with the divine
Persons and the heart of Jesus for which without a perfect purity
the ardor of love does not suffice — which, without requiring it
however, are, so to speak, connatural with chastity of the body.

The vows of religion

The preceding remarks can help us, I believe, to understand
that the vow of chastity, and the two other vows to which it is
joined, constitute for the man who consecrates himself to the religious state a veritable *holocaust*, in which beforehand and for always
he gives himself to God body and soul — and in what expectation,
if not in the expectation of advancing here on earth to perfection,
under the regime of mad, boundless love for God and for Jesus?

The promise of the subdeacon in the Latin rite

From the vow of chastity, which by essence is for the sake
of the one who makes it, for the sake of his own easier and more
rapid progress towards the perfection of charity, it is clearly necessary to distinguish the promise which in the Latin Church the
subdeacon makes at the moment of his ordination.[1] When the bishop
towards whom he has advanced informs him that for the service of
God it will henceforth be necessary for him to observe chastity if
he perseveres in his intention to receive the subdiaconate, the ordi-
nand simply takes a step forward (he takes *the* step). In itself this
promise[2] is (like the priesthood itself), not for the sake of the one
who makes it, but *for others* (in order that, once he is ordained a
priest, the one who has made it may be able to accomplish *better*
— with an entire devotion which no other attachment and no other
obligation impede or diminish — his mission, his ministry in the

1. At the time when these pages were written, the subdiaconate had not yet
been abolished. Today it is in receiving the diaconate that the promise in question is made.
2. Or this vow, if one prefers to call it thus — the name matters little. In any
case the reality thus designated differs in nature from the vow of chastity properly so called, made with a view to an interior perfection to be acquired.

service of the souls to whose good he is dedicated). The promise made by the subdeacon is so far from being identical with the vow of chastity that when a man who is already a priest enters into a religious order he makes at this moment the vow of chastity, together with that of obedience and of poverty (it is therefore, very clearly, because he had not already made it). The promise of the subdeacon of the Latin rite is not intended to contribute to a holocaust of the human individual, it is a sacred *wound* accepted for the better exercise of a function towards others. And it is up to the individual to keep this wound open while putting up with it as best he can (in a difficult life in which he can no doubt be a «*good priest,*» but also a mediocre priest or even a more or less vanquished priest), or to heal and transform it into a source of graces (for himself and for others) by devoting himself freely, while remaining in the world, to mad, boundless love for God. Then only will he be able to become a «*holy priest,*» through his personal response to the precept addressed to all to advance towards the perfection of charity, and to the call which this precept contains.

CHAPTER EIGHT

APROPOS OF THE CHURCH OF HEAVEN

This chapter emerged from a seminar held with the Little Brothers of Jesus, students in Toulouse, the 28th of May 1963. It was a question there of desultory reflections, which I have left in their original form of a completely informal talk.

I. OUR ATTITUDE TOWARDS THE CHURCH TRIUMPHANT

It seems to me that an extreme negligence prevails among Christians concerning the Church of Heaven and therefore that there is progress to be made here, not, of course, in dogma or doctrine, but in growth in awareness.

1. The Church triumphant and the Church militant are but a single Church, a single and unique mystical body under two essentially different states; the Church militant is *in time* and, as Abbé Journet says, under the journeying and crucified state; the Church triumphant is *in eternity*, under the state of glory.

The living link and the living relation between the two are manifested in the public life of the Church here on earth by the liturgy. The liturgy is wholly turned towards Heaven. And Heaven listens to it. However, the feasts of the cycle of time are above all centered on the states of Our Lord during His earthly life; and, in the feasts of the saints, each is commemorated only once a year. And it is always a prayer of petition which we address for what we here on earth think to be our good, and for the intentions of the Church militant (and it must be like this, it is absolutely normal in the prayer of the Church militant, who is like a beggar-woman in relation to the Church triumphant). And the liturgy and the breviary assure and maintain in this way a continuous communication between earth and Heaven.

But in our private prayer, in our personal spiritual life? Heaven, it seems to me, is very distant, abstract, impersonal. Naturally I am not speaking of the Holy Trinity, nor of Jesus and of the Blessed Virgin. Yes, we think of them, in a habitual and profound manner. But the Mystical Body, the angels and the innumerable saints, all the humanity who populate Heaven and who constitute the Mystical Body of which Christ is the head, all of this remains hidden, in general, as though behind a curtain of azure. This is due, without doubt, in part to the fact that Heaven is *unimaginable* and that Revelation teaches us only a minimum of things concerning *the other world*. Why? Because we would not understand. We have no landmark. (We are as it were primitives whom one trots round in a universal exposition or before an electronic machine; not having any landmark, any common measure, they are not at all astonished, they do not understand. I think that it is a little like this with regard to Heaven and the other world.) But this is due also to our stupidity and to our reluctance to attach ourselves to the *invisible*, to seek in it our daily bread.

Here I am going to introduce a parenthesis: I have just said that Revelation teaches us only a minimum of things concerning the other world. This is true. However, though still without anything accessible to our imagination, we know a little more about it, I believe, than we think, but our attention is not drawn to it enough.

We naturally think that what constitutes the beatitude of the blessed is the vision of the divine essence; this is clearly the essential; but it is not the whole of their life.

Just as the Word Incarnate had on earth a life divine and human at one and the same time, so also the blessed in Heaven have entered into the divine life itself through the vision, but they also lead there, outside of the vision although penetrated by its radiance, a glorious and transfigured human life.

They love God, from the moment that they see Him, by a necessity of nature, without their free will having to exercise itself in this. But with regard to all the rest, with regard to the whole universe of creatures, they continue to exercise their free will; they act freely without being able to sin.

On the other had, there is between them, and with the angels in the midst of whom they are as equals, there is intellectual communication (wordless, of course) dependent on the free will of each. Each blessed is master of the thoughts of his heart and opens them freely to whomever he wishes. And all are co-citizens of the heavenly Jerusalem, over which the Lamb reigns.

Therefore, there is a *human life* of glory and of human inter-actions of glory for the separated souls, as there will be after the Resurrection for the risen human persons, who will not be content with walking about with palms in the avenues of Paradise. They will be the masters of a nature henceforth without anguish, to carry it along into the great human life of the city of the saints and into the adoration of God.

Already before the Resurrection, there is in Heaven an immense and perpetual conversation. (And I think that in this conversation the angels will tell us the stories of this poor earth, for, how can one think that all that has passed in the flux of time, charged with so much beauty, so much love and distress, will be lost forever? There is the memory of the angels.)

And in Heaven, at each instant of discontinuous time, which is the time of the pure spirits, there are *events* which take place: new blessed arrive constantly from earth to be born to eternal life, they are welcomed by the others, friendships are established; and from Purgatory also souls newly delivered arrive unceasingly; and each time that a sinner is converted on earth, there is joy and thanks-giving among all the saints of Heaven. All of this makes a great history, in a duration different from that of our history.

And this world which they have left, the blessed know it now without shortcoming, and its relation to God and to the eternal purposes, and all the modes of participation of the creature in its Uncreated Principle. And the higher spirits, whose knowledge is more simple and more perfect, illumine the other spirits. And they instruct each other in what God expects of them and of their prayer in the great combat for the salvation of souls.

And in this world which they have left to live where the glori-ous bodies of Jesus and Mary exist (outside of and beyond the whole universe and its space) the blessed intervene, they are still present in it by their love and by their action, and by the inspirations which they give us and by the effects of their prayers. And the love which they had on earth for their loved-ones, they have kept in heaven, transfigured, not abolished by glory; and if it was a love of charity, this love was already on earth what it is now in Heaven. You remem-ber the saying of St. Theresa of Lisieux: «I wish to spend my Heaven doing good on earth.» This saying goes singularly far — in the direction of what one could call the humanism of the saints even in Heaven.

All of this amounts to saying that the creature and the created reflections of the uncreated Goodness also have their role in the beatitude of the blessed. They add themselves to it without adding anything to it; they add absolutely nothing, not the thickness of a hair, to that beatitude which comes to the saints of Heaven from the vision of God and which deifies them, transfers them into the very order of divine Transcendence, but the spiritual riches which come from the created are something *more* which is integrated in the joy and in the supreme actuation of the blessed without rendering them greater. Somewhat as, from the fact of creation, there are *beings* over and above (numerically) uncreated Being, without *being* itself being (intensively) increased by the thickness of a hair.

My parenthesis is finished. You will pardon me this digression, I hope it «was not useless,» as Bergson liked to say.

Before this long parenthesis, I had remarked that in general in our spiritual life Heaven, the other world, the Chruch triumphant are very distant, very ignored, and that this is largely because we neglect to turn our attention in this direction, and are reluctant to attach ourselves to the invisible.

2. And yet *the other world* is present in our world, it plunges into it like lightning — invisibly. In each tabernacle there is Jesus in glory in His humanity and His divinity. — And there is also Heaven, according as in the Eucharist the Body of the Lord is itself the sign of His mystical body.

They are all there, to crowd behind Him, not sacramentally present, certainly, but present by their attention, their adoration of Jesus and their love for Him, and also by their love for us. «Where the body is, there the eagles are.» Virtually, all the saints of Heaven are in your chapel, around the tabernacle. And, actually, in a more special manner, those who love you and whom you love in particular, and who adore Jesus with you.

And if we cannot imagine them, we can love them. And if there is a terrible curtain between the invisible world and the visible world, love enables us to pass behind, it is the same love of charity which is in them and in us; through our love we attain them as they attain us and through our prayer also.

From this point of view we can well understand the importance, disregarded by more or less archaizing liturgists, of the exposition of the Blessed Sacrament and of the hours of adoration which are devoted to it. It is the door of Heaven open on the earth. And we look through this door with the eyes of faith.

3.   Formerly, in a more or less primitive and superstitious mentality, there was a great and profound familiarity between the saints and the Christian people. Each saint, as you know, had his specialty, generally a specialty of healer for such or such illness or infirmity of men or of animals. Recourse was had to them all the time in the particular circumstances of life. Today there is scarcely any of this except the devotion to St. Anthony of Padua to find lost objects.

This familiarity with the saints was, moreover, terribly egoistic. We importuned them with our miseries and our needs. We turned to them only to beseech them to make happen what *we* wanted here on earth, to help us to do *our* will. The saints put up with it nevertheless. At least there was a permanent contact with them.

This more or less primitive mentality has been drastically purified. It is certainly not necessary to regret it. But it has been replaced by a self-styled rational mentality — in reality an anemic and aseptic one — in which in fact there is no longer any lived contact with the saints.

And this seems to me disastrous.

For at a lower rank, certainly, and *below* the liturgy, *popular piety* plays an essential role in the life of the Church, because it expresses the direct and spontaneous movement of souls, with regard to their daily life and to their particular destiny in the world, and varies according to the epochs like the life itself of the world.

In this sense one can say that the liturgy, while being absolutely necessary, nevertheless does not suffice. In the first place because lived participation in the liturgy will always be, whatever one does, reserved to a relatively restricted number of laymen.

Next and above all because, in liturgical prayer (am I about to speak heresies?), it seems to me that its grandeur and its superiority come from the fact that as a general rule *my* prayer *effaces itself* in the universal prayer of the Church — the Church, not only of all places on the earth but also of all times, with her immense memory. That is why the Old Testament has such a cardinal place in liturgical prayer. Each is there as *part*, each prays the prayer of a whole which covers the whole earth, which covers all times since Abraham and before.

Of course, there are moments — Christmas, Holy Week, Easter — in which *my* prayer is fully engaged in the liturgical prayer and nourished by it. Of course, there are in the Mass of each day responses to *my* needs. Of course, there are psalms which sometimes become the life of *my* flesh and of *my* blood. — But finally, I do not think that this is the general rule. And when I recite the Divine Office, not only does the astonishing bad taste of certain hymns recall to me relatively recent epochs which I would prefer to forget, but even in the psalms, well, personally I do not have much desire to crush the new-born children of Babylon on stone, nor to see the sons of the impious reduced to beggary and chased from their houses, nor to annihilate a lot of kings whose names mean nothing very clear to me.

Whereas popular piety, the piety of the Christian people, of the little people of God, has to do with the petitions and with the initiatives which issue spontaneously from the very heart of people, in the particular circumstances and the particular adventures and in the whole temporal context of their existence, and with the motions of the Holy Spirit which pass through all this. And it is an indispensable piece of the life of the Church militant. And as I said just now, it is more and more neglected. There are indeed Lourdes and the great pilgrimages, and a few particularly famous saints like the Curé of Ars or St. Theresa of Lisieux, and also and above all that kind of para-liturgy of popular piety which is the adoration of the Blessed Sacrament. But with regard to all that immense multitude which is the mystical Body in the state of glory, popular piety has fallen into dust. One would think that we believe stupidly that this multitude sleeps in the beatific vision and no longer wishes to see us, and has forgotten us. And as for us, to the extent that we can, we do everything to encourage this.

4. The idea which I would like to propose to you is the following: Since the Church triumphant is but a single Church with the Church militant, and since the saints continue to occupy themselves with the things of the earth and to interest themselves in them (they see all this in the beatific vision itself), well, they surely have their own idea and their own intentions concerning these things,

concerning the life and the behavior of each of us, and the events of the world, and the progress and the expansion of the kingdom of God.

And without doubt each of them also has his ideas on what more especially concerns the *mission which he had here on earth*, and those whom he loved and was entrusted with protecting here on earth. The founding saints, certainly, have their ideas on their religious order, the patron saints have their ideas on the countries or the cities which are under their aegis. St. Thomas Aquinas on the progress of theological truth and of the truths which he himself established and defended on earth, St. John of the Cross on the progress of the contemplative life; Father de Foucauld on the vocation of those who bear witness for Jesus without preaching or teaching but through fraternal love, and who must be, like Foucauld, universal Little Brothers.

Therefore, is not the true manner in which we have to *exist with them* and maintain a living communion with them — still more than to pray to them for *our intentions* and to explain *our* needs and *our* desires (which is necessary, of course, and will always continue) — to pray to them for *their intentions*, for the accomplishment of their aims and of their desires concerning the things of here below, in order that in this way the will of Heaven may be accomplished more on earth? We say in the *Our Father*: «Your will be done,» and in this sense we pray to God for God, well, what I am saying is that we ought to pray to the saints of God for themselves also, in order that their will may be realized by the idiots that we are.

If the Dominicans all over the world said thousands of Masses *for the intentions of St. Thomas Aquinas*, well, the things of the intelligence would perhaps progress a little better here on earth. — And likewise for the things of the apostolate and of Catholic Action, if all priests said Masses *for the intentions of St. Paul.*

5. I have just spoken of canonized saints.

But there are in Heaven lots of other saints — and not only canonizable saints who are not yet, or never will be, canonized — and all of these are *exemplary* saints, who are beacons for humanity, and who have lived under the habitual regime of the gifts of the Holy Spirit, so that one can say (I take up again a theme of «Love And Friendship») that they have not lived like everybody, in this sense that, even sometimes in their external behavior, the measure of their action, being that of the gifts of the Holy Spirit, is higher than that of the acquired or infused moral virtues; this is why they surprise us, disconcert us in some manner; their heroism, however secret the sources of it may be, cannot not manifest itself publicly in one manner or in another.

Well, and it is on this that I would like to insist, besides these exemplary saints, canonized or canonizable, there are in Heaven, not only all the elect who have passed through the sufferings of Purgatory and have been delivered, but also all those elect, whom I believe immense in number, who have been on earth *unapparent* saints, I mean that, except as regards the heart's secrets, they led among us a life like everybody. If there was heroism in their life, and there was without any doubt, it was a perfectly hidden heroism. And they passed straight to Heaven, because they died in an act of perfect charity. It is for them also, for them above all, I believe, that each year the Church celebrates All Saints' Day. It is of the immense mass of the poor and of the little people of God that it is necessary to think first of all here, I say of all those who practiced to the end self-abnegation, devotion to others and firmness of the virtues.

And these saints concern each of us more closely, in this sense, that there are some among them who have been our close relatives on earth, among the deceased members of our own family, and among our ancestors, and among our friends, and among the people whom we have met. Surely there are some among them, as among your deceased Little Brothers — God is not so sparing of His grace; it is we who do not have enough practical faith and are not attentive enough to the glory of those whom we no longer see. I remember that when the Curé of Courneuve used to tell us the story of Notre-Dame-des-Bois, and how he carried a statue of the Blessed Virgin through the woods to the little old house which he was going to make into a chapel, he would tell us that the saints accompanied him in procession through the trees — the saints, that is to say, not St. Peter and St. Paul, but the holy souls in their glory of certain deceased whom he had known, peasant-men and peasant-women who had belonged to his family and to his village. And these saints who concern us and whom we have known — do you believe that they have forgotten us? that they do not desire to help us, and that they do not have a better idea than we do about what is best for us, and that they do not have their own intentions concerning the things of the earth and their friends of this earth?

II. THE DECEASED

The second part of my exposition, which is only a natural continuation of the first, concerns the deceased and what we think about them.

6. Here I would like to begin by a small parenthesis concerning language. There is something which scandalizes me: it is the manner in which Christians speak of their deceased. They call them the dead — they have not been capable of renewing the miserable human vocabulary on a point which nevertheless concerns the essential data of their faith. The dead! One attends masses for the dead! One goes to the cemetery with flowers for the dead; one prays for the dead! As if they weren't billions of times more living than we! As if the fundamental truth stated in the Preface of the Burial Mass: *vita mutatur, non tollitur* — life is changed, it is not taken away — was itself a dead truth, incapable of fecundating and of transforming the common routine of our manner of conceiving and of speaking.

Villiers de L'Isle-Adam used to say that death was an invention of the undertakers.

In actual fact, I think that this word «death» has its proper use when it serves to designate the terrible moment when the soul separates itself from the body — at that time, yes, one is in the presence of death, of that death which horrifies our nature, so much so that it is unthinkable, and one can say that a man «is dying»; and after this one can mention this man as «dead» in the registers of the civil State, or of the police, whose vocabulary is not that of truth, but of sordid appearances.

But those who have left this earth to enter into the other world are not the dead. If they are in Heaven and see God, they are the living *par excellence*; if they are in Purgatory where they suffer but with the certitude that they are chosen and that they will see God, they are — through this very certitude, and through the very pure and very ardent love with which they accept and bless their sufferings — much more living than we are. And even if they are in Hell, in the abyss of the second death, at least they are through

with the mutabilities and the equivocations of earthly life and with
the dark recesses of the unconscious; they have made a definitive
choice freely and they see clearly into themselves. They are perverse
and chastised living beings, they are not dead.

7.   Let us now leave this parenthesis, and return to the consideration of the behavior of Christians with regard to the Church
of Heaven.

The second thing which scandalizes me is the sinister and
lugubrious apparatus which surrounds the funerals of Christians;
it is all this black and this mourning which adorns our churches,
our walls, the prie-dieus, the altar (they tell me that this is beginning
to change in certain parishes, so much the better, but so far it is not
very noticeable) and it is even these black vestments which the priest
puts on to say Mass.

Things were not done like this in the first centuries of Christianity. As one notes in Martimort's remarkable Introduction to
the Liturgy, *L'Eglise en prière*: «The spirit of the Christian funeral
is profoundly different from that of the pagan funeral. On the one
hand, Christians do not attach to the funeral, like the pagans of
the ancient world, an absolutely decisive importance for the survival
of the deceased; above all, the certitude of salvation and of the
resurrection of the dead invites Christians to proclaim that Christ
has conquered death and that their hope and their joy are stronger
than their pain. Ancient Christianity manifests this reaction in
diverse ways, in the funeral inscriptions, in the costume, in opposing
to lugubrious vestments *white, the color of immortality*; above all
in the very liturgy of the funeral, in which the dominant note is faith
in the resurrection rather than mourning. This note, in part masked
in the present Roman liturgy by late additions or exterior details,»
(it would be very interesting to know just when these late additions
were made) «is expressed in a striking manner in the Oriental litur-
gies, for example, in the Byzantine funeral liturgy, which makes use
in these circumstances of the *Allelulia*.»

One could add that, in France, the manner in which for several
centuries past the Roman funeral liturgy has been applied goes
far beyond the reservations expressed in the passage which I have
just cited. How are we to explain this dreadful invasion of mourning and of affliction into rites in which faith in the redemption and

in the resurrection should be the dominant note? There would be here subject-matter for useful studies of historico-sociologico-theological erudition. If you asked me my opinion (as a mere working hypothesis, for I'm not worth anything when it comes to erudition), I would say to you that I see there first of all a kind of naturalist revenge of *human society*, with its imperatives and its traditional costumes, on supernatural faith. It is a kind of duty of etiquette towards the deceased, a duty which the family and social group would consider it dishonorable to shirk — if not to utter for some days shrill lamentations, at least to manifest one's sorrow by black vestments and apparent signs of mourning. And in truth, how much ashes and mourning would be necessary to express, if this could be expressed, the true, the authentic pain caused by separation from a being whom we loved more than our life? *Et Rachel noluit consolari*, Rachel would not be consoled.

Well, it is this pain so natural to our heart, and it is this black of human mourning that people wish at any cost to find again in the funeral rites, and that they have succeeded in superimposing on the Christian rites, at least as to the color — even to that of the vestments of the priest — and to the exterior details of the ceremony. And this phenomenon of *naturization* is so related to the inclinations of man and of human society as such, that one finds it not only in the bourgeois parishes, in which the brilliance of the silver tears on the dark draperies illustrates and magnifies the sorrow of the rich, but also in the poor country parishes, where the faithful absolutely oblige their curé to celebrate requiem Masses, humbly and uniformly lugubrious, all through the year, with that parody of a coffin draped in black and surrounded with miserable cardboard candles on which, flanked by a bewildered altar-boy, he throws the holy water of absolution.

It would seem then very incongruous to think that the poor deceased for whom all this sadness is required has any chance of exulting in the joy of Paradise and of being a part of the Church triumphant.

8. But I think that there are still other causes — more specifically religious this time — for this prevalence of mourning and of black, and of a sort of somber apprehension in the ordinary attitude with regard to the deceased, and for the ordinary practical indifference with regard to the Church of Heaven.

Just before the advent of rationalist and anthropocentric humanism, and of the enthusiasm which it entailed for the material conquest of nature, infallibly necessary progress, indefinite prosperity and indefinite fun, there was at the end of the Middle Ages then in process of dissolution a period of distress and despair which makes one think a little of the existentialism of today. If I remember well, it was in the fifteenth century that the great vogue of the Dance of Death began. And this spiritual state penetrated into religious sentiment. In Martimort's book we are told that the *Dies irae* is an Italian work of the twelth or thirteenth century. (I would think it rather of the fourteenth.) This central piece of the Catholic funeral ceremony of today, which shakes up the congregation a little bit and where the singers enjoy bellowing false notes to make the thunder reverberate, Martimort's book assures us that it is «the only hymn of the Mass which deviates from the ancient Christian piety,» because it is wholly «absorbed in the fear of the Last Judgment.»

In actual fact, the *Dies irae* is one of the most beautiful poems in the world, a work of extraordinary and admirable poetry, and admirable Christian poetry — think of the strophe «*quaerens me, sedisti lassus,*» and the sequel — but it is a Christian poetry which becomes ambiguous and which is engulfed in terror. I would like nevertheless to defend the *Dies irae* a little, for Moses also felt terror, and terror is essential to Christianity also, and to every religion, even in the purely natural order. But it is the terror of the infinite majesty of God, the fear and the trembling before the Presence of Him Whom no name can name, before the divine transcendence which overthrows all our measures, before the *Deus excelsus terribilis.*

But where the ambiguity slips in is that this terror now descends into the universe of the human — terror before the manifestation of all the secrets of our miserable hearts on the day of the Last Judgment, terror of human destiny, of chastisement and of Hell.

Then it is indeed true that to describe the Second Coming of Christ and the Last Judgment as a day of anger, of calamity and of misery, a day of tears and of unfathomable bitterness, *dies magna et amara valde,*[1] *lacrymosa dies illa,*[2] is a strange way of

1. *Dies illa, dies irae, calamitatis et miseriae, dies magna et amara valde*: these words of the *Libera*, in the absolution, which begin in the same manner (inverted) as the *Dies irae*, recall and accentuate further the somber grandeur of it.
2. *Lacrymosa dies illa*: — in the 18th verse of the *Dies irae.*

singing Christian hope. The mercy of God is not forgotten, but it consists in drawing those who are its objects from a lake of perdition to which all men seem destined.

Is there a theological idea in the background of this terror of the Judgment — and of human destiny — of which I have just spoken? Yes, in my opinion: the Augustinian idea of the mass of iniquity, of anger, of death, and above all the idea which seems linked with it of the *small number of the chosen*, which, in later centuries, was to grow still worse with Jansenism.

Here, I immediately meet a difficulty which comes from St. Thomas himself. St. Thomas (see *Sum. theol.* I, q. 23, a. 7, ad 3) seems to accept the interpretation, in my opinion very contestable, of the words of Jesus concerning the narrow gate and the hard road (Matt. 7:13-14) as referring to eternal salvation; in my opinion it is a question there of the earth. on the one hand, of those who engage themselves *on earth* in the wide and spacious road of sin and perdition (this does not mean that they will be lost); on the other hand, of those who engage themselves *on earth* in the narrow road of eternal life *already participated in here on earth*. In other words, St. Thomas seems to follow the pessimistic views of St. Augustine, and he seeks to justify them by a philosophical argumentation drawn from what takes place in nature. The good proportionate to the *common state* of human nature finds itself, he tells us, in the *greater number;* for example, a knowledge sufficient to «manage» in life is denied only to the mentally defective. But on the contrary, if it is a question of a good *which goes beyond the common state* of nature, for example, of a profound knowledge of intelligible realities, this is reserved to a comparatively very small number. And likewise, because the vision of God exceeds the common state of human nature — which moreover and above all bears the wounds of original sin — *pauciores sunt qui salvantur*, the chosen are fewer in number than the damned.

Well, let me say that this argumentation seems extraordinarily unconvincing, and indeed turns against itself. For, salvation is not, like the profound knowledge of intelligible realities, a summit of *natural perfection* which goes beyond the common state of nature, it is something entirely supernatural and which belongs to an order entirely different from that of nature. And the law of nature is not abolished by grace, but there is *another law*, proper to the supernatural order — here the law of redemptive mercy and of the salvific will of God — which surmounts and carries along in its wake the law of the smaller number of successes going beyond the common state of nature, and which must reconcile, according to a relation of suitability, the number of the chosen with the victory of the redeeming Blood over evil and with the large measure required by the limitless mercy of God. — And moreover the wounds of Original Sin have less efficacy to impair our nature than the wounds of Christ to elevate us by grace to friendship with the God who pardons.

I am persuaded that the idea of the *greater number of the chosen* imposes itself and will impose itself more and more on the Christian conscience. Firstly, for a doctrinal reason. On the one hand, there is God who «wills that all men be saved» and who sends His Son to redeem them by the death of the Cross. On the other hand, there is man who through the nihilations of which he is the first cause evades the love of God. Who can be persuaded that man through his evasions is *stronger* than God through His love? This does not exclude there being perhaps a great multitude in Hell, but it does mean that there is surely a much greater multitude in Paradise.

Secondly, something which is in *practical* contradiction with the requirement of Christian life, I mean as to the unity of the Church militant with the Church triumphant such as it must be lived by us, cannot be true. The idea of the smaller number of the chosen translates itself practically, not among the theologians doubtlessly, but in the faithful people, by a prevalence of fear over hope, and by the more or less confused — but irresistible — feeling that Hell is, *in actual fact*, the place of destination which befits the *common state* of humanity, the greater number, and which one escapes only through the good fortune of an exceptional mercy. Here you have the terrors of the *Dies irae*.

But then, if there are without doubt the canonized saints towards whom the Christian people continue to turn, but as towards kinds of supermen foreign to the common human destiny, what about all the other chosen — in much smaller number, it is believed, than the damned — what about this small number of chosen who with the canonized saints constitute the Church triumphant, the mystical Body in Heaven? The Christian people are going to hold them to be survivors who have also been separated from the common lot, and who have nothing more urgent than to turn away from us and forget us in order to flee into eternal beatitude. The sense of the unity and of the living communication between the Church of the earth and the Church of Heaven is going to be irremediably broken, lost.

9.   It seems to me finally that one could point out a third cause of this prevalence of mourning and of black, of this kind of somber apprehension in the ordinary attitude with regard to the deceased, and this kind of practical indifference with regard to the Church triumphant, of which I have been speaking for a moment — too lengthily moreover, pardon me.

This time it is no longer a question of the latent and more or less confused idea that the common state of humanity would destine us to Hell, save a comparatively small number of exceptions; it is a question of the latent and more or less confused idea that the common state of humanity destines us *normally* to pass through Purgatory for a more or less long time, so that the souls which open directly onto Heaven enjoy a supra-normal privilege.

This idea certainly represents a great progress over the first one. For all those who are in Purgatory are chosen, who will one day be in Heaven. And thus the idea in question is not incompatible with belief in the greater number of the chosen.

One can ask oneself however whether from the time of St. Catherine of Genoa (end of the fifteenth century), Christian common conscience has not been so fixed on the thought of Purgatory, with respect to the deceased, that it has somewhat lost sight of other truths.

I am not arguing here about a question of *number*. It would require a great deal of presumption to ask oneself whether the chosen who wait in Purgatory are more or less numerous than those who enjoy the Beatific Vision. I am arguing about the question of what is, or is not, *normal*. And you know very well that between the notion of that which is *normal* and the notion of that which is *the more frequent in point of fact*, there is an enormous difference. The *more frequent* deportment of men is a sinful deportment. It is not the *normal* deportment of the human being, the deportment consonant with the law and with the proper exigencies of his rational essence.

Well, what I am saying is that even if the chosen who must pass through Purgatory are more numerous than those who go straight to Heaven, nevertheless it is these latter who are in the *normal* case of a humanity redeemed by the Blood of Christ. It is not only the saints, the heroes of the moral life, exemplary saints or unapparent saints, it is also the ordinary run of us sinners, who, even after the greatest strayings, open straight onto Heaven if before their death, or at the instant when they are about to die (or perhaps at the instant when the soul separates itself from the body) they make an act of perfect charity. Because they have had confidence in the infinite merits of Christ. Let us remember the *commendatio animae* of the ritual; let us remember the good thief: «This day you will be with me in Paradise.» What is *normal* for the Christian — is to go straight to Paradise, to rejoin the Lord. Not only rejection into Hell, but even also passage through Purgatory, however it may be with the question of number or of frequency, represent *abnormal* cases, the first very obviously, because it supposes revolt against God, the second because it implies that the soul has not let the redemptive work reach completion in it here below.

This remark seems to me important in connection with our relations with the Church triumphant, because it is likely to fortify the ardor of our hope for the souls of those who leave the earth. Because of the awesome transcendence and the inscrutable majesty of God it is an absolute duty to pray for the souls of the deceased; never will our compassion for them be great enough. But because of the infinite mercy of God and the infinite merits of Jesus, we do not hold ourselves practically at the height of our faith if our hope with regard to their eternal destiny does not reach almost to excess. But in actual fact, this hope is in general only a very small and timid pilot-light half buried in the ash of indifference.

In paradisum deducant te Angeli, sings the Church at the end of the funeral of the deceased, and she incenses their body: «May the angels lead you into Paradise; may the martyrs receive you at your coming, and lead you into the holy city of Jesus. May the choir of angels receive you, and may you have eternal rest with Lazarus, who once was poor.» In Paradise, with Jesus; not only is it normal not to hesitate to believe — with human faith, of course, and without forgetting the mystery of the divine transcendence — that such is the lot of those whose holiness of life is known to us, and in the measure in which we have been able to know it; but further we should boldly hope that it is so with all those in whom, at any moment whatever, any sign whatever of response to the kind attentiveness of grace has appeared. And even for those in whom no sign of this kind has been discernible we must hope for it also, so that our hope for them, more or less strong according to the cases, and however anxious it may be, remains in spite of everything stronger than our fear.

Why is it that I speak to you in this way especially of those whom we have known? It is because of a certain idea that I have in my head, concerning the Church triumphant. It seems to me that in turning towards the Church triumphant we must think first and above all, this is very obvious, of Jesus and Mary, and of the Holy Angels, and of the great saints whom the Church proposes for our veneration; but that there is also a certain special role to be recognized for the non-canonizable chosen, for the unapparent saints whom we have known and who have known us here on earth. They have carried with them to Heaven the memory of their friends. They continue to love them as they loved them, I mean that they do not love them only with the supernatural love which derives from the Beatific Vision, as St. Paul for example loved St. Thomas Aquinas, or as St. Thomas loves Abbé Journet — they love them also with human love, superelevated and transfigured by this supernatural love, and with the love of charity with which they loved them here on earth. It is experimentally, if I may say so, both humanly and divinely, that they interest themselves in their affairs and have views concerning them. In short, they continue in the vision the solicitude which they had for them on earth, and the prayer which they offered for them. — And on the other hand, inversely, we who continue to live here on earth, and who have known here on earth these non-canonizable chosen who begin their eternity while we are still on earth, we remember them, we can invoke them. Not being inscribed in any martyrology, who will remember them when in our turn we will have finished with this planet? They will enter into anonymity, no one here on earth will pluck them by the sleeve to ask them for a helping hand.

All of this in order to indicate that the blessed of whom I speak, the non-canonizable blessed who are in some manner our contemporaries, form a kind of fringe through which the Church of Heaven in still in contact in each generation with the passing time, and in physical continuity, so to speak, or, if you prefer, psychological continuity, with the Church militant.

It seems to me that it is important practically to be as attentive as possible to this. And for instance, if you will permit me to allude to what concerns you, to place great confidence in your deceased Little Brothers about whose death I recently read a beautiful and moving account.

In order to indicate the bearing of the remarks which I have just submitted to you in this second part, it would suffice, I think, to pose the following questions:

Does it not seem that after the apostolic times there took place, with regard to the common attitude towards the destiny of souls, a kind of slipping, which after the fifteenth century became a kind of progressive collapse, of the practical exercise of the virtue of hope — on the one hand under the weight of the consciousness of human dignity and of human misery, on the other hand under the weight of all the formulas and affectations of ready-made humility and of overwhelming self-accusation with which the Christian people have been nourished by manuals of piety whose authors were ordinarily persuaded that outside of the religious state (or more generally, with the French school, outside of the ecclesiastical state) one has the greatest chances of losing one's soul?

In reality however, is it not precisely because we are all radically unworthy of eternal life, and have *all*, except the Virgin Mary, a «heart hollow and full of filth,» as Pascal said, that in all and for all, hope founded not on us, but on the Blood of Christ, which is *divine*, must be greater than the fear due to our strayings which are *human*?

And concerning Christian laymen in particular, whose role and activity in the Church militant are now the order of the day, and indeed very justly (but not sometimes without certain misunderstandings), is a preliminary condition not required to understand well, theoretically and practically, this role and this activity (which, being of the Church, can have fecundity only through the virtue of the Holy Spirit)? By this condition I mean the fact of understanding that the laymen in question, if they die in a state of grace, are indeed exposed in actual fact, like everybody, and perhaps in very great number, to have to effect a more or less long detour through the purifications of Purgatory — but that, nevertheless, while leading a frankly and squarely lay life, and even if they are not enrolled in Catholic Action, they are called *normally*, like those who have left everything for the evangelical counsels, to pass, in leaving this life, directly into the Church triumphant? In other words, that the Christian lay life is, by the very fact that it is Christian, normally ordered, by virtue of the merits and of the Blood of Christ, to open straight onto Paradise?

III. ON PRAYER

10.   In the third part I would like to submit to you some reflections on prayer. That is to say that I would like to turn back to discuss a little more a point which I have already indicated.

I said at the very outset that we should pray and have Masses celebrated for the intentions which the saints of Heaven have with regard to us and with regard to the things of the earth.

A question arises immediately: do the saints of Heaven need this? They are close to Jesus; they are, through the Beatific Vision, of the very family of the Trinity; for their intentions with regard to the earth do they not have in their hands the weapon of prayer, of the prayer of the blessed, much more powerful than ours? Do they need, so to speak, the reinforcement of our poor prayer?

Well, I shall point out first that I have spoken not only of our own prayers, but of Masses to be offered, in which we have on earth the prayer of Christ Himself in His supreme act of oblation.

And moreover, I hold that our own prayers are required, and it seems to me that it is the whole treatise on prayer which is at stake here.

For it is indeed clear that God has no need of our petitions in order to will our good and in order to know infinitely better than we in what this good consists, and in order to exercise His power to cause it to happen. And yet He, the Almighty, wishes us to address our petitions to Him: and not only for ourselves, but also for Him, for His own intentions, as is the case with the first three petitions of the Our Father, especially when we pray that His will be done.

Quite obviously, He has no need of us or of our prayer for this. But as St. Thomas explains (see II-II, q. 83, a. 2), just as, in the things of nature, God has disposed that such and such an effect will happen because according to the proper laws of the essences in play such and such a cause will have produced it, so likewise, in human things, in the things of the *free* agent that is man, He has disposed that certain effects would happen *in consequence* of such and such acts freely accomplished by man, in particular, in consequence of his prayer. «It is disposed by divine Providence not only that such and such effects happen, but also that they issue from such or such causes and from such and such a determinate order. But among created causes human acts also are causes of certain things; whence it follows that men must accomplish certain acts, not in order to change by the latter the divine disposition, but in order that there be produced certain effects according to the order disposed by God. And it is the same with natural causes. And it is also the case for prayer. In reality we do not pray in order to change the divine disposition, but in order to obtain that which God has disposed as having to occur by reason of the prayers of the saints. . . .»

There is therefore an *order disposed by God* according to which certain things occur here on earth because we have prayed to God concerning them.

And it is very clear, is it not, that among these certain things which God wills that they happen but on condition that we ask Him for them, there are not only things which correspond to our own desires and intentions, there are also things which correspond to the desires and to the intentions of God Himself (think of the first three petitions of the Our Father) — moreover such is the case with everything that is good — and there are therefore also, clearly, things which correspond to the desires and to the intentions of the saints of Paradise.

There is a great number of things, concerning not only our desires and our needs, but also the desires and the intentions of the saints regarding the work of God on this poor earth, which happen only because human liberty here on earth turned towards God in order to pray.

11. There we have what is entirely certain, it only repeats under another form the very general truths taught by St. Thomas.

But it seems to me that it is necessary to try to be a little more precise, and here I enter into the field of hypotheses which I would like to submit to you, and which would require a more thorough study.

In the *ad tertium* of this same Article 2 (II-II, q. 83) which I have just cited (I would have many things to say concerning this *ad 3*, but this is not the moment), St. Thomas writes: «There are lots of things which we receive from the liberality of God even without having asked for them. But there are certain things which He wishes to give us at our request, and this is *for our benefit*: namely, in order that we may acquire a certain habit of confidence in having recourse to God — *ut scilicet et fiduciam quamdam accipiamus recurrendi ad Deum* — and in order that we may recognize that He is the author of all our goods.»

Yes, without doubt, this is very true. But is this all there is to it? Is it only a question, as one would run the risk of thinking if one stopped at that point, of an in some way educative or pedagogical disposition of Providence, destined to assure the equipment of our moral life, like the rules which a good father of a family establishes for the right moral formation of his children?

My idea is that we must go further. Did not St. Thomas himself, in the body of the article, take care to note that in the things of nature God has disposed a similar order between the effect which He wishes to cause to come into existence and the cause which produces this effect, according to the very laws of essences or the laws of nature? What I am thinking is that in what concerns prayer we do not have to do only with a disposition of the paternal Prudence of God aiming at the moral formation of man, but with a genuine *law* — I would willingly say ontological — not a law of nature but a law of the universe of the spirit and of liberty, and more especially of the supernatural order.

I am not sure how to express myself. One could say, it seems to me, that with regard, not certainly to all the things which depend on this universe, but to a certain ensemble of things which depend on it, the intentions of Heaven are accomplished on earth only by means of certain conditions, certain enticements, or certain openings which relate to dispositive causality and which depend on the prayer of minds turned towards God. But there is much more still: why is it necessary that the Sacrifice of the Cross which took place at a moment of time but with an infinite efficacy which is valid for all times, be again rendered present — the same sacrifice, in a non-bloody way — all through time, at all the instants in which a Mass is celebrated on earth, if not because it is necessary that on the side of the earth and all through time there be — and this time through the supplication and the immolation of the God-Man Himself, head of humanity — an appeal here below, a cry, an abyss

hollowed out in human liberty, which corresponds in the imper-
manence of our fleeting duration to the eternal merciful will of God?

Here is therefore what I would like to submit to you, without
being very sure of what it is worth.

It seems to me that in the laws established by Providence as
to the behavior of created things, there are three orders, or rather
three *regimes* to be considered:

In the first place, the *ordinary regime* of creatures not endowed
with intelligence, or of material nature. Divine Providence provides
for the good of all these creatures, It feeds the little birds, It clothes
with beauty the lilies of the fields, by means of the exercise of
natural causalities and of natural energies, without any petition
or prayer being addressed to God except by the very existence and
the needs of these things — the little birds open their mouths, and
do they!

In the second place there is the *ordinary regime* of intelligent
creatures insofar as they are *free agents*. These intelligent creatures,
because they are intelligent, know that God exists, and that everything comes from Him. Here, it is a law, a necessary law of this
regime, that the goods which the divine liberality wishes to dispense
to such beings be received from it by means of the causality *of their
prayer*, according as their liberty turns towards God and, in having
recourse to Him, opens in the soul — and not only in the soul which
prays, but at the same stroke in the invisible universe in which all
souls are in intersolidarity — the path through which the intentions
of the generosity of Heaven will pass in order to realize themselves
here on earth. It is as if there was at the summit of the soul a window
towards Heaven, a window which depends on the liberty of the soul
for the opening or closing of its panes and shutters. As long as the
shutters are closed the light does not enter. But if by a free act of
recourse to God the soul opens the window and its shutters, light
springs in, and with it an avalanche of the gifts of Heaven which
were pressing to enter.

I note, parenthetically, that if it is a question of man, who
is a part both of the world of nature and of liberty, the exercise
of his liberty having recourse to God through prayer concerns
also his natural life itself. One can contrive to feed oneself and
to feed one's family without praying to God, such is the case with
a multitude of human beings, as of all the beasts of nature. But
Jesus tells us to pray for our daily bread, *our* bread, that of all

our brothers as well as our own; and if there were a greater number of men to make the fourth petition of the Our Father, and a greater number of Christians to make it *better*, there would be less famine on earth.

Finally in the third place, there is the *extraordinary regime* of intelligent creatures insofar as they are *free agents: to receive without having asked*. Extraordinary regime, not, certainly, on the side of God, who always gives first; but extraordinary regime on the side of created spirits, because it is according to *the nature of things* that created spirits ask Him whom they know to be the author of all good — ask before receiving. And it is a good thing that it is there, this extraordinary regime, and that it produces its effects with great frequency! Then, through exceptions which can sometimes be miraculous, but the majority of the time they are only outside of the ordinary course of things — through exceptions to the laws of the *ordinary* regime, the goods of which free agents have need are given to them *without having been asked for*, without the free agent having had recourse to the First Cause of all good. This is an extraordinary regime, because then the gifts of Heaven, instead of penetrating into the soul and into the world through the ordinary way, through that freely opened window of which I spoke, penetrate into them by burglary, so to speak, without the soul having opened of itself in asking God for what is good. The word «burglary» which I have just used is moreover only a paltry metaphor: there is no violence, because the causality of the Almighty never does violence to the creature. It would be more true to say that the force of Heaven is so strong that it penetrates through the walls of the soul with its gifts.

The soul receives then without having asked. This is the case for example with certain natural or supernatural inspirations, with prevenient graces, with a multitude of blessings which escape our consciousness or our attention and which are due sometimes to fortuitous meetings — and above all with that sovereign work of God which is the «justification of the impious.»

Let us add immediately that if the impious person, by the very fact that he is impious, has not turned towards God to ask to be cured, there are other souls who have prayed and suffered, and have perhaps been crucified, and have perhaps given their life for this. St. Theresa of Lisieux prayed for Pranzini. And there are all the prayers of the saints which God uses as He likes for the benefit of such or such individual. So that finally what I call the *extraordinary regime* – unless one understands it of the goods given to a specific individual person without having been asked for *by the latter* – reabsorbs itself for the most part (and even entirely if it is a question of the supernatural order and of salvation) in the *ordinary* regime which befits free agents as such, in this sense that the goods which they receive from God *have been asked for* if not by their own prayer, at least by the *prayer of the saints* and of the mystical Body in its entirety and above all by the prayer of Jesus and of Mary.

12. I would like to make still another remark: If all that I have just said is correct, one sees that what is the *ordinary regime* for material nature (to receive without having asked) is the *extraordinary regime* for free agents (for such and such a given free agent): and inversely, what is the *ordinary regime* for free agents as such (to receive after having asked and because one has asked) is for material nature an *extraordinary regime*, which is in play, for example, when an event of nature occurs by reason of the prayer of a free agent – cure of a sick person, deliverance of a man escaping from his persecutors, end of a war, fall of a tyrant, successful harvesting of the fruits of the earth, etc., without forgetting the petition for daily bread.

What matters above all in this affair is to understand that prayer is not something good without doubt, recommendable and pious, but *more or less optional*; it is a *necessity* in the world such as God has made it. It is as necessary to pray as to sow in order to reap, or to employ any source of energy in order to make a machine work. Even in the things of nature according as they serve the human being, the humanity which does not pray will indeed be able to attain by its science and its technique to a formidable mastery of matter, but if it does not pray this will finally turn out badly for it; it will be enslaved by matter instead of employing it for its own liberation, and in fissuring the atom it will become the slave of dust. This is indeed why a great nuclear physicist whom I knew said to me one day that some lines of Baudelaire announced this whole pretty work of the atomic bomb and its true significance. I still see him going and getting *Les Fleurs du Mal* in his library, and showing me these lines from the poem entitled *L'Imprévu:*

Whereupon appears One they had all denied —
their gloating accuser: . . . .
'Hear my laugh and welcome Satan home,
    huge and ugly as the earth itself! . . .
Now you will learn just how much misery
    loves company — *come down!*
down with me through layers of mud and dust,
down through the rubble of your rotting graves
(It is this verse which had struck the physicist.)

into my palace carved from a single rock
    without one soft spot in its heart,
made as it is of universal Sin:
it holds my pain, my glory and my pride!'

And now I would also like to read to you the end of the poem,
first of all because there are, in my opinion, singularly beautiful
lines here, next because they refer as it happens to the Church
triumphant:

— Meanwhile perched above the universe
    an Angel trumpets the victory
of those whose hearts exclaim: 'O Lord, my God!
I bless Thy rod, I thank Thee for this pain!
My soul in Thy hands is more than a futile toy,
    and Thy wisdom is infinite.'

That trumpet's sound is so magnificent
on solemn eves of Heavenly harvesting,
that like an ecstasy it gladdens those
    whose praises it proclaims.[1]

Well, what is it that I was saying myself? That if one does
not pray one will be able to gain empires and to gain much money,
but that with regard to that which matters most to man one will
not be able to bring anything to consummation. If one does not

1. From *Les Fleurs du Mal* by Charles Baudelaire, translated by Richard Howard
Copyright © 1982 by Richard Howard. Reprinted by permission of David R.
Godine, Publisher, Boston.

pray one will be able indeed to be a great painter and a great musician, but there will be something dead in this grandeur. If one does not pray one can be a great philosopher, but one will betray philosophy and will pass by the side of truth — one can be a remarkably erudite and more or less daft expert in theology and in exegesis, one cannot be a great theologian or a great exegete. If one does not pray one cannot advance in the Christian life or receive all the good things, true fraternal charity, interior peace and interior joy, and the dunghill of Job and its vermin, through which one enters here on earth into eternal life.

To conclude, if I wished to sum up in a single phrase what I would have liked to be able to show in this «seminar,» I would say that for a singularly greater part than we believe, the intentions of Heaven with regard to the earth and its goodness for us are frustrated or paralyzed by our neglect to pray, and especially to pray to the saints of the Church triumphant — exemplary saints and unapparent saints — and especially to pray *for the intentions* of these saints and for the purpose of the Church of Heaven.

APPENDICES

Appendix To Chapter Five
Appendix To Chapter Six
Appendix To Chapter Seven
French Text To Poems

APPENDIX TO CHAPTER FIVE

I

TWO APPROBATIONS

1. *Letter of J.M. to Mgr. Gibier, Bishop of Versailles,*
   and approbation of the latter.

Versailles, 21 rue Baillet-Reviron,
April 10, 1922

Your Excellency,

Permit me filially to ask the approbation of Your Grace for a Study Circle whose members, preoccupied with the necessity of maintaining and of propagating in the world, and particularly among laymen, the doctrine of St. Thomas in its purity, strive to mutually aid each other in the knowledge of this doctrine by means of monthly meetings, while trying also to practice, each to the best of his ability, the life of prayer, without which they are convinced that the study would not bear its fruits.

With regard to the spirit of this group, it will suffice for me to tell Your Grace that Fr. Garrigou-Lagrange, professor at the Collegium Angelicum, in Rome, consented, with the approval of the Fr. Provincial of France and of the Most Reverend Fr. General of the Dominican Order, to assume the chief intellectual direction of our studies.

In a spirit of absolute deference to ecclesiastical authority, we ask Your Excellency to kindly approve the director of studies he has chosen, who is the signer of this letter.

We also ask Your Grace to kindly permit us to ask Fr. Garrigou-Lagrange to preach a retreat for us at Versailles, between the 5th and the 10th of next October.[1]

We ask Your Excellency to grant us your paternal blessing, and to accept the expression of my veneration, of my gratitude and of my affectionate devotion for Your Grace.

[*Beneath my signature, Mgr. Gibier wrote in his hand:*]

I approve most heartily and I bless affectionately Monsieur Maritain and all those who will join him for the study of St. Thomas.

† Charles
Bishop of Versailles

2. *Letter of Mgr. Mariétan, Abbé of Saint-Maurice d'Agaune*

[In this letter, dated the 17th of April 1922, Mgr. Mariétan spoke to me first of another project for organizing the «new brothers,» — «those who are in the process of advancing» or «who have not yet found their way» — a project which did not continue. He added:]

The project of the Thomist study group appears to me no less worthy of attention. It is assuredly one of the most necessary works. For truth alone, truth drawn from its authentic sources will deliver our sick souls. Those who come or will come to us, to our faith and to our Catholic life, have the right to require that we be men and Catholics who passionately love truth and desire nothing so much as to communicate it to the world which has such a pressing need of it.

And what surer means of conquest by truth than that of prayer? It is this which you have so admirably understood. The idea of the *vow of prayer* is full of the richest promises. And I greet with a particular joy this holy and fruitful daring. Is it not proper that

---

1. In actual fact, at the request of Fr. Garrigou, this date was advanced, and the first retreat took place from the 30th of September to the 4th of October (1922).

the devotees of St. Thomas, in imitation of the Master, expect more from prayer than from study, more from the Crucifix than from the masters of human thought?

Believe therefore, my dear Sir, that I thank God for all that He has inspired in you and that I ask Him heartily to give you His divine grace. May the blessing which I send you so gladly be a deficient pledge of it!

Affectionately yours in Jesus Christ and in His divine Mother.

† Joseph Mariétan
Titular Bishop of Bethlehem
Abbé of Saint-Maurice d'Agaune

II

STATUTES OF THE THOMIST STUDY CIRCLES

†

O SAPIENTIA

"O Sapientia, quae ex ore Altissimi prodiisti, attingens a fine usque ad finem fortiter, suaviterque disponens omnia: veni ad docendum nos viam prudentiae."

THOMIST STUDY CIRCLES

I. – General Principles

I. – God, in making of St. Thomas Aquinas the common Doctor of the Church, gave him to us for leader and for guide in the knowledge of truth. The doctrine of St. Thomas is the doctrine which the Church recommends behond all others, and which she enjoins her masters to teach. It imposes itself on reason as a chain of demonstratively linked certitudes, and it accords with dogma more perfectly than any other. It has for itself the pledges of a holiness which is inseparable from the teaching mission of the Angelic Doctor, and which proceeds even to a kind of effacement of his human personality in the radiance of the divine light. Because he profoundly venerated the Fathers of the Church and the holy Doctors who preceded him, St. Thomas, as Leo XIII wrote, «in a certain way inherited the intellect of all.» He so lost himself in truth that one must say of him, with one of his great disciples: *Magis aliquid in sancto Thoma quam sanctus Thomas suscipitur et defenditur*, «in St. Thomas it is something greater than St. Thomas that we receive and defend.» Heir of the past and treasurer of the future, he alone can teach us to become, by his example and according to the measure of our weakness, transparent to truth, docile to the Spirit who gives understanding, open to the common and century-old wisdom with which the Church is

divinely instructed. An active, progressive and conquering fidelity
— but absolutely pure and entire — to the principles, to the doctrine
and to the spirit of St. Thomas, is therefore the means *par excellence*
of serving the Truth which is Christ, and it is specially required for
the salvation of the intelligence threatened today on all sides.

II. We believe moreover that the human intelligence is so weak
by nature, and so weakened by the heritage of Original Sin, and
that on the other hand the thought of St. Thomas is of such a
lofty intellectuality, from the metaphysical as well as the theological
point of view, that in order for this thought to be given to us, all
the supernatural graces of St. Thomas were needed. The eminent
sanctity and above all the unique mission of the Angelic Doctor
assured him of the help of these graces. We believe that in order
for his thought to live among men, a special assistance of the Holy
Spirit is and will always be needed.

In particular, in our epoch so full of errors, and especially
where the discipline and the graces proper to the religious state
are lacking, we believe that it is impossible for Thomism to be
maintained in its integrity and in its purity, without the special
aid of the life of prayer.

We know besides that this union of the spiritual life and of
the life of study was not only practiced to an eminent degree by
St. Thomas himself, but also by his most authoritative commentators, for example by Bannez, who was the director of St. Theresa,
and by Gonet, who dedicated to the great contemplative his *Clypeus thomisticae theologiae*, and by the Salmanticenses, who remained so perfectly faithful on all points of Thomist theology,
and who saw in it the foundation of the great spiritual doctrines
taught by St. Theresa and by St. John of the Cross.

III. But Thomism, by very virtue of the powerful impulse
given by Leo XIII, has already begun to win minds *in the world
and amongst laymen*, and it is called to spread in this way more
and more. Otherwise how could it win the modern intelligence?
It surely must spread throughout the dough to cause it to rise. In
order to penetrate the world, in order to renew philosophy, to
assimilate the materials which it has acquired since the Middle Ages,
to direct its progressive advance in all domains, in order to disengage
the true significance of all the partial truths and of all the researches

accumulated by the particular sciences, in order to animate and enlighten the intellectual renaissance which is preparing itself in the order of letters and of the arts, whose role can be immense, finally in order to inform common intelligence, which has more than ever need of a general theological and philosophical culture, it is indeed necessary that Thomism pass into the intellectual life of secular priests and of laymen, and that it find workers among them.

But its very diffusion can give rise to certain dangers. To the degree that it is studied by minds insufficiently prepared and armed, and more or less influenced by modern prejudices, it will run the risk of being studied without suitable light, and consequently of undergoing diminished, piecemeal and distorting interpretations. Experience shows that this danger of a materialization of Thomism is not imaginary.

IV.   In order to promote in the world the doctrine and the spirit of St. Thomas, while guarding against the danger which has just been pointed out, and while maintaining the Thomist synthesis in the superior light which it requires, it seems useful and opportune therefore to associate the souls of good will who, through love of Truth and of the Church, desire to work for the diffusion of Thomism or to draw their inspiration from it, in study circles which would help them to improve in the knowledge of St. Thomas, and to make it better known, and which would aim to perpetuate in lay circles, through a lasting institution, the living tradition of the masters of Thomsim.

V.   But since the principal element here is, as we have seen, the spiritual and supernatural element, and since such an association can only have value and effectiveness if those who compose it are dedicated as fully as possible to the action of the Holy Spirit, each of its members would bind himself by a private vow to practice the life of prayer. Thus this association of secular priests and of laymen would have at the base of its activity a very intimate and very profound gift of oneself to God, and would offer to souls who desire perfection while remaining in the world a very real help, without however encroaching at all upon the liberty of each, since the vow of prayer concerns only the absolutely personal relations of God and of the soul.

It happens that the usefulness of these study circles would be twofold: on the one hand, they would help to maintain the required integrity and purity of the renewal of Thomist studies in our time, through the means of prayer; and on the other hand they would also help to maintain the required rectitude and purity of the renewal of spirituality in our time, through the means of Thomism.

In a time when the majority of minds are interested in everything except in God, and seem to have lost the strength to reascend to the first cause, it seems desirable that, among their intentions, the members of these study circles include that of *intellectual reparation*. For if it is true that intellectuals especially have the duty of recognizing in God the supreme object of the intelligence and of scrutinizing with love and reverence the depths of natural and supernatural theology, it is equally true that God is in our day especially offended by them. It is important therefore that intellectuals apply themselves in a special manner to rendering to God the homage which the majority of modern philosophers refuse to Him, and to interceding at the same time for all those who are the voluntary or involuntary victims of error.

II. – Organization

VI. There is constituted, under the patronage of the Blessed Virgin Mary, Seat of Wisdom, *Thomist study circles* open to persons who, living in the world, wish to work for the diffusion of Thomism or to draw their inspiration from it, while remaining strictly faithful to the doctrine of St. Thomas and to his thought, which lives in his great disciples, such as Cajetan, John of Saint-Thomas, or the Salmanticenses.

These study circles will not comprise solely philosophers and theologians by profession; they are open to all those, whoever they may be, who desire to take St. Thomas for guide, and it is desirable that they bring together minds having the most varied cast, artists and scientists in particular.

Even persons who would not have the means of regularly studying St. Thomas, but who would offer their prayer in order that the influence of the Angelic Doctor might act on souls according to the will of God, could be a part of this grouping.

VII.   The members of these study circles bind themselves to study St. Thomas as far as possible, and they make the private vow to practice the life of prayer, as much as their way of life and their practical duties permit.

The normal order which the members of the circles are invited to follow, with the approval of their confessor, is to carry out in practice the substance of this vow for one year before pronouncing the vow itself; then the vow is to be annual and renewed twice, and after these three years it is to give place to a perpetual vow.

This vow, either annual or perpetual, does not bear on a materially determined exercise, which must last a precise time each day. A time so fixed could only be a minimum, and all the persons whom the study circles will bring together generally give to prayer, in actual fact, much more time than could be fixed in such a commitment. If the object of the vow is not determined in a material manner, it is in order to have it bear on the essential, the vital, not to belittle things, and also not to give occasion in certain cases to all kinds of scruples. It bears therefore solely on the *general orientation* given to life, so that only the act of *explicitly revoking* the intention to practice the life of prayer can constitute the violation of it.[1]

The formula of this vow could be the following one: «In the presence of the Holy Trinity, of the Blessed Virgin, of St. Thomas, of my patron saints, desiring to tend, in spite of my weakness, to union with God and to the perfection of charity, without obliging myself to a daily exercise of a determined duration, I make a vow to devote myself (here the indication of the duration of the vow) to the life of prayer to the extent that my way of life and my practical duties permit.»

VIII.   The general director of the Thomist study circles will always be a monk of the Order of St. Dominic. The first general director chosen by the Very Reverend Father Provincial of France and approved by the Most Reverend Father General, will be Father Garrigou-Lagrange, professor of theology at the Angelicum, Rome. It is from him that the first members, who had the idea of forming

---

1. If moreover this vow, even so worded, became an occasion for difficulties of conscience for certain members, they could have themselves dispensed from it by their confessor.

a group, desire to receive the original directives, as much from the point of view of doctrine as from the point of view of spirituality.

The successor of the general director will be proposed beforehand to his Superiors by the latter, or in case of major impediment, by the directors of studies assembled for that purpose. Since the study circles comprise members in different regions of France and abroad, this general director will have to be approved by the Most Reverend Father General of the Dominicans.

IX.   The general director guides and supervises the studies of the diverse groups by keeping in touch with the directors of studies; he also gives a general orientation concerning the spiritual life, thanks above all to an annual retreat preached, theoretically, by him, according to the approval of the Ordinary of the place. It would be good to profit from the annual retreat by having, outside of the exercises of the retreat itself, a general meeting presided over by the general director, who could then give instructions concerning the studies and the intellectual work of the year.

The study groups which can be formed in different places will each have a director of studies. It goes without saying that they will function only according to the rules of the Catholic hierarchy. The director of studies, who will have to give full evidence of knowledge, piety and competence, will be chosen by the general Director from among the members of the circle, and approved by the local bishop. He will occupy himself exclusively with studies, neither he nor the study group will need to interfere at all with what concerns an individual's spiritual life, a domain in which each person (especially in a group such as this which does not in any way have the character of a religious institute) depends only on God and has but to consult his own director or confessor. In this order the usefulness of the group will be limited to facilitating for each member the reading of the masters of the spiritual life.

The general Director being charged with maintaining the integrity and the purity of Thomist teaching, will have the right to depose or to replace as he wishes the directors of studies. He will see to it that the latter are in thorough agreement on the essential points of the doctrine of St. Thomas. If against all probability it happened that a group persisted in an intellectual direction judged by him as dangerous, he would also have the right to dissolve it.

Each year, the secretary or the director of each study group will send to the general Director a report on the activity of the past year. This report will have been previously read in a meeting of the group and approved by it. If a member has personal observations to be formulated, they will be added to the report.

Every follower of a study circle will have to be presented by two members of this circle, with the approval of the general Director and of the director of studies.

X.   The Thomist study circles have in nowise the character of a Third Order. It is desirable that their members be a part, as tertiaries or oblates, of a religious family. But the most diverse religious families can be found in them.

XI.   Each group will have at least a monthly meeting devoted to the study of St. Thomas or his commentators.

The members will occupy themselves in these meetings with strengthening themselves in the knowledge of Thomism and with helping each other to realize as far as possible an intellectual collaboration: for example, by sharing with one another information useful for each one's work, and by keeping each other acquainted with the movement of ideas. They will also occupy themselves with preparing the work which could be done for the diffusion of Thomism, above all by indicating to the various groups the points which it would be useful to concentrate on.

The members of the study circles will ordinarily be very burdened with occupations, since they live in the world. So care will be taken that the Association shall be an aid for them and not a supplementary burden. Thus, outside of the study meetings, there will be no other meetings, such as monthly Masses, however desirable in themselves, but which would occur in addition to the Masses and the meetings of the Third Orders to which the members of the circles might belong. Likewise in the study meetings, it is in general the director of studies who will do the principal work, by himself preparing the topic of the meeting.

Each group will have a secretary who will keep note of its activities, will act as liaison among the members of the group and between it and other groups, and will devote some time to organizing the intellectual collaboration just mentioned.

XII. It will be necessary to assure regular communication among the groups.

XIII. It will be necessary also to envisage the creation of a library for each group: above all books and periodicals concerning the doctrine of St. Thomas and the spiritual life.

It would be advantageous for each group to meet its general expenses through regular contributions, establishing the amount according to the necessities.

XIV. In the study meetings, each member will strive not to rest content with an elementary initiation, but to reach a truly intimate knowledge of the highest principles of Thomism. In particular a great effort will be made to deepen at one and the same time the knowledge of the philosophy and theology of St. Thomas, and to develop in all members the superior light of theology. This insistence on theology is all the more necessary for the formation of minds since in external works and publications, on the contrary, it seems more useful to disregard the theological point of view in order to show in the face of modern ideas the value and strength of Thomist philosophy as philosophy.

In the study meetings not only the members can take part, but any of their friends who on any grounds whatever are sincerely interested in the thought of St. Thomas.

XV. In addition to the vow of prayer, and the commitment to study St. Thomas as far as possible, the members of the study circles are only required, in order to strengthen the spiritual bond which unites them, and to ask for the graces which they need, to recite each day the prayer of St. Thomas: *Deus, qui Ecclesiam tuam,* etc., preceded by the antiphon: *Collaudetur Christus Rex Gloriae, qui per Thomam lumen Ecclesiae mundum replet doctrina gratiae,* and by the verse: *Ora pro nobis, beate Thoma, ut digni efficiamur promissionibus Christi,* and to add to the Angelus the invocation: *Doctor Angelice, ora pro nobis.*

APPENDIX TO CHAPTER SIX

APROPOS OF GWENDOLINE AND
AUGUSTUS JOHN

Augustus John was one of the most brilliant among the English painters of this time. As enamored of silence as he was of notoriety, his sister Gwen (1876—1939) is far from having the same celebrity, but it seems that justice has not been done to her, and it appears probable that the researches of the historians of art will make, with time, her value better recognized.[1] At any rate she certainly had an exceptional talent. In this appendix I shall give some somewhat more detailed indications concerning her than in the chapter.

Sir John Rothenstein devoted a chapter to Gwen John in *Modern English Painters;*[2] Augustus John spoke of her in his *Memoirs*[3] and in his Foreword to the *Memorial Exhibition* of 1946, Wyndham Lewis in an article written on the occasion of this exposition.[4]

The date of the conversion of Gwen John to Catholicism is not exactly known. Sir John Rothenstein thinks that after about a year of inner struggle and meditation she was received into the Catholic Church at the beginning of 1913. She already lived in Meudon at that time.

Our relations with her and her friendship with Vera began in 1926, just after the death of Rilke,[5] whom she knew well, and to whom she was very attached. I recopy here the reply that Vera made in 1951, from Princeton, to a letter in which John Rothenstein, then director of the Tate Gallery, asked me for information concerning

1. "I believe her to be one of the finest painters of our time and country," wrote Sir John Rothenstein (*Modern English Painters*, Grey Arrow, p. 180).
2. *Modern English Painters*, Vol. I, *Sickert to Grant*, Eyre and Spottiswoode, 1952; Grey Arrow (paperback), 1962.
3. *Chiaroscuro, Fragments of Autobiography*, Jonathan Cape, 1952; Grey Arrow (paperback), 1962.
4. *The Listener*, October 10, 1946.
5. Rilke died on the 29th of December 1926.

what we knew about Gwen John, for the work on *Modern English Painters* which he was preparing. (It was Vera who replied to him, for it was she — and not Raissa or myself — who had been the friend of Gwen John and had received her confidences. But as she feared to commit a breach of discretion, she wrote in the briefest possible manner.)[1]

«Miss Gwen John,» Vera wrote, «came to see us for the first time the day after the death of Rilke, who was one of her friends; she was very anxious concerning the soul of Rilke, wanted to aid it by her prayers, and wondered whether she could do so while remaining in Meudon, where she lived, or whether she had to go to pray where he had died.

«I know nothing about her conversion, but she was great friends with the Superior of the Soeurs de la Présentation, in Meudon — this Superior is dead — but perhaps the present Superior could give some particulars regarding Gwen John.

«Gwen John was a very practicing Catholic, she received Holy Communion every day. She was very reserved and secret. She suffered a great deal in her life, she was extremely sensitive and touchy.

«She did not wish to look at paintings, she told me that she did not know the Louvre Museum and did not wish to visit it.

«She lived in a very penurious manner, she saw no one, yet she showed me much sympathy. She told me that she had known Rodin.»

Sir John Rothenstein said more concerning the relations between Gwen John and Rodin, who, while being affectionately concerned about her health (of which she took absolutely no care) seems, after she had entered into his friendship, to have quite rapidly treated her with the condescending superiority peculiar to men of genius (and who know it).

Vera spoke to us very little of her conversations with Gwen John, because of the discretion to which she felt herself bound with regard to what had been said to her in confidence. It was after Mass that Gwen John talked with Vera. She wrote her a great number of letters, many drafts of which were found in her papers. I reproduce two passages of these letters among those which Augustus John

---

1. The draft from which I copy this letter of Vera is not dated; it is certainly of 1951 (the reply which John Rothenstein made to it is dated the 15th of June, 1951).

published in *Chiaroscuro*. «Dear Mademoiselle, I need your eyes, but mine do not wish to look at them. I told them to look at them but they do not wish to do it. I love you as I love flowers.» — «One has tenderness for the little animals which one has saved from death, does one not? You must have tenderness for me because you saved me from death. . . .»[1]

After the visit in which she spoke to us of her anxieties concerning the soul of Rilke, Raissa and I saw Gwen John only very rarely. (Having taken only Vera into her confidence, she seemed to avoid us as much as possible, and slipped away quickly when she happened to meet us.) She had appeared to us from the outset as both timid and fierce. She spoke only by murmuring in a low voice. One felt that the solitude in which she enclosed herself — with an unheard-of passion for her art, to which she sacrificed everything — sheltered tempests.[2] We knew that she had only her cats for companions and the endless reverie on which she nourished herself, in such a manner that it was doubtless difficult for her always to distinguish fiction from reality. Sir John Rothenstein tells us that among the mass of papers which she kept, there were not only copies made by her (sometimes several copies) of prayers and of meditations, of extracts from the writings of Catholic authors and of the saints, «as well as from Bertrand Russell, Baudelaire, Dostoievski, Oscar Wilde and Diderot,»[3] but also drafts of her own letters and, in addition to a certain number of autographic replies received by her, many copies of replies of which the originals are missing.

To judge according to what Vera let one guess, and according to what Augustus John and Sir John Rothenstein say, one must admire in Gwen John a rare natural magnanimity joined to a passionate violence from which she was the first to suffer. But her affection was intolerably engrossing, and it was because of this,

1. *Chiaroscuro*, Jonathan Cape, p. 253.
2. "Nobody suffered from frustrated love as she did," writes her brother (*Chiaroscuro*, p. 248). And again: "Gwen John's apparent timidity and evasiveness disguised a lofty pride and an implacable will. When possessed by one of the 'Demons' of whose intrusions she sometimes complained, she was capable of a degree of exaltation combined with ruthlessness which, like a pointed pistol, compelled surrender: but the pistol would be pointed at herself. . . ." (*Ibid.*, p. 256).
3. *Modern English Painters*, p. 162. — Augustus John mentions also Schopenhauer and William James (*Foreword*, p. 8).

as also because of the impossibility of remedying the need she had
of torturing herself, and the tyranny of her sentiments, that Vera
finally had to recognize the necessity of ceasing to see her. Such a
decision surely cost her very much, and was not taken without
the certitude that it was in Gwen's own interest that she must act
thus. At what date did this rupture take place? As far as I remember,
in 1932, but after two years, I believe, of difficult and fruitless
efforts to pacify the situation.

I see in the book of Sir John Rothenstein that Gwen John had
attended the courses of the Whistler School in Paris, but had retained from them only an extreme concern for science and for technique in her painting methods, and had quickly freed herself from
all influence. He writes also — following Augustus John[1] — that she
was «familiar with the National Gallery and the Louvre.»[2] She herself however told Vera that she did not wish to see anyone's paintings and had not even visited the Louvre. Is it necessary to take this
assertion literally, and to think that Augustus attributed to his sister
what he himself considered as going without saying? It appears more
probable that in speaking to Vera Gwen John somewhat exaggerated
things, in her desire to affirm her ideal of absolute solitude and of
absolute independence. The assertion in question remains however
significant, and shows that she was so attached to her own vision
that she forgot the works which she had formerly seen, and certainly
refused, at the time in which we knew her, to visit any museum and
any exposition of contemporary painters.

In the article which he devoted to the *Memorial Exhibition* of
1946 Wyndham Lewis tells us that «one of her great friends was
Jacques Maritain» (which is entirely incorrect), and that she belonged to the «Catholic Revival in France» (which, considering
her total solitude, is *senseless*). He says also (which has all the appearance of an absurdity) that this alleged friendship with me and
this alleged belonging to a cultural movement of her time partially
explain why she succeeded so well in «isolating herself from the
influences of her time.»

The *Foreword* and the *Memoirs* of Augustus John have much
more interest. What he writes about Gwen shows that there was
in her a great deal of authentic grandeur, of nobility and of courage,

1. *Foreword*, p. 3.
2. *Op. cit.*, p. 163.

an ardent instinct for the absolute,[1] and a lively and fervent faith. When however he comes to speak of us, his Preface contains errors[2] which I must point out.

Thus, for example, he does not doubt that I am the author of a letter (in English) found among his sister's papers, in which the most imperious counsels are dispensed to her with a ridiculous arrogance. But at the time in which Vera (and indirectly Raissa and myself) were in relations with Gwen John, I did not know a word of English (I learned it later), and would have been incapable of writing to Gwen John even in the kitchen English of the letter in question. Whether I wrote once or twice to Gwen John, after the visit in which she spoke to us of her anxieties concerning Rilke, I have no recollection. At any rate the letters which Augustus John cites are certainly not from me.

A supplementary proof of this (supposing that one wants one) is furnished by the researches of an art historian who is particularly interested in Gwen John and is preparing a work on her. Mrs. Mary Taubman kindly wrote to me − I am grateful to her for having thought of doing so − that in examining the papers of Gwen John she had found in them, not the letter quoted by Augustus John, but several others which are exactly in the same style and in the same English, and whose handwriting has no resemblance to mine. The author of these letters, whom she has not yet succeeded in identifying, but of whom some idea can be formed according to what he writes, was, it seems, a bit cracked, and considered himself to be «the Master» to whom obedience was due. Some of the letters in question are, it appears, signed, Y.M. (Your Master),[3] and these,

---

1. He relates for example that one day when his son Henry Elfin, who had been converted to Catholicism, was having a try at an attempt at proselytism with regard to Augustus himself by expounding to him the diverse advantages which he would find in embracing the true faith, "my sister Gwen appeared, and hearing this argument, at once contradicted her learned nephew with the statement that one accepted the truth, not as a business transaction, but for the love of God, even if it meant disaster or death itself − 'As if *that* mattered,' she added contemptuously and left the room." (*Chiaroscuro*, p. 212)

2. Taken up again in *Chiaroscuro*, pp. 251-252.

3. I suppose that Gwen John, in writing to him, also called him "Cher Maitre," − this is doubtless why Augustus John does not hesitate to affirm that she always gave me this name. "Jacques Maritain was a neighbour at Meudon. Gwen always addressed him as 'Dear Master'." He affirms likewise that "the brilliant Neo-Thomist adopts a highly authoritative style in his communications with

initials are easy to confuse with J.M. All of this (including the tone of absurd authoritarianism which one must expect, must one not, from a «neo-Thomist») expalins why Augustus John did not hesitate to attribute to me the letter he quoted, as also the other letters of the same type, with a lack of reflection which was doubtless candid but doubtless also not very cordial.

But what I am anxious above all to point out is the entirely unjust, and, to tell the truth, quite vulgar manner in which Augustus John expressed himself concerning Vera (whom he took for my niece). How moerover, let us say in his excuse, would he have been able, not being at all acquainted with Vera, and in the presence only of a few poor lifeless papers, to have the slightest idea of the affection and of the devotion with which, in order to aid the soul which had appealed to her, she had taken under her responsibility a friendship very heavy to bear? How would he have been able to understand the reasons for the ungrateful role which she had assumed in striving to put a little peace in a heart so sensitive and so constantly exacting and constantly troubled? He supposed (and I confess that for me, who knows that Vera's compassion, her clearsightedness with regard to souls and her limitless understanding never failed, these lines are not easily tolerable) that she was «what we call a 'sensible' girl» — a reasonable *petite bourgeoise* seeking «to keep her admirer's conduct within the bounds of reason and propriety.» Concerning which he declared not without pride: she might as well have tried to restrain a whirlwind. In actual fact Vera spoke to a Christian; and when she told her to turn her sensibility towards the Lord, not towards creatures, she was not stating a rule of propriety.

As to Gwen John's habit, which greatly shocked the parish priest of Meudon, of bringing her sketchbook to church and of sketching people there, Vera found it very innocent. And if she refrained from contradicting Gwen's confessor, she did so, along with the wisdom which was fitting, with a tinge of humor, and a smile, which it is not, all the same, so difficult to perceive. «You told me,» Gwen John wrote to Vera, «that you do not think that it is a very great sin to work in spirit at my drawings during the High

Gwen and enjoins complete obedience which his pupil is only too eager to render." (*Foreword*, p. 4) All these assertions are, in that which concerns me, pure invention.

Mass. I told you the Curé told me that it is a sin. Then you said gently, 'If he said that, it is a sin.'

«When the Curé said this to me, I felt neither contrition nor fear . . . but I shall draw only at Vespers, Evening Services and Retreats. I like to pray in Church like everybody else, but my mind is not capable of praying for long periods at a time. . . . The orphans with those black hats with the white band and their black dresses with the white collars charm me, and other creatures charm me in Church. If I cut out all of this, there would not be enough happiness in my life.»[1] One can be very sure that Vera loved that letter.

1. *Foreword*, p. 5.

APPENDIX TO CHAPTER SEVEN

TWO SYNOPTIC TABLES

Those who do me the honor of reading me know that I have an immoderate liking for synoptic tables and schemas. It seemed to me that the topics discussed in the seventh chapter of this book, and the distinctions which I propose there, are sufficiently complex to merit that a general view be presented of them in the form of a table. Hence the two synoptic tables — the first concerning the analogical notion of love, the second relating to the perfection of charity — which will be found in this Appendix.

TABLE NO. 1: *On the notion of love*

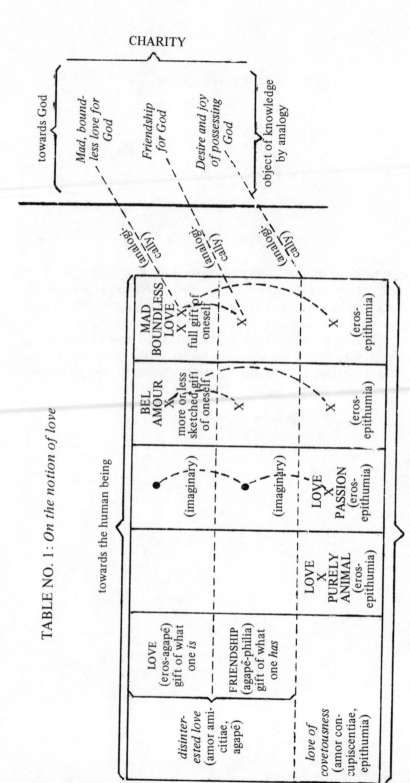

TABLE NO. 2: *On the pursuit of the perfection of charity*

Regime of Life	Mystical State	Kind of Life	Contemplation	Predominant Exercise of the Gifts	Mad, Boundless Love for God	Mystical Inspiration	Perfection of Charity (supposed attained here on earth)
of *mad, boundless love* (including friendship)	threshold passed	contemplative life (mystical)	more often typical and open	of *Wisdom* and *Understanding* (and *Knowledge*)	habitually pre-dominant	in the habitual state	under all relations
		active life (mystical)	more often atypical and masked	of the other Gifts			
of *friendship* (in which mad, boundless love is buried)	threshold not passed	active life without habitual mystical inspiration	fugitive touches	fugitive touches	fugitive touches	fugitive touches	under the relation of intensity only

Pursuit of the perfection of charity:

- as to the power of alienating the soul from itself and as to intensity — called by right to pass the threshold
- under the relation of intensity only — in actual fact remains the regime of a great many

Page 11:

> O les steppes; les déserts.
> La contemplation.
> Mourir à Jérusalem.

Pages 12-13:

> Le pauvre infirme
>
> va.
>
> Il est laid et dégoûtant à voir.
> On a pitié de lui et on lui laisse croire qu'il est
> aussi beau que les autres hommes.
> Il est méchant sans le savoir.
> On a pitié de lui; on lui laisse croire qu'il est bon,
> qu'il aime et qu'on l'aime.
> Il boîte et trébuche à tous les ruisseaux.
> On a pitié de lui; et on lui laisse croire qu'il marche
> droit, comme les autres hommes marchent droit.
> Il est aveugle et ne voit que des hallucinations folles.
> On a pitié de lui; on lui laisse croire qu'il voit
> comme voient les autres hommes.
> Il est sourd et n'entend que des hallucinations folles.
> On a pitié de lui et on lui laisse croire qu'il entend
> de belles harmonies, et que telles sont les harmonies
> qu'entendent les autres hommes.
> Il est muet et ne profère que des sons inarticulés.
> On a pitié de lui; on lui laisse croire qu'il parle,
> et que telle est la parole des autres hommes.
> Il est malade.
> On a pitié de lui et on lui laisse croire qu'il est sain
> comme sont les autres hommes.
>
> Il est mort.
> On a pitié de lui; on lui laisse croire qu'il est vivant,
> et que telle est la vraie vie.
> Mais parfois n'entend-il pas, au loin,
> comme un rire?

Page 13:
Vois, le jardin se meurt lentement sous la pluie;
       Vois-tu se creuser les grands trous?
Nous enterrerons là notre âme et notre vie,
       L'ombre dormira près de nous.
Vois les fleurs se faner lentement sous la pluie.
Vois, l'eau coule à travers les chemins défoncés
       Entraînant des feuilles pourries.
Tel sera bien le fleuve où nos félicités
       Vogueront aux villes bénies.
Vois nous passer parmi les chemins défoncés.

Vois nous passer parmi la jeunesse gâchée.
       Les fruits du verger sont tombés.
Le soleil s'est couché au fond de la vallée.
       J'entends courir des vents glacés
Et j'ai peur de partir vers l'aurore gâchée.

Page 19:
Il faut porter la mort avec gaieté. Il est heureux
       à jamais; veut danser toujours.

Et peut-être il y aura des beaux jours; les jeux de
       la vie voudront-ils imiter le souvenir.

Sa douleur est à lui, c'est le néant de l'œuvre,
       pour le passé, le présent et l'avenir.

Sa douleur infinie, c'est la fureur des servitudes,
       qui venues depuis les temps, font pleurer Dieu lui-même.

Sa volonté est à Dieu. Sa liberté est totale.

Tout ce que donne Dieu, il le reçoit avec bonheur.
Si Dieu le croit un jour à sa ressemblance et l'appelle,
alors, il viendra.

Ainsi il est mort, et presque rien n'est changé à sa vie,
ni à son action, ni à son bonheur. C'est comme un homme
qui continuerait la veille par le rêve, et y ferait
les mêmes choses. Il rêve pourtant.

En voilà assez pour lui.

Il faut que Dieu soit libre.

Page 54:
. . . Comme un navire fortuné
Qui s'en revient au port sa cargaison intacte
J'aborderai le ciel le cœur transfiguré
Portant des offrandes humaines et sans tache.

Pages 194-195:
Le bœuf escortant la tortue
songe au paradis perdu.
Entendez-vous le carillon des Antilles,
les essaims des fleurs trépassées?
Le long des mares des licornes chantent
l'histoire des brebis.
Toutes les pierres de l'univers sont attendries
et les larmes coulent le long des cratères.
O mes amies ce sont des chants
d'amour et d'agonie.

Page 195:
Agneau aux yeux bleus — poussière impossible,
diamants lumineux — tête dure, serrée comme la
vérité, douceur des anges, tendresse implacable,
goutte d'eau qui creuse les rocs, imprenable, paisible,
tranquille.

Protège ton bonheur par des actions de grâce
Entoure-le d'une haie de roses,

Et l'Esprit qui le suit dans son pèlerinage
Pleure de le voir gai comme un oiseau des bois.

Page 199:
L'être étonne dans les yeux de l'enfant
et refuse de voir le monde . . .

Page 282:
Et puis, Quelqu'un paraît que tous avaient nié,
Et qui leur dit . . .
Reconnaissez Satan à son rire vainqueur,
    Énorme et laid comme le monde . . .
Je vais vous emporter à travers l'épaisseur,
    Compagnons de ma triste joie,
A travers l'épaisseur de la terre et du roc,
A travers les amas confus de votre cendre,
(C'est cette strophe-là qui avait frappé le physicien)

Dans un palais aussi grand que moi, d'un seul bloc
    Et qui n'est pas de pierre tendre,
Car il est fait avec l'universel Péché,
Et contient mon orgueil, ma douleur et ma gloire!

Cependant, tout en haut de l'univers juché,
    Un ange chante la victoire
De ceux dont le cœur dit: «Que béni soit ton fouet,
Seigneur! que la douleur, ô Père, soit bénie!
Mon âme dans tes mains n'est pas un vain jouet,
    Et ta prudence est infinie.»

Le son de la trompette est si délicieux,
Dans ces soirs solennels de célestes vendanges,
Qu'il s'infiltre comme une extase dans tous ceux
    Dont elle chante les louanges.

JACQUES MARITAIN: HOMAGE IN WORDS AND PICTURES
by John Howard Griffin and Yves R. Simon

A beautifully produced testimonial by two of his close friends. John Howard Griffin has contributed the notes from his diary of his meetings and friendship with Maritain and over thirty striking photographs of the philosopher, from Princeton to Toulouse, several full page. Yves R. Simon shows Maritain's importance in a perceptive biography and personal history. A unique and moving tribute. Ninety-six pages, printed in duo-tone, oversize 8 1/2 X 11 inches.

John Howard Griffin's works include the very influential *Black Like Me* and several other photographic essays, especially, *A Hidden Wholeness: The Visual World of Thomas Merton*. Although known as a forceful writer and diarist, he was also a master photographer, and a member both of The Society of Photographers in Communications and of the Royal Photographic Society of Great Britain.

Yves R. Simon was a longtime friend of Maritain and a philosopher in his own right. His works include the *Philosophy of Democratic Government* and in the philosophy of science, *The Great Dialogue of Nature and Space*. Maritain said of him, "All his books, whether in French or in English, have been fraternal companions for me."

"Griffin portrays in reverential portraits and words, the final edges of the aged and gentle life. A handsome memorial, in sepia on cream paper."

Booklist

"... reveals the person, the old man, this small packet of flesh and blood and bone who carried immensity inside his head."

Spiritual Life

"The Griffin/Simon book on Jacques is another treasure."

National Catholic Reporter

"A lovely, unforgettable book." **The Church World**

"A welcome memento. The volume would make an attractive gift."

Review for Religious

CATALOG ON REQUEST

MAGI BOOKS, INC. 33 BUCKINGHAM DR. ALBANY, N.Y. 12208

RAISSA'S JOURNAL
presented by Jacques Maritain

Shortly after Raissa Maritain's death from cerebral thrombosis in 1960, her griefstricken husband, Jacques Maritain, began to go through her papers. Among them he found a set of journals Raissa had kept over the 54 years of their life together. Jacques knew that she kept diaries, just as he did, but he had no idea of their true nature until he read them after her death.

The journals so overwhelmed him that he had a selection published in a small private edition for their friends. Jacques asked each recipient to help him decide whether or not these intimate pages should be made public through a regular book edition.

Few people have written more starkly and vividly of the spiritual life. Few have had the perceptions that come from a life of utter and absolute abandonment to the will of God, perceptions in Raissa's case supplemented by very high poetic gifts and philosophical learning.

The initial reaction of such friends as Thomas Merton was that these notes were too powerful and too searing to be made public, even though he felt enormously privileged to read them himself. Others expressed much the same reaction. In almost case, however, such friends had second thoughts and encouraged Jacques to allow a regular edition of *Raissa's Journal*.

They appear here for the first time in English, in a translation corrected, revised and approved by Jacques Maritain before his death in 1973. A book of 425 pages, with six pages of photographs.

"An intense document of contemplation and revelation . . . includes notes on poetry and letters to close friends."

Booklist

"Perhaps the spiritual classic of our century." **America**

"*Raissa's Journal,* in its faith and love, belongs with Pope John XXIII's *Journal of a Soul*, with the *Markings* of Dag Hammerskjold, and with the writings of Soren Kierkegaard."

Sign

"The one book of this decade certain to be recognized sooner or later, as a great spiritual classic of the century."

The Church World

"Spiritual journals arresting in their own right."

Christianity Today

"A reminder of the debt we owe to the Maritains."

Commonweal

CATALOG ON REQUEST